FR. VINCEN'

Rendezvous
with
GOD

SOPHIA INSTITUTE PRESS
Manchester, New Hampshire

Rendezvous with God

*And beholding Jesus walking, he saith: "Behold the Lamb of
God." And the two disciples heard him speak, and they followed
Jesus. And Jesus turning, and seeing them following him, saith
to them: "What seek you?" Who said to him, "Rabbi ... where
dwellest thou?" He saith to them: "Come and see." They came
and saw where he abode, and they stayed with him that day.*

(John 1:36–39)

Contents

FIFTH DAY

SIXTH DAY

SEVENTH DAY

EIGHTH DAY

Author's Preface

With desolation is all the land made desolate;
because there is none that considereth in the heart.

(Jer. 12 :11)

OURS IS A society sorely in need of prayer yet deeply inimical to it. Everything around us wars against the spiritual life: An obsessive careerism rules our workaday world, demanding more and more of our time and attention and allowing few to opt out without being trampled. What remains of our free time is dominated by a kind of frenzied self-indulgence that hardly deserves the name of "recreation" and that leads not so much to refreshment as to besotted stupefaction. Television and movies inflame our passions while they corrupt our minds; magazines and newspapers traffic in propaganda, sleaze, and gossip; most modern books are more suitable for burning than for reading.

Those sectors of society that we might expect to defend against this war of moral and spiritual attrition, such as our courts and schools, have instead become its spearheads, aggressively promoting every manner of godlessness while ruthlessly stamping out every public manifestation of religion. Even our religious institutions must share some blame — perhaps most of it: when churches become hotbeds of activism instead of houses of worship, when seminaries exalt politics and psychology over doctrine, when priests and religious follow after the latest secular trends rather than Christ — no wonder, then, that religion in general is discredited, and prayer in particular is devalued and made more difficult.

In such a war, surrender is not an option. Retreat, however, is more than an option—it is a recommended practice of long-standing tradition in the Church, going back to our Lord Himself, who often withdrew from the fray to reflect and pray. And in spiritual as in actual warfare, such retreat has a tactical aspect: to recover our strength, to refurbish our defenses, and to heal the wounds sustained in battle with the Enemy. In such retreat, we surrender ourselves, as it were, more fully to our heavenly King, that by the grace thus gained we may return with Him to vanquish the Prince who would rule our hearts and our world.

Such retreat, however, cannot be fully accomplished in a book. Without the sacraments of Confession and Holy Communion, which would be available on most actual retreats, our healing and recovery can at best be partial; important, too, is silence and solitude. In fact, the present volume would perhaps ideally serve as spiritual reading to take along on a retreat; in any case, it is certainly not intended as·a substitute for one.

Still, prayerful reflection is always profitable and should be undertaken whenever possible. This book, then, is especially intended for those whom time and circumstance may prevent from going on retreat any time soon.

A few words about this book's form and the recommended manner of reading: In adapting it from a retreat I once gave for fellow priests, I have chosen to preserve its original format; thus, each of the eight chapters is a "day" comprising of four separate "meditations" or "conferences" such as were actually given at different times of an actual day. While the sub-chapters do, therefore, have a certain independence of one another, they are closely related in theme and are part of a necessary sequence. It would perhaps be best, then, to set aside sufficient time to read at least one chapter at a sitting.

At the same time, I would recommend against reading too much at a gulp. This is a book to be grasped by the heart and imagination as much as by the intellect, to stimulate prayerful contemplation as much as to deepen understanding. To some extent, it requires your participation. More than most, it does not benefit from speed-reading.

—Fr. Vincent P. Miceli
Orange, California
Holy Week, 1991

Rendezvous with God

FIRST DAY

Purpose: To consider the end of Creation

Patron: The Sacred Heart of the Incarnate Lord

Points for Self-Consideration:

- The supernatural and its control of my life.
- Does the supernatural permeate my general habits of thought and action?
- Does the supernatural pervade my intentions and motivations?
- Does the supernatural control and elevate my use of creatures?

Suggested Readings:

Luke 8:9–15

Imitation of Christ, bk. 3, ch. 1 and 2

Spiritual Exercises: Annotations 1–10

Aspirations:

"O Lord, make me know my end. And what is the number of my days: that I may know what is wanting to me." (Ps. 38:5)

"Thou art worthy, O Lord our God, to receive glory and honor and power: because thou hast created all things; and for thy will they were and have been created." (Rev. 4.11)

FIRST MEDITATION
Life with God in the Divine Family

WE MAY IMAGINE St. Paul coming into our midst with the words: "The Kingdom of God is ... justice, and peace, and joy in the Holy Ghost" (Rom. 14:17). "For whosoever are led by the Spirit of God, they are the sons of God" (Rom. 8:14). We ask to appreciate and love the divine family to which we belong so that we might enjoy the justice and peace of God.

Back home to God. Our annual retreat is a furlough back home. It is a leave of absence from the fighting front. It is a call to come home to our Heavenly Father and "rest a little." A retreat should be predominantly a time of peace, peace for body and mind. The soldier on leave puts aside the daily duties of his army life and turns to the rest, joy, and refreshment to be found in the love of his family. The retreatant drops the ordinary occupations of his day and turns to the rest, joy, and refreshment to be found in the silent recollection of God's eternal love for him. St. Mark relates how the apostles returned from the marvelous works of their first mission in these words: "And the apostles coming together unto Jesus, related to him all things that they had done and taught. And he said to them: Come apart into a desert place, and rest a little" (Mark 6:30–31).

Today Christ invites us to that solitude that is the audience chamber of God. We need this time of solitude: we need the peace, the strength, and the joy of dwelling lovingly with the family of God. Hence, we appreciate the loving kindness, we gratefully accept the tender condescension of God in allowing us not only to know of His inner life in the temple of His divinity but also to become adopted sons, sharers of His divine nature. For as St. Paul tells us: "Because you are sons, God hath sent the Spirit of his Son into your hearts, crying: Abba, Father" (Gal. 4:6).

Here, then, are the members of the divine family with whom a retreatant is lovingly united in silent prayer during his annual retreat: God the Father, God the Son, and God the Holy Spirit. One God in one divine nature and three distinct, divine Persons. Let us prayerfully turn our minds and hearts to the study and love of these inexpressibly loveable divine Persons.

The divine Persons. In the family of God, there exist three divine Persons — the Father, the Son, and the Holy Spirit — and these three Persons are really distinct; yet all three Persons equally subsist in and possess the one divine nature. "Nature" answers the question: "What is it?"; "Person" answers the question: "Who is it?" Were we to ask in reverent humility of the infinite majesty of God, "Who are you?" three would answer. The one would say: "I am the Father"; the second would say; "I am the Son"; and third would say: "I am the Holy Spirit."

If we continued our childlike questioning and asked, "What, then, are you?" each of the three would answer: I am God, the one self-subsisting, eternal, infinite being that knows no partner or second. Behold the mystery of all mysteries. We are amazed at a truth that seems to go counter to a fundamental principle — one thing cannot be three things. Yet we know that in God there is no contradiction. For the Father is equal to the Son; both Father and Son are indeed equal to the Holy Spirit; for all three are God, and there is no inequality in God. Yes, all three are equal in *what* they are — that is, in their nature — but that does not prove that the three are identical in *who* they are.

The Father is the well-spring of the Deity; He is the common root, source, and principle of divine life and love. The Father is the Father because He is eternally begetting His Son. The Father brings forth His Son as a person in His own image and likeness; He gives His own Godhead to the Son while remaining God Himself. The Father begets His Son by an infinite act of self-knowledge, utters Him as an infinite object of His thought. Herein lies a wonderful mystery of divine life: the divine mind is a two-fold subsistence or Person, that of divine Sayer and that of the divine Word Said — eternally distinct in infinite otherness yet eternally together in absolute equality.

How is this divine generation like human generation? What has it in common with human generation? Quite naturally, we get our notion of generation from creatures. Yet we know that in God is found in perfection all the good that is found scattered in creatures. This is true of generation. "I bow my knees to the Father of our Lord Jesus Christ, of whom all paternity in heaven and earth is named," says St. Paul (Eph. 3:14–15). Divine and human generation have this in common: the production of a living thing by another living thing from its own substance, conveying thereby its own nature to the thing produced. In God, the sameness of nature is sameness in number and therefore identity; in man, it is only in kind and therefore only similitude. We say "conveying thereby" in order to indicate the very purpose, aim, and direction of the act of production. In generation, the very originating act must have for aim and formal object the production of this sameness of nature, the very imparting of the nature of the giver to the one who receives the gift. The Second Person in the Godhead is produced because the Father wills to utter and attest Himself, to express and manifest His own nature. The Son receives the Father's nature in order to exhibit and manifest it in Himself. The Son is a real, substantial, personal image of His Father. Here we have the infinitely perfect ideal of all generation, the infinitely perfect ideal of all fatherhood in God the Father. Created fatherhood here below is but a lightsome shadow, a faint outline and replica of the everlasting, great reality above. In the human title of "father," there is but a created similitude of the might and majesty, the dignity and awful grandeur, the tenderness and understanding that lies in the divine name "Father" as known by the only-begotten Son of God. A ray of the glory of that fatherhood has travelled the infinite distance between God and man and shone on our world here below. In the prism of our materiality, this ray has been broken and divided that it might be shared by men and women in a distinct way, thus displaying the riches of the parenthood of God.

The Son is the living image of His Father, the Word so called because He is the thought of the Father. He is the Son only because He is being eternally begotten of the Father. The Son is indeed the second Person of the Blessed Trinity, but He is neither second in time nor second in nature. He exists co-eternally with His Father. Nor is the Son dependent on the Father, for the Son could not not-exist. He exists by the same divine, eternal necessity as the Father Himself. Hence, the Son is neither inferior nor unequal. The Son is not outside the Father, but His is within for His being within the bosom of the Father. The Son is the brightness of God's glory and the figure of His substance, upholding all things by His power (see Heb. 1:2–3).

The third Person of the Blessed Trinity is a Spirit of Holiness. Holiness in God is the will and enjoyment of His own infinite goodness. It is the love of His own infinite being. Now love seems to demand some duality of lover and beloved. Our human reason might have faintly surmised that perhaps this might be true even of the Godhead, but we could never have known the fact. God has deigned to reveal that it is indeed so, and that it is so in a way beyond our understanding. God as Holiness—that is, as love or will—is a distinct Person breathed out by the Father and Son. We human beings, when speaking of such ineffable things, must use analogies and metaphors. We picture to ourselves, as it were, how out of the embrace of the Father and the Son—i.e., the infinite knower and the infinitely known—there leaps forth the third—the infinite beloved—and each of the three is the same one God, with all the fullness of divine intelligence and will. Thus, we have the infinite, eternal life of the three-in-one being, knowledge and joy. The Holy Spirit is the breath of love, the life of love, the bond of love, existing between the Father and Son. He is the Person of the Trinity who proceeds from the inner intensity, the inner activity, and the inner effusion and torrent of love in which the Father and the Son fuse and pour forth their divine nature. That is why the Holy Spirit is symbolized in the roaring wind that shook the house of the apostles and in the darting, flaming tongues that hovered over the heads of these same holy men. He is the subsistent will, love, and bounty of God. Hence also, He is another Paraclete, the supreme gift of God to God and of God to man. He completes the infinite unity of knowledge and love in the family of the Holy Trinity.

Unity, peace, and love in the life of the Holy Trinity. The divine nature and substance is one in all three Persons, and these in turn are one with the essence from which they are really distinct, just as they are not distinct from one another in essence. They are one supreme Being, *una summa res.* The union and the community among the Persons appears in higher relief when we reflect that not only are any of the two Persons immediately related and united to each other but that each of the three Persons is in His own way a center and focus to which the other two are related, and in which They are united to each other.

The Father unites the other two Persons with and in Himself as their common root and source, for He is the common principle of both. He alone is the principle of the Son, and together with the Son is the principle of the Holy Spirit—not only mediately, not merely through the Son, but immediately as one principle with the Son. Contrariwise, the Holy Spirit unites the Father and the Son with and in Himself, not as Their principle, but as the product of Their mutual love, in which They manifest Their unity and show Themselves to be one Spirit of love. The Holy Spirit is the crown, the seal of unity in the Trinity, as the Father is its root and source. Lastly, the Son is neither principle nor product of the two other Persons. He is the product of the Father and the principle of the Holy Spirit. As such, He occupies a central position and is thus a link that joins the other persons in Himself to form a golden chain. His birth from the Father is the essential prerequisite for the procession of the Holy Spirit, so much so that the Holy Spirit's relationship to the Father cannot even be conceived without the Son. The union of the Holy Spirit with the Father, like His distinction from the Father, is conceivable only in the Son and through the Son.

Nowhere in the Divine Family do we perceive a division, a partition, a separation, or even a distinction that does not imply the principle of union and unity. Everything in the Holy Trinity is unity in the highest and most beautiful sense of the word, embracing the concepts of harmony and love. The Trinity does not destroy unity and simplicity in God: rather, the ineffable unity and simplicity of God is gloriously manifested in its full force and grandeur only through the unutterably lovable Persons of the Trinity. Such is the marvelous life of God; such is the immeasurable ocean of power, light, and love that dazzles our minds and overwhelms our hearts.

We are called to be partakers of this divine nature. We are called to live in the depths of God's life, to experience the inexpressible delights of the Godhead. We men are slow enough in admitting our fellow men to the intimacy of our soul. We show the outside, but not many are permitted to see the innermost truth about ourselves as we ourselves know it. Only the dearest friends are invited to enter into the secrecy of our mind and will. We zealously guard the full reality against all intruders; only in close confidence do we allow our bosom friends sometimes to see us as we are, when all veils are drawn away.

When God, who stood aloof from sinful mankind for many generations, at last came to redeem mankind and make them again His darling children, He bethought Himself and admitted them to the secrets of His divine intimacy. He revealed that within the Godhead there were three divine Persons: that there was the Father and His Son and the love between Them both, the Holy Spirit. God allowed us to discern the Trinity that we might adore God not merely for what He has done for us but for what He is in Himself. He told us the truth about Himself as far as mortal mind could understand it, or perhaps a bit beyond our grasp. He spoke to us about Himself as only a friend dare speak to a friend. But, marvel of all marvels, He came to dwell within us. "Know you not," says St. Paul, "that you are the temple of God, and that the Spirit of God dwelleth in you?" (1 Cor. 3:16). And our Blessed Lord has said, "If any one love me, he will keep my word, and my Father will love him, and we will come to him, and will make our abode with him" (John 14:23). Hence, we read in St. John: "He that abideth in charity abideth in God, and God in him" (1 John 4:16). For "In this we know that we abide in him, and he in us: because he hath given us of his spirit" (1 John 4:13). And when he depicts the purpose of the Incarnation, St. John says it was "that ... our fellowship may be with the Father and with his Son" (1 John 1:3).

A retreat is a time of fellowship with God. Let us walk before God these days and be perfect, that we may live with the Holy Trinity within us. Let us beg God to increase our love and to give us a deep appreciation for the divine family to which He has raised us. Let us relish the eternal unity, love, and wisdom of God by turning our minds and hearts calmly yet seriously to the God who dwells within us. For during these days especially, we are the Temple of God. During these days especially, "the charity of God is poured forth in our hearts by the Holy Ghost, who is given to us" (Rom. 5:5). During these days especially, all we who are making this retreat are to be "careful to keep the unity of the Spirit in the bond of peace" (Eph. 4:3). For we who are to be led in this retreat by the Spirit of God are indeed the sons of God (see Rom. 8:14).

Confer: Matthias Joseph Scheeben, *The Mysteries of Christianity*.

Arendzen, *The Holy Trinity*.

SECOND MEDITATION

The End of Man

"What doth it profit a man, if he gain the whole world,
and suffer the loss of his own soul? Or what exchange
shall a man give for his soul?" (Matt. 16:26).

SOME FOUR HUNDRED years ago, a wounded veteran lay bored to
death in a hospital. He was an ambitious, brave soldier, proud of his
noble lineage in the house of Loyola. Yet he had all the failings of the
ordinary soldier of his day. He called for the latest popular romance
stories. There were none on hand. Fretfully, he snapped; "Give me
anything you have then." He was handed two books—a *Life of Christ*
and the *Lives of the Saints*. Disgusted, he threw them aside. Finally,
in a desperate attempt to conquer his boredom and take his mind off
the pain in his wounded leg, he reluctantly began to read.

As he read, a wonderful change took place in the soul of Ignatius
of Loyola. He compared the magnificent lives of Christ and the saints
with his own life, thus far miserably and selfishly spent in the pursuit
of the empty military glory of a professional soldier. He thought of his
boredom over his confinement in this hospital with "nothing to do
and no place to go." And suddenly, with the inward light of grace, he
saw how much he really had to do to save his soul and how, whether
he liked it or not, he *was* going somewhere. It all depended on which

place *he* chose. For the first time in his life, Ignatius realized to the depth of his soul the meaning of life: Man is a pilgrim and is made to praise, reverence, and serve God and thus to save his soul. What was he, Ignatius, doing about it now; what was he going to do about it in the future? We know what he did about it. The sick soldier rose from his bed a sinner, but he began a life that made him a great saint.

"God created me." Have you ever thought of the love, power, and goodness of God that is shown forth in those three words: "God created me"? Not many years ago, certainly less than a hundred, all here present were nothing. We did not exist, we just were not, we were *no thing*! Yet here we are today, alive and sitting in this beautiful temple of God. We are enjoying existence and know we will continue to exist forever. We have minds that can soar beyond the conditions of space and time. Our souls are restless and unsatisfied and hunger for eternal happiness, reaching out to possess God Himself. We run and rule this earth, with millions of creatures obeying our commands.

Let us reflect. Why was there nothing and then suddenly something? Why was there nothing and then magnificent man? Why was there nothing and then lucky I? Did God have to make something? No, He is, was, and always will be supremely and infinitely happy all alone. He needs nothing. Was God perhaps lonesome that He sought the company of men when He said: "Let us make man to our image and likeness" (Gen. 1:26)? From all eternity, God lives in the Blessed Company of the three divine Persons: a Father of infinite power, a Son of infinite wisdom, and a Holy Spirit of infinite love — three infinitely lovable Persons in the family of the Holy Trinity. No loneliness in that glorious family! What, then, could God want from me to make Him create me?

That's just it! God does not create to *get*; He creates to *give*! "Because He is good," says St. Augustine, "we exist." God created us to share His infinite goodness with us, to communicate His divine perfections to us. Because goodness is diffusive of itself and tends to pour itself out on others, God, who is infinite goodness, created other beings to pour His goodness into them so that they could in some degree share His happiness with Him.

But how did God create all things? From nothing. There was first a void, then at God's will there was something. We can't explain the mystery of creation; we have no experience of creation in our lives; everything we make, we make out of something already existing. Creation is a truth beyond and above the power of our intellects. No wonder! Infinite power alone can create; our finite minds cannot understand infinite power. Yet God used His infinite power to create me. Yes, but why me? Because He loved me. This is the mystery of infinite love for me. He alone knows why He chose me. Yet God gives testimony that His divine love made Him choose me: "Yea, I have loved thee with an everlasting love, therefore have I drawn thee, taking pity on thee" (Jer. 31:3). Isn't it wonderful! God drew us out of the black abyss of nothingness because He loved us. From all eternity He has loved us. Since we were nothing, certainly we had nothing in us to make God love us. Why, then, did He love us? His infinite goodness alone can solve this mystery. All we can do is repeat with St. Augustine: "Because He is good, we exist." Behold how completely we depend from our very first beginnings on the power, the love, and the goodness of God! "God created me" means that I exist because God has infinite power over me, infinite love toward me, and infinite goodness to share with me. I came from God; I am proceeding from Him continually as a ray of being from an infinite fountain of being. As St. Paul says: "In him we live, and move, and are" (Acts 17:28). On Him we depend for our existence, for our life, for every one of our vital activities. We belong to God, to God solely, to God always, completely to God.

We are the handiwork of God. Our bodies were formed through those powers and processes of generation with which God endowed living matter when He called the world and all things in it out of nothingness. Our souls, when their vesture of clay was once prepared, came into existence by an immediate *fiat*, an act of God's will. Hence, we belong to God far more than a slave does to his master, a subject to his king, a child to his father. This explains why we owe God the greatest loyalty in all the world. For God, besides being our Owner, our King, and our Father, is also our Maker. We owe Him the loyalty of a creature to its Creator, a loyalty in harmony with the intelligent nature given to us by our Creator.

One fine spring day, the Curé of Ars was walking in the fields visiting some of his parishioners who were tilling their farms. It was blossom time, and the whole countryside was beautiful to behold. In the budding trees, the birds were singing gaily and profusely. Quite pleased with their songs, the Curé remarked to his companions: "All nature blesses God, and the birds are singing his praises." Then he sadly shook his head, adding, "Only man refuses to love God."

Just as the whole realm of nature and the birds praise God by using their powers and perfections, so we, too, must praise God with the powers He has given us. Irrational creatures necessarily praise God, for they have no spiritual soul or free will to choose to act against their God-given natures. But we humans are much higher creatures. "What is man," asks the psalmist, "that thou art mindful of him? Or the son of man that thou visitest him?" And the answer given is: "Thou hast made him a little less than the angels, thou hast crowned him with glory and honor: and hast set him over the works of thy hands" (Ps. 8:5–6).

"A little less than the angels." That means we have an animal nature; we have vegetative and sensitive life in common with the other living things on the earth. Yet we are also made to the image and likeness of God. That means that like God we are spirits; we possess an intellect and a free will. Hence, when we praise God, we must use our faculties of soul and body in His service. We are the only creatures on this earth who are capable of reading the book of creation, of interpreting how God has revealed Himself in it, and of actively and freely proclaiming in thought, word, and deed the perfections and goodness that their Creator wished to show forth.

We praise God when we freely acknowledge Him as our Lord and Creator. We praise Him when we use our minds to learn more about Him, when we use our free wills to love Him and to follow His laws. We praise God when we use all other creatures to help us in our journey to Him, and when we subordinate our love of these creatures to our love of God. We praise God when we adore Him, when we thank Him for all He has given us, when we ask Him for favors in prayer. We praise God when we offer sacrifice or gifts to Him to show Him that we love Him and wish to serve Him. We Catholics praise God when we lead good Christian lives every day. When we use our faculties to praise, reverence, and serve God, we save our souls. For to do all these things is to follow after the most important law of God: "Hear, O Israel, the Lord our God is one Lord. Thou shalt love the Lord thy God with thy whole heart, and with thy whole soul, with thy whole strength" (Deut. 6:4–5). This is the first and greatest commandment because it expresses the primary purpose of our creation.

We must all be awakened to this fundamental purpose of our existence. We are not to live on this earth forever. This is a place of pilgrimage; we are on trial. We can either accept God's invitation to love and serve Him in this life, and thus ensure eternal happiness for ourselves in the next, or, since we are free creatures, we can reject this invitation. But God, who has poured His blessings upon us, is not mocked. He desires our welfare and salvation, and He does all He can to make our path sweet and easy unto it. But woe betide those who scorn His vast mercies! If we do not accept His love, we will have to endure His justice. If we fail to fulfill the purpose of our existence, we shall show forth the perfections of God in a way that will cause us sorrow for all eternity. For instead of partaking in the intimate life and love of God for which we were created, we will be separated from God in terrible pain for all eternity. We will mirror in ourselves that divine justice that cannot approve evil, for since evil freely rejects God, it cannot find a place in the presence of the divine goodness or in the Kingdom of Heaven.

Remember this: God created all men for Himself and Heaven; He never wills any man to be condemned independently of that man's own free will. Because men are free, they can and do reject God's love. Yet God gives all men, even the most evil, all the graces and helps necessary to save their souls. Men must freely accept these graces. Men lose their souls because they reject God, not because God rejects them. God, who has made us without our consent, will not save us without our cooperation. God does not sentence us to Hell as much as we sentence ourselves. When the cage is opened, the bird flies out into the open air that it loves; when the body dies, the soul flies out into eternity for which it was made. But the soul in the state of sin at the moment of death flies out into the place of sin, which it loves just as naturally as a stone released from my hand falls to the ground. It does this freely, for it has freely chosen sin. God has not a different mood for those who go to Hell and for those who go to Heaven. The difference is in us, not in Him. The sun that shines on wax softens it; the sun that shines on mud hardens it. There is no difference in the sun but only in that upon which it shines.

Hence, we must follow God in doing what is good and avoiding what is evil. Like Him, we must wish that all men be saved, detesting sin whether in ourselves or in our neighbor. We must try to root out all evil in ourselves so that we may better be conformed to God's holiness. In proportion as we do this, we shall also be working good in others. We Catholics are called to be the outward expression, the very embodiment of God's goodness to man, that through us and in us, all outside the Church may come to know and love Him who has loved them first. And the crown of this holiness is salvation; the end set before us is that we should finally be sanctified by the vision of God Himself. Not satisfied in merely revealing to us some perfections of the family of the Holy Trinity, God wishes to reward us, after faithful service in this life, by bringing us into the inner and supreme joys of His divine family, making us new children of this family, "partakers of the divine nature" (2 Pet. 1:4).

We Americans especially must realize the truth of why we are on this earth. Material success and even good health often more readily persuade men to live as if they were not pilgrims traveling on to reward or punishment. This false sense of security is common to many of our people. Because they have their own position, their own home and car, and trust that their insurance and other investments will take care of the future, many men live as if this life were the be-all and end-all of their existence. The truth is that a man's whole life, from birth to death on this planet, is but an infinitesimal fraction of his future, which is eternity. That is why our Blessed Lord warns us in these words: "What does it profit a man, if he gain the whole world, but suffer the loss of his own soul? Or what return will a man give in exchange for his soul?" (Matt. 16:26).

And so we Americans, as a nation, are guilty of the sin of indifference; we don't deny God as much as ignore Him. We are secularists, immersed in the things of this earth to the exclusion of God. We are too busy to find time for God and the things of God. Housewives are busy running their children all over town, washing, scrubbing, and cooking, and they have little time to take sides with God against the forces of evil. The tensions of a hurried world leave the working man or woman exhausted and with little time or energy to devote to the care of his or her soul. Yet we must stop and reflect on how short and transitory this life is. We realize with St. Paul that "we have not here a lasting city, but we seek one that is to come" (Heb. 13:14).

Today, at the start of our retreat, is a good time to check up on our lives. Are we living such that we realize where we are going? Is the place we are headed for the right one? Is it God we are seeking or our own selfish interests on earth? Are we bored with life because we don't understand the wonderful destiny for which we have been made? I'm afraid many of us are. Sadly, I often see young men and women just graduated from college who no sooner set out on the seas of life than they are disgusted with the journey. No wonder! With a secular education behind them that ignores God, they know nothing about the purpose of life. Can anything be more unbearable than to sail into an awful void, not knowing where one is going or whether there is another shore? People without purpose in life suffer from anxiety, frustration, and psychoses. They often try to satisfy the infinite longing of their hearts for happiness by feeding on the husks of sin. They do not know the true explanation of the purpose of life; or if they do, they ignore it to their own destruction. When will they realize that man is composed of soul and body and that he is specially placed in the environment about him? When will they realize that the mind was meant to know all truth; that the body was meant to enjoy its pleasures for the sake of the soul; and that the world was made to serve the body and soul for the sake of God? This is the only true order that banishes boredom, anxieties, and fears. This is the only order that gives peace, the peace of being a friend and child of God. This is the peace St. Ignatius found when he realized and began to live for the sublime destiny for which God created man.

Don't expect perfect happiness here in this world, because creatures cannot satisfy the infinite longings of our souls. Only God can do that. Hence, don't waste time chasing impossible wealth or passing pleasures. You can't take them with you into eternity. Why, then, allow such creatures to prevent you from attaining eternal happiness? A moderate use of creatures as steppingstones to God is in accordance with our end of life. Our friends, the joys of marriage, the thrill of possessions, magnificent sunsets, masterpieces of music and art, gold and silver, our industries and the comforts they give us—all these and millions of other creatures are gifts of God, dropped on the roadway of life to help us attain the Infinite Beauty who draws us to Himself through the beauty He has placed in them. All these are bridges over which we must cross to God. The only conceivable reason why God could create us men and all things is to diffuse His own inexhaustible perfections upon us, to shower down upon us from His bosom "the depth of the riches of the wisdom and of the knowledge of God," the depths of the riches of His goodness and love (Rom. 11:33). It is God for whom we were made; it is God whom our souls desire. St. Augustine perfectly expresses the end of man when he writes: "Thou hast made us for Thyself, O Lord, and our hearts are restless until they rest in Thee" (*Confessions* 1:1).

The Filial Spirit of the Children of God

PERHAPS THE MOST important Christian dogma, but not well understood by the faithful, is the dogma of our divine adoption as children of God. All know the Trinity, the Incarnation, and the Resurrection, but very few seem to realize just why the Word became flesh and what it is that He has bought back for us. As a matter of fact, although Christ poured out His Blood for the sins of the world, the Lamb of God first of all offered Himself to expiate the very first sin ever committed and from which all other sins flowed. We know that Adam had been elevated to the supernatural order, that is to say, he constituted an adopted son of God. He was to transmit this marvelous destiny, this gift of divine sonship, to all his children, a great privilege and one that was the marvel of the angels and of all of Heaven. If Adam had obeyed His Creator, he would have had the rights and the inheritance of the only-begotten Son of God, the Second Person of the Blessed Trinity. But when he sinned, Adam rejected this sublime destiny and fell from the exalted state of divine sonship, dragging his whole family, the human race, with him. Yet God in His goodness did not want to cancel forever the marvelous plans He had for the human race. So St. Paul tells us: "But when the fullness of the time was come, God sent his Son, made of a woman, made under the law: that he might redeem them who were under the law: that we might receive the adoption of sons" in order to restore these lost privileges to us (Gal. 4:4–5). For the Apostle also writes: "You have not received the spirit of bondage again in fear; but you have received the spirit of adoption of sons, whereby we cry: Abba (Father)" (Rom. 8:15). This spirit of adoption is the harmony of those supernatural dispositions that give a Christian the desire and ideal to imitate Christ, his elder brother, his model, as a son of God. In order to develop in ourselves this filial spirit of children of God, we must understand what opposes it, what traits of souls are characteristic of it, and whence it comes.

The spirit of soul that opposes the spirit of divine adoption.

1. It scarcely needs mentioning that the spirit of independence and revolt is not filial. This was the crime of Lucifer — "I will not serve" — and the spirit with which he seduced our first parents: Eat this fruit, "and you shall be as Gods" (Gen. 3:5). Instead, when we know the truth, we become like God — through grace, through humility, through docility, through imitating Christ.

2. The spirit of servitude and of fear is opposed to the filial spirit. Notice well that there is a servile fear of a slave through which a slave obeys his master for fear of chastisement or the rod, yet the slave wishes in his heart to violate his master's laws, if only he could get away with it.

Then there is simple servile fear. This fear has at least the beginning of respect and love. Here the servant not only renounces the evils forbidden but even does not wish or desire such evils in his heart because they displease his master, who has been benevolent to him. This fear aids the servant to perform his duties faithfully; this reverential fear is said to be the beginning of wisdom. God instilled this fear in His Chosen People under the Old Dispensation through the promulgation of His Law on Mt. Sinai, through the threats of His prophets, and through the severe chastisements for the people's idolatry. It was necessary to use these punishments and this type of servile fear to maintain this "stiff-necked" people in obedience to His laws. These times that preceded the first coming of Christ are called the times of "the law of fear." Not that many of the just of the old Law did not appreciate and experience God's tender love as a Father, but the masses of the people scarcely ever looked at God as more than a severe and exacting master. This fear, as you can see, leads one to act from less noble motives in serving God. Hence, it never inspires those it rules to great deeds of love, generosity, or heroic self-sacrifice. Moreover, such fear deprives God of the homage and glory that belong to Him as a Father who loves tenderly all His creatures, especially the sons of men.

All this was changed when Christ came to be one of us, to teach us of the tenderness of the Father. "Behold what manner of charity the Father hath bestowed upon us," says St. John, "that we should be called, and should be the sons of God" (1 John 3:1). And St. Paul writes, "And if sons, heirs also … and joint heirs with Christ" (Rom. 8:17). Hence, we must change our attitude; we must not be ruled even by that simple servile fear. That is why St. Paul says: "You have not received the spirit of bondage again in fear; but you have received the spirit of adoption of sons, whereby we cry: Abba (Father)" (Rom. 8:15).

Adopted sons of God as we are, elevated to an incomparably high dignity, can we continue to preserve the mentality of a slave? What are the sentiments we ought to cherish to drive out this spirit of servile fear?

The traits of soul characteristic of the filial spirit. Let's suppose that some wealthy Croesus finds an army of slaves living in hovels and squalor. Without any merit on their part, and simply because he dreams of making them happy, he says to these slaves: "I will not only free you from slavery, but I also adopt you as my children. From now on, consider me your father. At my death, my immense riches, beyond all calculations, are yours." What would be the reactions of these poor creatures? Would they prefer to remain in their squalor and destitution?

Only the mad or insane would. What a tremendous privilege to become the sons of the king! And of course the treasures of the king would also bring joy to their hearts. As a matter of fact, no human king of such tremendous generosity has ever been found. Yet God Himself, with the one purpose of making man happy, has decided to make us sharers of the one divine nature even in this life, and He holds out to us happiness with Him not for a hundred years, not for a thousand, and not for a million, but for all eternity. "As many as received him, he gave them power to be made the sons of God, to them that believe in his name" (John 1:12). With this offer, how can we be children of servitude living in fear? To become filial sons, we must be motivated by the spirit of gratitude, submission, and love of God, our Father.

The gratitude of a child of God. We have been honored by God; we have been lifted above ourselves to God's level of dignity; we have been made the brothers of Jesus Christ. Of ourselves, we are nothing; now, with Christ, we enter the very presence of the Trinity. What must be our gratitude! God retouched all our faculties to bring us to Himself; He has transformed us; He has divinized us by infusing sanctifying grace into our souls and coming to live in us with His gifts and all His graces. In our second birth through Baptism, we have become children of God. Such a favor is even above the rights of the seraphim and the cherubim; it was given to us. To show our gratitude to God, we ought to think often of our divine sonship. The remembrance of it will warm our daily lives with the love of so good a Father. We should make frequent acts of thanksgiving, asking God to make us loving children, children of deep devotion and complete dedication to Him and His cause in this life. We should now say the Our Father with renewed love and appreciation. Now when we pray, "Thy kingdom come," we should remember that that kingdom is ours too: our sublime destiny.

The second characteristic of filial spirit is absolute obedience to our Father. We owe God this obedience on the score that He made us creatures; how much more now that He has made us His sons! Our obedience should be inspired and performed with the affection that all true sons have for their father. "My meat is to do the will of him that sent me," says our elder brother Jesus (John 4:34), and we must imitate Him by performing cheerfully and thoroughly whatever is the will of God for us. To obey is to love, and children prove their love through their obedience. "Did you not know that I must be about my father's business?" asked Jesus of His Holy Mother (Luke 2:49). Even in this life, a father who adopts a child has true authority over her and seeks her love in her devotion to him through obedience. How much easier can we be obedient, for, as our Lord tells us: "My yoke is sweet and my burden light" (Matt. 11:30). And St. Gregory says: "It is not hard to obey where we love Him who commands." God our Father commands; resolve to love and obey Him in all piety and filial devotion.

Whence comes this filial spirit? This childlike love and devotion of God, so recommended by our Savior, is infused into us at our new birth in baptism. It comes not from earth but from Heaven. "God," says St. Paul, "hath sent the Spirit of his Son into your hearts, crying: Abba, Father. Therefore now he is not a servant, but a son" (Gal. 4:6–7). "Whosoever are led by the Spirit of God, they are the sons of God" (Rom. 8:14). The Holy Spirit, the Spirit of Jesus, is given to us in order to assist us, to, as it were, be at our service, just as the love of parents is placed at the service of children. The Holy Spirit stirs up our love, our confidence, and our childlike trust in God, our Father. The Holy Spirit produces in our souls the three theological virtues of faith, hope, and charity and all the moral virtues. Uniting Himself to our faculties, the Holy Spirit penetrates them, elevates them without destroying their nature, and makes us constantly live and think and act and love the way Jesus lived and thought and acted and loved. "Let this mind be in you, which was also in Christ Jesus" (Phil 2:5). That is what the Holy Spirit is working to produce in us with His grace and our cooperation with this grace. Hence, when we allow the

Holy Spirit to have His way in us, he so perfects us as children of God that the Father, looking down on us, sees Jesus in us and says: "This is my beloved Son, in whom I am well pleased" (Matt. 3:17). The Father Himself cannot refuse to help us become more like His Son, since He sent His Son and the Holy Spirit to us precisely to make us become like Himself through the imitation of His Incarnate Son.

"He who is joined to the Lord," says St. Paul, "is one spirit" (1 Cor. 6:17). When we cling to the Holy Spirit by our cooperation with His inspirations and illuminations, we become one spirit with Him, and children like to Jesus. In order, then, to become worthy of increasing in this filial spirit as children of God, let us meditate often during this year on this truth: We have been made partakers of the divine nature; the Holy Spirit has been sent into our hearts, thereby making us children of God; no longer are we under the law of fear, but under the law of love. Keep your eyes and desires fixed upon your elder brother Jesus Christ, who has come to earth not only to repair our sins, but also to reveal to us by His preaching and by His own goodness the ineffable goodness of His Father and ours in order to show us by His example how to love as children of God. Beg the Holy Spirit, the Paraclete, to teach you how to pray, to help you in every duty of your religious lives, and to inspire you to obey the way Jesus obeyed, with fidelity and with the same intentions: not of fear but of filial love. If we live in this way, then the words of St. John will be happily verified in us: "When he [Jesus, our elder brother] shall appear [at the time of the particular and general judgment], we shall be like to him: because we shall see him as he is" (1 John 3:2). St. Bernard says: "To see Him as He is, is nothing else than to be just like Him, to have imitated Him so well that now while still keeping our own personalities, we are lost in God, absorbed, drowned in His Infinite Goodness and happiness, with Jesus, as His most darling children."

Confer: Pinard de la Boullay, S.J., *Exercices Spirituels*, vol. 4, pp. 3–20.

THIRD MEDITATION
Creatures

LET US STAND, with reverence and love, in the spirit of our Blessed Lord, on a very high mountain. Above, we see our Creator and Lord; at our feet are all other created beings, all the kingdoms of the world and the glory of them (see Matt. 4:8). Listen to the inspired voice of St. Paul: "for all things are yours ... and you are Christ's; and Christ is God's" (1 Cor. 3:22–23).

All creatures are good; we must love them. "The other things on the face of the earth are created for man to help him in the pursuit of the end for which he is created," says St. Ignatius. Creatures will best help us only if we fully appreciate and properly evaluate them. The good and wise Catholic loves all creatures first of all because they come from God. All things and persons, and all their innumerable activities, spring from the creative power of God, and consequently, they are all good—that is to say, full of the power and sap of being, consistent, nutritive, invigorating, desirable, and capable of enriching and exalting man. "And God saw that it was good"—that is the refrain that punctuates the account of creation in Genesis, and St. Paul echoes it back: "for every creature of God is good, and nothing to be rejected that is received with thanksgiving" (1 Tim. 4:4). From the very moment that anything exists, that thing is good and worthy of our love. Every reality is an image of God. Before He brought it into being, He conceived it in

His mind; it was born of His knowledge and of His love; and that is why it always carries with it—for those who have eyes to see—a reflection of His beauty. There is an indestructible reflection even in the sinner, who in spite of his sin is still called by God and is still a son of God in expectation and hope. There is a reflection even in the damned, who are still spirits and tragically destined to know and love the God they have rejected. All activity reflects the divine activity. God gives existence and gives life, and the effort by which man discovers, makes, and brings anything to realization is a distant image of the divine activity. God knows Himself and loves Himself; and human knowledge and love are an image of God's life. From the very beginning, all creatures were stamped with the supernatural, at least in their use. They were destined to serve men, the created adopted sons of God. No wonder there is no thing or activity incapable of attracting us. True, sin came upon the scene. But if sin wounded everything, it has corrupted nothing. In spite of the original transgression, everything still bears the divine imprint, everything remains capable of true orientation and a genuine, holy use; what is wounded can be healed. All is redeemed in Christ in principle; and the divine benediction redescends on things and men and the actions of men. The Church has never thought that things are bad; it is man's heart that is bad when he uses things ill and makes them groan beneath a perverted yoke. Yet we know that the heavens never cease to declare the glory of God; man has received his vocation as a son of God, and God still insists that he retain it. Human activity remains always destined to perfect the universe and to save souls. Creatures and temporal activities may be wounded and dangerous because of sin, yet they remain innocent and always worthy of love.

In the beginning, before sin, man was one with creation, and it was for him to give it its meaning and to effect its fulfillment. As long as man's heart remained within the divine order, creatures also worked harmoniously with him in the service of God. From the day when his heart was turned away from God, when his interior powers were dislocated because he no longer loved God above all things, when his eyes were blinded to the light that lit up things with all their meaning—then, for him, all things fell apart into disunity and disorientation, each reverted to its own brute value and became pliable to any and every end. Since that time, our love of creatures has had to be a love at grips with evil. The root of this mischief lies in the fact that by sin, creatures have been severed from God. Man, instead of being content to give his love to creatures, gave them his preference over God, made them his be-all and end-all, so that his love, now become idolatry, ended in a positive exclusion of the divine and the eternal from his life. Hence, he became like a beast governed not by his divine aspirations but by his lusts: carnal lusts for money or for pleasure, spiritual lusts for power over matter or over his fellow man. His cult of money issued in general misery; his cult of pleasure in physical or moral collapse; his cult of power in war. In the present meditation, we are not asked to hate creatures but rather to purge all idolatry from our love of creatures, to return whole-heartedly to the one absolute love of our lives, the love of God and of beatitude in God. He is asking us to love all "the other things on the face of the earth" with a love in accord with our first love, animated and safeguarded by our supreme love, a love that prefers God above all things.

For Christians, Christ, the God-man, is the perfect example of one who had true love for creatures. How often Christ showed His love for creatures, and how often His brotherly heart went out toward His Father's creatures! In each of them He read the message left by the touch of divine love. Birds and flowers spoke to Him of the creative goodness; the harvests ripened in His eye to the image of another harvest; the cockle mingled in the corn pictured that other terrible mingling with which His own would have to live. And when He recited the psalms, it was all the universe that glorified God on His lips; for He alone, the center of all cries, desires, and supplications, could sovereignly gather up the praise of the whole creation and offer it to His Father in one immeasurable act of homage. He did not sing the glory of work, but He worked at the carpenter's bench to the point of being identified with His profession. He gives us a glimpse of His taste for good work in some of His parables. In one (the wheat and the cockle; see Matt. 13:24–43), we have the misery of work spoilt; in another (good and bad servants; see Matt. 24:45–51), the need for religious earnestness in the daily task; in yet another (talents; see Matt. 25:14–30), the call to serve with all our strength. He chose His apostles from the ranks of the workers; and for the last, the thirteenth, He would have a Hebrew of the Hebrews, a Greek in formation and withal a Roman citizen, thus combining all human resources—religious, cultural, political—in him who was to be the conqueror of the Greco-Roman world. He made a point of sharing men's sufferings, of providing for their humblest needs, of healing all their most fleshly ills. He knew affection and friendship. He acknowledged his racial ties with His own people and, foreseeing the doom of Jerusalem, He did as the weakest among us would do and wept at her fall.

The Lord Jesus loved and sanctified every creature. His attitude toward them is our law and our rule of life. The love of God's creatures, of human joys, of human endeavor, is not merely permitted us but commanded: we, too, have to love these things if we would be like Christ and accomplish our task. Like Christ, we must not condemn creatures but attempt to rectify and transform a strayed love of creatures into a God-ward love of them.

The Rule of Indifference. Christ has taught us: "Seek ye therefore first the kingdom of God, and his justice, and all these things shall be added unto you" (Matt. 6:33). "What shall it profit a man to gain the whole world and lose his soul?" (Matt. 16:26). "No man can serve two masters" (Matt. 6:24). "It is better for thee with one eye to enter into the kingdom of God, than, having two eyes, to be cast into the hell of fire" (Mark 9:46). The meaning is clear. God must be the first desired, the first sought, the first served. Toward all other creatures, man must adopt an attitude of liberty of heart. Although he loves them, he will only use them in so far as they help him to attain His God. Should they hinder him from this end, man will restrain himself from their use, remembering always the wise words of St. Paul: "For the rest, brethren, whatsoever things are true, whatsoever modest, whatsoever just, whatsoever holy, whatsoever lovely, whatsoever of good fame, if there be any virtue, if any praise of discipline, think on these things" (Phil. 4:8).

The active spirit of detachment and indifference frees man's love from bondage to the creature because his love goes first to God and the eternal; in attachment to God, man finds freedom from the world; in adherence to God, man enjoys deliverance from the yoke of creatures. Instead of becoming bad masters, creatures become for men good servants in the hands of rightful love. When a man habitually suspends the choice of his will in choosing creatures until he sees which choice is better for his advancement to God, he practices that evangelical love of creatures that is a love of the visible based on a love of the invisible; a love of things created straining past things to the Creator; a temporal love proclaiming the eternal love. This is the love and use of creatures that our Blessed Lord expressed when He said: "My meat is to do the will of him that sent me" (John 4:34).

There will be natural attractions and repulsions in our relations to creatures. These are involuntary, the instinctive dislikes and likes of our nature. True liberty of heart and indifference toward creatures is quite consistent with these indeliberate movements of the will. For indifference is not apathy, nor does it lead to a leaden nature. Our blessed Lord, prostrate in an agony of fear and sorrow, could yet pray and make the following heroic choice: "Father, if thou wilt, remove this chalice from me: but yet not my will, but thine be done" (Luke 22:42). Here is the perfect spirit of indifference and liberty of heart from all creatures, that self-poise and equilibrium of the will that is ready to choose all that is most repugnant naturally—even a most cruel death—if such be the will of God.

Sometimes, creatures are dangers and obstacles on the path to God, and they have to be sacrificed. Cut off thy hand, pluck out thine eye, if so it must be to enter into life! Sometimes creatures help us to rejoin God. That is why St. Ignatius advises indifference to all creatures. He writes:

> For which purpose [to attain our eternal destiny] it is necessary to make ourselves indifferent to all created things, in all that is allowed to the freedom of our free choice and is not forbidden it; in such sort that we do not desire on our part health rather than sickness, riches rather than poverty, honor rather than dishonor, a long life rather than a short one, and so of all the rest, only desiring and choosing that which better leads us to the end for which we are created.

The true Christian loves creatures because he loves God, whom they reflect. Yet as a clear-sighted and decided man, he knows that because of sin, all creatures stand in need of purification. He knows, too, that in Christ and through Christ all things are capable of being purified. He recognizes that the universe has but one principle of consistence, of movement, and of fulfillment, and that principle is Christ: "For in him were all things created in heaven and on earth, visible and invisible ... all things were created by him and in him. And he is before all, and by him all things consist" (Col. 1:16–17).

Christ is thus the great Assembler who works in the depths of souls and in the depths of creatures to sanctify all, to unify all, to consecrate all to the glory of God. To this gigantic work the true Christian freely pledges himself—at this place, in this hour, and with all his resources. Remember, you do not work alone; you collaborate.

Confer: Jean Mouroux, *The Meaning of Man*.

SECOND DAY

Purpose: To attain a sense of my own sinfulness

Patron: The Holy Angels

Points for Self-Consideration:

- Am I influenced at this stage of my life by any worldly ideals and principles?
- Is there evidence of any disordered attachment in my life?

Suggested Readings:

Romans 6

Imitation of Christ, bk. 1, ch. 21

Spiritual Exercises: Additions and Notes

Aspiration:

"For everyone that doth evil hateth the light, and cometh not to the light, that his works may not be reproved." (John 3:20)

FIRST MEDITATION

Sin

ST. JOHN CHRYSOSTOM, the famous Archbishop of Constantinople, brought down upon his head the hatred of Queen Eudoxia. He had courageously stigmatized the evils of her court. The queen decided to put away this plain preacher. Calling her counselors, she said: "Tell me the best way of getting rid of this brash bishop." "Banish him," suggested one. "Take away all his property," advised another. "Put him in prison," said still another. "Put him to death," recommended a fourth. Finally, one who seemed to know the saintly archbishop well spoke: "Your Majesty, to banish Chrysostom is useless: he already considers this life a banishment. Take away everything he has, and he will be as happy as ever; he hates the things of earth. Put him in prison, and he will be just as cheerful as ever; he is already in prison in the cage of his body. Kill him and he will consider it a service; death to him will be but the door to a better life. If you really want to do him harm, to punish him, devise some means of leading Chrysostom into sin. Sin is the only thing he dreads, the only evil he fears."

What did St. John Chrysostom see in sin to make him dread, despise, and shun it? He saw and deeply abhorred the nature of sin: an act by which a creature rebels against His Creator, offends Him, and refuses Him reverence and love. What does this rebellion imply? When God made us free, He took a chance on us, just as any father takes a chance when he gives freedom to his children. Will they abuse their precious gift of freedom and become rebels? God made us to choose only what is right, but we are able to choose what is wrong. To fully understand sin, we must fully understand God's original plan for our happiness. Let's reconstruct the scene.

In the very beginning, God, in His infinite love, made man a child of His own family. Adam and Eve were created in holiness; sanctifying grace adorned their souls. In them the human race was elevated by this grace to the dignity of partakers of the divine nature. Yet in freely and generously making us His sons and daughters, God would not force His happiness upon anyone. It was as if God said to our first parents as He walked with them in the garden: "Children, I have created you as free, intelligent creatures after My own image and likeness. But over and above your natural powers, My love for you has induced Me to give you the supernatural gift of sharing in My divine nature. By reason of this divine sanctifying grace, you are not merely My subjects; you are My darling children. I live within you, and you live in Me. To help you preserve this divine life with Me, I have also added some lesser gifts that do not strictly belong to your human nature. These are: you will never die; your passions will never rebel against your reason; and your mind will be free from error. You *will* preserve your dignity as My children for yourselves and your race — if you obey only one easy commandment. And that commandment is that you must love Me of your own free will. How can you prove that you love Me? Well, love is not love unless it is free. Hence, you can prove that you love Me by abstaining from the fruit of this one tree. For how else is love proved than by an act of choice, by choosing the one we love over something or somebody else? It is only because you are able to say 'No' that you prove you love Me when you freely say 'Yes.' If you choose Me, Heaven and happiness are yours forever. If you reject Me, you lose Me and all My supernatural and lesser gifts. No longer My children, you choose to suffer and die. Will you love Me or reject Me?"

The tragedy of Original Sin is that our first parents rejected God. Despite the infinite love God had generously showered upon them, these adopted children of God rose up against their divine Father; they drove Him and His wonderful gift of sanctifying grace out of their souls. Our first parents, in a most disgraceful and unnatural manner, disavowed their supernatural dignity as children of God. They desecrated and outraged the sublime holiness of God and cut the bond of love that had joined God to creatures.

In insulting God, our first parents also dishonored and disgraced themselves. How? The right relationship to God under all circumstances constitutes the creature's highest dignity and destiny. Sin destroys this right relationship with God; hence, sin also destroys the creature's dignity and destiny. Actually, the sin of our first parents was not unlike suicide. It killed and annihilated the divine, supernatural life of God in the soul, a life that is immensely more precious than the soul itself, to say nothing of the life that the soul imparts to the body. This sin destroyed the most glorious work of God's supernatural grace in the soul. Here again we see the terrible malice of sin. But besides destroying the divine life, it also brought on the death known as the separation of the soul and body, with the body disintegrating back into the dust from which it was taken. Once the supernatural gift of grace and sanctity was lost, those other lesser gifts of bodily immortality, immunity from concupiscence, and freedom from error were all lost. Here we see that Original Sin was a double suicide, for it destroyed natural as well as supernatural life. Do you wonder why St. John Chrysostom abhorred sin? Sin is the greatest evil in all the world. So vast is its wickedness that St. Paul calls sin "the mystery of iniquity" (2 Thess. 2:7). In very truth, sin is a mystery: a mystery whose unfathomable wickedness only He whom it offends can fully understand.

But you will perhaps say: "Granted that Adam sinned and that sin is the most heinous evil in all the world. What have I to do with Adam? Why should I be punished because of his sin?" When the father of a family squanders a millionaire's fortune and dies a pauper, his children suffer the loss of a rich inheritance; they live as paupers. They are treated as paupers by society. The father is the guilty spendthrift, but the children suffer the dire consequences. Adam, our father, was a spiritual millionaire. God gave him the supernatural gift of sanctifying grace, not as something personal but as a good common to the whole human race, a good that all the members of the race were to receive through Adam and from Adam. If Adam had preserved this gift, it would have been preserved for all; but since he destroyed it in himself and discarded it from himself, it was, in consequence, taken away from the whole race. Adam committed the personal Original Sin of destroying sanctifying grace in himself. There, he alone has full responsibility for the physical act of Original Sin. Yet since Adam was the trustee of this common good, he acted with reference to sanctifying grace as the family head of the entire human race. His deed in this connection is considered as the act of all, much like the act of declaring war by the president of this nation is considered an act of war by the whole nation and all its members whom he represents. Hence, Adam's sinful act is imputed to us, his children, and we suffer its dire consequences. Hence, too, we lose sanctifying grace not by any personal guilty act of our own but by reason of an offense common to all the members of the race. At birth, we stand in the sight of God destitute of sanctifying grace, a gift we must have to be pleasing to God, for it was God's original plan that we all be born as his children. Hence, He is displeased to see us born without His grace.

It is this estrangement that constitutes Original Sin. We stand before God as sinners not through any act of our own but as sinners by heredity. Here we see that Original Sin has a double definition: the act of Original Sin that is Adam's personal act, and the state of Original Sin that is our poor inheritance. We are spiritual paupers at birth because of a spendthrift father.

Was it unjust of God to deprive us of His sonship and His other wonderful gifts simply because our first father sinned? No, for these gifts are supernatural gifts. That means that they are goods that are way above our human nature. Hence, we have no right to them either as human beings or as persons. If God does not restore them to each person at birth, He does no man any injustice, even as you do me no injustice if you fail to give me an Easter gift. I have no right to receive, and you have no obligation to give a gift. That is what the word "gift" means: a free offering. All God is bound to give us, granted He once decides to create us, are the perfections demanded by our human nature—our souls and bodies with their respective faculties.

Hence, we see how from birth we are all sinners, even before we are capable of committing our first act of personal sin. The human nature we inherit, although good in itself since it comes from God, is nevertheless disorganized because it has lost those special gifts that were to keep it in perfect harmony within itself and lead it to perfect happiness with God. Sin has weakened our will and darkened our intellect. We have inherited a nature that is turned away from God and has a strong bias toward evil, with a reluctance to do good and a tendency to rationalize our evil. We are aware of a terrible war within us: our passions, like unbridled horses, plunge forward in mad haste to attain their pleasures, so that our reason and our will can scarcely hold them together and assert their rule against them. St. Paul complained of this struggle within himself when he wrote:

For the good which I will, I do not; but the evil which I will not, that I do.... I find then a law, that when I have a will to do good, evil is present with me. For I am delighted with the law of God, according to the inward man: but I see another law in my members, fighting against the law of my mind, and captivating me in the law of sin that is in my members. Unhappy man that I am, who shall deliver me from the body of this death? (Rom. 7:19, 21–24)

Here St. Paul vividly depicts the inner struggle that goes on in all human beings between the lower sensual nature and the higher aspirations of the soul. Because man rebelled against God, his own lower nature rebelled against man. Sin has destroyed our integrity, has blasted that unsullied and undisturbed healthy state that previously had made the life of man so pleasant. Such are only some of the vile and hideous effects of sin in our souls. I pass over quickly the sufferings, sicknesses, wars, and thousands of other disasters that sin has brought down upon the human race.

I prefer to look at what sin has done to the angels, to study it under that aspect. What has sin done to the angels? First of all, sin expelled the angels from Heaven. "I saw Satan like lightning falling from heaven," our Blessed Lord tells us (Luke 10:18). And St. Peter says: "God spared not the angels that sinned, but delivered them, drawn down by infernal ropes to the lower hell, unto torments" (2 Pet. 2:4). These most beautiful creatures in an instant were deformed into hideous devils. They were created holy and of surpassing excellence. Yet in a single act of pride, they loved themselves more than their Creator, rejected God for their own beauty that was a gift of God, and thus sinned. Isaiah tells us of their leader: "And thou saidst in thy heart: I will ascend into heaven, I will exalt my throne above the stars of God ... I will be like the most High" (Isa. 14:13–14).

And of this same Lucifer, the strongest spirit that fought in Heaven and the fairest that lost it, the prophet Ezekiel tells us:

> Thou wast the seal of resemblance, full of wisdom, and perfect in beauty. Thou wast in the pleasures of the paradise of God: every precious stone was thy covering.... Thou a cherub stretched out, and protecting, and I set thee in the holy mountain of God, thou hast walked in the midst of the stones of fire. Thou wast perfect in thy ways from the day of thy creation, until iniquity was found in thee.... Thou hast sinned: and I cast thee out from the mountain of God.... And thy heart was lifted up with thy beauty; thou hast lost thy wisdom in thy beauty. (Ezek. 28:12–17)

Sin created Hell for thousands of God's most beautiful creatures — children of God become rebels, angels become devils.

But the full malice of the mystery of iniquity is seen in what sin did to God. What did sin do to the incarnate Son of God? Sin had destroyed our family relations with God. Man had committed an infinite offense against an infinitely good Father. How could man re-establish his friendly relations with God? Obviously by making amends for his sin, by offering God an infinite apology for the infinite insult, an infinite atonement for the infinite reproach, an infinite payment for an infinite debt. Every insult is measured in seriousness and grievousness by the dignity of the person insulted. Man offended God, hence the insult was infinite. But as creatures who are finite, we are incapable of restoring the infinite dignity of God. Hence, left to ourselves, we could not give God infinite acts of atonement, for atonement is measured in goodness and value by the dignity of the person making the atonement. It was, therefore, simply beyond man's power to win his way back to God's friendship, unless God came to his aid. In His divine love and mercy, God did come to our rescue. He did not condemn us to eternal separation from Himself as He did to the bad angels. The most loving Trinity decreed that the divine Son, the second Person, should become man and rescue His fellow men from sin, thereby restoring man to the sonship of God. Christ became the new Adam: a man like ourselves, yet God, and hence capable as both man and God of offering complete and infinite atonement for the sins of the human race. Our Blessed Lord willingly and lovingly accepted the terrible task of destroying sin. "Having joy set before him, [he] endured the cross, despising the shame" (Heb. 12:2). "Christ Jesus: who being in the form of God, thought it not robbery to be equal with God: but emptied himself, taking the form of a servant, being made in the likeness of men, and in habit found as a man. He humbled himself, becoming obedient unto death, even to the death of the cross" (Phil 2:5–8). "Him, who knew no sin, he hath made sin for us, that we might be made the justice of God in him" (2 Cor. 5:21). For our salvation, the sinless Son of God, in the Person of Christ our Redeemer, became identified with our sins; so that God "suffered Him to be condemned as a sinner, and to die as one accursed" (St. John Chrysostom). The prophet Isaiah truly said of Him: "he was wounded for our iniquities, he was bruised for our sins … and by his bruises we are healed. All we like sheep have gone astray … and the Lord hath laid on him the iniquity of us all" (Isa. 53:5–6). To atone for sin, the all-holy, all-perfect Son of God had to, as it were, besmirch His infinite holiness; and by becoming sin, which as God He infinitely hates and abhors, had to die a horrible death on the Cross. The enormity of sin had to be atoned for by the death of the Son of God. It was through His death on the Cross that Christ reconciled the world to God and restores to us those supernatural gifts that Adam lost in the Fall. God so loved the world that He sent His own Son to save it (see John 3:16).

Now that it is possible to be reunited to God, we must show our gratitude and love to God and Christ by hating and avoiding sin. We are still free creatures. God still wants us to love Him of our own free will. Unlike the angels, we have been given another chance to prove our love for God. Yet the Cross of Christ will not save us without our cooperation. It offers us the chance for forgiveness. Surely we will accept it, now that we appreciate something of the infinite horror of sin. If St. John Chrysostom was willing to suffer the loss of personal liberty, his property, his fatherland, and even his life rather than commit even one venial sin, surely we Catholics will do our best to hate and avoid all sin, for we are the children of the saints and must prove ourselves worthy of them in the Kingdom of God.

The Bible, the inspired Word of God, stigmatizes sin with the following names: abomination, iniquity, work of darkness, disobedience, work of the devil, rebellion. Our Holy Mother, the Church, the eternal rock upon which all truth is founded, calls sin these names: death, wound, stain, fall, ruin, shipwreck of the soul, poisoned cup, forbidden fruit. Will we choose this hated evil in preference to God?

For the love of our Lord Crucified, the friend of sinners, let us turn away from all sin forever. We must hate and be sorry for our own personal sins and for all sins. Let us transform our guilt for our sins into sorrow for them — a poignant, personal sorrow that rends the soul until we cry: "O God, be merciful to me, a sinner." From the Cross, divine love looks down upon us to lift us to His Sacred Heart. His death irresistibly attracts our love. Can we stand at the foot of the Cross and resist His broken heart? Peter could not; all the days of his life, tears flowed from his eyes when he remembered that he denied his God. Magdalene could not; she clung to the nailed and bleeding sacred feet. The good thief could not: "Lord, remember me when thou shalt come into thy kingdom," he cried, throwing himself full of hope on his crucified companion (Luke 23:42). We cannot, for our Lord has invited us to receive forgiveness: "Whose sins you shall forgive, they are forgiven them" (John 20:23).

Make use of the wonderful Sacrament of Penance frequently, seeing that it cost Christ His life's Blood. Confess your sins in sorrow; tell God you have chosen Him freely as the love of your life. Promise Him your best efforts to avoid sin, and finally, throw yourself upon His strength to attain the victory over sin. "For God is faithful and will not permit you to be tempted beyond your strength, but with temptation will also give you a way out that you may be able to bear it" (see 1 Cor. 10:13). "The Lord is gracious and merciful: patient and plenteous in mercy" (Ps. 144:8).

SECOND MEDITATION
Personal Sin

WE EAGERLY DEFEND and indeed glorify our past, glorify it, perhaps, more than the truth allows. Let us now deliberately recognize that we have committed both faults and follies, saying to the Lord like King Hezekiah on his bed of sickness: "I will recount to thee all my years in the bitterness of my soul" (Isa. 38:15). Let us say like David unto the Lord: "Evils without number have surrounded me; my iniquities . . . are multiplied above the hairs of my head" (Ps. 39:13). "My soul is filled with evils: and my life has drawn nigh to hell" (Ps. 87:4). "Unless the Lord had been my helper, my soul had almost dwelt in hell" (Ps. 93:17).

We want now to look ourselves and our sins squarely in the face. We shall not dwell upon our sins for their own sake but to shake our self-complacency, to cool the ardor of self-adulation, and thus to prepare ourselves in the spirit of shame and humility for the spectacle of our real faults. Thus alone can we attain a deep and practical contrition that is the present object of the tale of our sins.

Let us pray for the grace of profound sorrow for our sins. We can never bewail them too much, even though they should be but venial. St. Ignatius tells us to ask "for ever-growing and intense sorrow and tears for my sins." Tears of heart and of will — that is essential. Tears of the eyes if it please God to grant them, for certainly there is matter for weeping. From our holy sorrow will come the resolve to trust in His boundless mercy, to help us live for otherwise in the future.

Suppose that for every sin you have ever committed God had struck a leaden token, marking the nature and gravity of the sin, the date, and its circumstances. Imagine a large hall with casements in which these tokens are arranged in chronological order, like coins in a museum. Below each coin is a document recording the absolutions and pardons you have received and the acts of contrition you have made. Walk into this Hall of Infamy — all yours — and look around. Here are your *opera omnia* recorded on the coins — what you've done on your own by breaking away from God. The briefs of pardon represent what you did with God's grace. You have been pardoned often and freely. Surely you cannot feel less ashamed on that account. Walking around in his Hall of Infamy, St. Augustine cried out:

> So tiny a tot was I, and even then so great a sinner. How ugly I was and how crooked, and filthy and spotted and ulcerous! I saw, and I was struck with horror, and I had no escape from myself.... I put it down to Thy grace and mercy that Thou hast loosed my sins like melted ice. To Thy grace also I put down whatsoever evil deeds I have not done. (*Confessions* 8:7; 2:7)

The Tale of Sins. Some sort of division of our lives is useful. Consider first the years of childhood from the dawn of the use of reason to the day of our First Communion; secondly, the period lapsing from our first reception of our Lord in the Blessed Sacrament to the day when, through the loving vocation of God, we settled our state of life; lastly, our lives subsequent to that great turning point. In each of these periods, I consider all my sins not with the arid statistical precision as to number and species, but all I want is a summary view so as to arouse shame and sorrow in a humble and contrite heart. We should consider our sins as though until now we had done nothing to expiate them, in order to see not what through the divine mercy we may actually have become but what through our own fault we should have made of ourselves. How great has been the malice and foulness of all my sins. Like stupid Esau, I have sold my brilliant birthright of sonship of God in sanctifying grace for a mess of pottage.

What degradation in every mortal sin! "Man, when he was in honor," says the psalmist, "did not understand; he is compared to senseless beasts, and is become like to them" (Ps. 48:13). Every mortal sin is of its nature a triumph of some lower element of our nature over the law of God within us; usually some animal instinct that has for the time claimed supremacy and usurped the place of God in our lives. We quarrel with one of God's laws in our lives; hence, we wish to dethrone God. We are like the citizens in the parable who said of the Son of God, the Son of the Lord of the Vineyard: "We will not have this man to reign over us" (Luke 19:14). But in dethroning God, we dethrone ourselves; we give up the right to be what God made us — lords over creation — and we become slaves to our lower nature. And if our sins have been habitual, how horrible is the description that Holy Scripture, the inspired Word of God, gives of us: "As a dog that returneth to his vomit, so is the fool that repeateth his folly" (Prov. 26:11).

Probably at no time is the repulsiveness or the degrading character of sin more clearly seen and felt than immediately after its commission — that is, in the soul not too hardened to sin. The reaction of the soul seems to excite reason to the fullness of its powers, and we experience a vague and painful sense of shame and humiliation. An oppression and unrest takes hold of us that is more intolerable at times than physical pain. A consciousness of discomfort and dishonor in the soul weighs us down; and often, when the habit of sin is gross and enslaving, sickens the sinner, driving him not unfrequently to self-horror and suicide. When sin has been consummated, all the bewitching attraction or maddening impulse that incited us to evil has passed away, and only the naked infamy remains. All the glamor has been dispelled, stripped of everything but its actual hideousness, and this must always be, as long as man is a reasonable being.

Who am I to offend God? The sinner is like a child looking out from the windows of his Father's wonderful house and wishing he were back in the gutter. Who is this child, anyway, that he opposes himself to Almighty God? An insignificant creature whom the Lord God formed out of the slime of the earth; as far as his body is concerned, he is no better than the beasts and birds, not even any better than the lifeless clay under his feet. We are matter, we are potentiality, we change as the years go past—every particle of the material tissue in our bodies. And when we die, we rot in the ground; we decay like dead leaves or fungus and pass into the general stock-pot of inert matter.

Because of our souls, though, we are nobler than inert matter. But we are spirits made by God out of nothing. "My substance is as nothing before thee," says the psalmist, "and indeed all things are vanity: every man living" (Ps. 38:6). From nothing my soul came, and out of nothing it is kept by the preserving hand of the God whom it dares to offend. It is preserved in the very act of offending Him.

My intellect cannot grasp, let alone solve, some of the commonest problems of existence, yet it dares in the pride of its impotence to exalt itself against the omniscient intellect of the Creator.

My will cannot exercise power enough to restrain passion. It is often a slave in the kingdom that it should rule. It is at times so weak, even when reason sees the light, as to be a wonder and a cause of affright even to myself; yet it rises in rebellion against the

omnipotent will of Him whose *fiat* called me and all things that
are out of nothing and sustains us in the hollow of His hand. My
will asserts itself and its independence against the Supreme Will of
the Universe. And when I look at myself in comparison with God's
other creatures, how puny am I! What am I in comparison with all
mankind; what in comparison with the beauty and brilliance of the
angels and the saints? Whence my swollen pride in sinning? How
miserable is a sinner. If he dies in his sin, "it were better ... if that
man had not been born" (Matt. 26:24).

Whom do I offend? I have sinned against God! It is a matter between God and myself. Other creatures show me my insignificance.
And yet myself against God! Who then is God? He is the infinite being
possessing all infinite attributes. He has three infinite attributes: goodness, wisdom, and omnipotence. Reflecting on these, I see the malice,
folly, and imbecility of my sins. I oppose my ignorance, stupidity,
and blindness against His infinite wisdom; my weakness, instability,
and nothingness against His omnipotence; my malice and perversity
against His perfect goodness.

Consider, first, the infinite goodness of God: so immeasurable
that if another infinite love were possible, it would all be due to
Him; so overpowering that it would be absolutely and metaphysically
impossible to see it as it is and not fall into an uncontrollable ecstasy
of adoring love. The seraphim and the cherubim, the most perfect
created intelligences, find the fullness of their being in worshipping
and praising His goodness: "And the four living creatures ... rested
not day and night, saying: Holy, holy, holy, Lord God Almighty,
who was, and who is, and who is to come" (Rev. 4:8). And I, a sinner, have despised and rejected the infinite goodness for the sake of
some created semblance of it!

Consider secondly the infinite wisdom of God, by which He
knows all things created or to be created, all things that under any

possible conditions could become creatures, and by which He knows Himself; incomprehensible in His judgments and unsearchable in His ways; who only has immortality and inhabits light inaccessible; whom no man hath seen or can see (see Rom. 11:33; 1 Tim. 6:16). He knows the secrets of human hearts: "the works of all flesh are before him, and there is nothing hid from his eyes. He seeth from eternity to eternity, and there is nothing wonderful before him" (Sir. 39:24–25). "His eyes are upon the ways of men, and he considereth all their steps. There is no darkness ... where they may be hid who work iniquity" (Job 34:21–22). Contrast my own ignorance as a sinner. When I sin, I virtually say in my heart the words of the fool condemned by Holy Scripture: "I shall be hidden from God ... in such a multitude I shall not be known: for what is my soul in such an immense creation?" (Sir. 16:16–17).

> Whom do I fear? The most High will not remember my sins ... and he [the sinner] knoweth not that the eyes of the Lord are far brighter than the sun, beholding round about all the ways of men, and the bottom of the deep, and looking into the hearts of men, into the most hidden parts. (Sir. 23:26, 28).

Lastly, consider the omnipotence of God, whose power is without limit in fact and without measure in thought. Only by the concurrence of that power is it possible to initiate the physical act by which I sin. Without that power, I could not desire the object of sin, nor could that object attract my will, nor could I execute my desire through the faculties and organs that I call mine. Without the concurrence of that omnipotence, my hands or feet could not move, my eyes see, nor my mind know. Yet in my native impotence as a sinner, I oppose myself to the will of the omnipotent God and use God's very omnipotence to offend my Creator and Father.

How can God and his holy creatures tolerate me in mortal sin?
How can the holy angels, the sword of divine justice, still bear with
me, watch over me, and, with the saints, pray for me, who has so
grievously offended God? How can the earth and sky and the beasts
still serve me? St. Leo, speaking about how the earth revolted against
the crime of deicide when our Savior was killed, says: "In detestation
of such a crime, all the elements uttered one sentence: the lights of
heaven were darkened, the day was turned into night, the earth shud-
dered with unwonted quakings, and the whole creation withdrew
itself from the service of the ungodly" (*Sermon 8 on the Passion*).
How has not the earth opened up to swallow me, creating new hells
so that I might suffer forever in them? Here we must remember that
God's mercy has been greater than the multitude or the heinousness
of our sins. St. Ignatius asks us to throw ourselves, like the Prodigal,
upon the loving goodness of the Father who has so far spared us. We
have no claims to urge, nothing but evil to confess—evil for all His
benefits. Let us extol His mercy in still preserving us alive, for bringing us once more before Him, for all the graces that He has given
us—and is still ready to give us.

Confer: Timothy Broshnahan, S.J., *Searchlighting Ourselves.*
Cuthbert Lattey, S.J., *Thy Love and Thy Grace.*
Joseph Rickaby, S.J., *Waters That Go Softly.*

CONFERENCE

Mental Prayer

Whoever is in earnest about attaining perfection must make use of a means absolutely necessary for perfection. Like our Blessed Lord, the good Catholic must hurry back at times to a more intimate union with God in mental prayer, leaving for a time the many good works of the day, even though they be clamoring for him. In order to renew in our hearts the zeal and love of mental prayer, we will today rapidly review its necessity in our lives, its difficulties, and the remedies for these difficulties.

The necessity of mental prayer. First of all, we must clearly state that the official prayers of the Church — those in the Mass, in the Breviary, and liturgical prayer — are all of the highest dignity and of the greatest esteem. We must love them and pray them fervently, for they unite us to the Spouse of Christ in the public worship of God through Jesus Christ. Now, without diminishing our esteem and respect for these prayers, we must affirm what is very easy to prove also, namely that these prayers are insufficient without mental prayer. That is to say that to these prayers must be added the prayer that wells up from the depths of each individual soul, whether one be praying in his private room, as our Lord counsels, or in a common church, holding private prayer alone with God. As a matter of fact, a minimum of personal meditation is necessary in order that the vocal prayers may be said at least with some intelligence and under-standing of their meaning. Is it not true that even the most excellent formulas of prayers from constant repetition become mechanical and lifeless? How many times, alas, does this monotony not attack such wonderful prayers as the Pater and the Ave! Mental prayer consisting in serious reflection on the truths that these formulas contain will freshen them up, deepen their meaning in our souls. When we say such prayers in the future, thanks to mental prayer, it will be our inmost souls that we will be stirring up and pouring out to God, not just words of a sing-song formula.

An even stronger reason for the necessity of mental prayer is that such prayer plumbs the depths of truth and the profound spiritual meaning that the Church wishes to express in her vocal and liturgical prayers. This spiritual taste, this filial understanding, this putting on of the mind of Christ are not conferred upon us by any sacrament, nor are they attained by using official texts of the Church's prayers, nor even by studying these prayers. The reason is that these graces are reserved for those who ask for them in prayer, or who, like Mary, keep the words in their hearts, pondering over them, in mental prayer. St. Francis of Assisi could go into ecstasy repeating a simple prayer like: "My God and My all!" Why? Because he saw and tasted the infinite riches of truth present in those words; he daily spent hours in mental prayer with his Lord and his all.

Mental prayer affects our whole lives and our outlook on things. Notice the case of priests: those given to mental prayer are powerful in their preaching, in their direction of souls, using the simplest of language in doing their work. The fire of love is coming from within. The Curé of Ars is a wonderful example. But of priests who have all the technical skill, the marvelous voice, and the commanding appearance, yet who are not given to mental prayer, an unbeliever made this remark: "He preaches like a priest who does not pray; his style is very proper, but hardly persuading." Moreover, mental prayer is essential to assure us a reform and renovation in our spiritual lives. Mental prayer helps us to see what causes us to fail to realize and appreciate the wonderful truth of our faith. Without it, our purity of heart and spiritual sense is dull; we are spiritually stupid, lethargic, lazy. If we do not pray, sin is not the horrible reality it should be to us; our faults we consider picayune; we drift and are not on fire for the better things. Such would not be our state of soul if we viewed ourselves every day in mental prayer under the gaze of God. "Mental prayer," says St. Francis de Sales, "places our understanding under the brilliant light of God and exposes our will to the heat of His celestial love." These are enough to reform our lives. "There is nothing," continues the saint, "which purifies our understanding of its ignorance and our will of its depraved affections like mental prayer." And St. Alphonsus Liguori has this to say: "Whenever a good confessor finds a penitent who detests mortal sin and who desires to make progress in divine love, the very first thing that confessor should do is to bring that soul to the practice of mental prayer." And he gives a reason: "Other exercises of piety can be practiced without sin being rooted out of the soul, but as for mental prayer, this cannot be consistently practiced without excluding mortal sin. Either the prayer will be abandoned, or sin will be abandoned; they cannot exist together." That's quite a strong statement, but experience bears it out. The Rosary, the breviary, vocal prayers—yes, and even the celebration of the Holy Mass—can all be practiced by a soul clinging to serious sin. In periods of spiritual decadence in the Church, history shows that priests and nuns lived sacrilegious lives because they did not practice mental prayer. What's the psychological explanation of this tragedy? Well, in all the above-mentioned exercises, even when a priest is standing at the altar, while the lips are reciting the formulas, the heart can be far away from the meaning;

hence, no good will come to the reciter from what he is doing, but rather more sin and sacrilege. Our Blessed Lord scolded the Pharisees and scribes for this very type of dead service: "This people honoreth me with their lips: but their heart is far from me" (Matt. 15:8).

How completely different it is with mental prayer! It is impossible to remain in mental prayer and persevere in mortal sin, because when one is not what he ought to be, he is embarrassed in a heart-to-heart talk with God; his conscience reproaches him; his faults and sins rise up before him; he sees his hypocrisy and understands the utter inconsistency and impossibility of his position — seeking God in prayer and yet clinging to sin. Perhaps he can stand this struggle one day, or two, but very soon, it is insupportable. A choice has to be made: either prayer will have to go or sin. No man can remain under God's gaze in this incompatible state. But if we persevere in mental prayer, our pardon is assured, for we will come to see sin the way God sees it, and we will reject it. Then in our prayer with God we will see the Father of all mercy, we will experience His pardon and peace, and our lives will be reformed.

Another motive for exacting from ourselves strict fidelity to mental prayer is the following: "Divine love alone binds a soul to its Savior and keeps it united to Him." But the furnace in which this divine love is enkindled and fed is mental prayer and meditation and contemplation. The psychological explanation of this truth is clear too. In order to have our truths and convictions about God take deep root in our souls, we must reflect on them often. They must pass from the head and the intelligence through the heart and into the fire of love. In mental prayer, we mull over these truths, we chew them, we digest them, and we are refreshed with their sweet taste. Once attained in this thorough assimilation, they drive us to lead the holy lives that logically must follow from the marvelous truths of our Faith. St. Alphonsus Liguori tells us what the inevitable result will be: "All the saints became saints through mental prayer." Convinced of this truth, our Holy Mother the Church acts on it. After centuries of experience, she tells her priests in her laws to celebrate Mass several times a year, at least on Sundays and the principal feasts. But when she speaks of mental prayer, she exacts some time devoted to it every day. She obliges the bishops and superiors of religious orders that all their priests and religious subjects perform this duty.

The difficulties of mental prayer. First, we have difficulties arising from our nature. We always avoid as much as possible whatever will cost us in suffering. We are tempted to substitute for mental prayer the reading of a good religious book. If the author is interesting, the time passes quickly, and we are pleased. But what have we got to show for our efforts? Little. We know by now that we reap in proportion to our efforts. Sure, read good books, but not during mental prayer time! Only personal reflection, pleadings with God, and companionship with Him in mental prayer will bring to life the Faith in our actions. Believe me, there is no substitute for communing with God in mental prayer!

Second, we have difficulties arising from the trials we have to undergo in mental prayer. Such are spiritual dryness, aridities. They could, of course, be punishments for our dissipated or worldly lives. In this case, use mental prayer to reform. Then there are those other trials, very hard and prolonged, despite the fervor of a good soul. These are extraordinary. Usually they are the prelude to some mystical favors. Their true test is if the generosity of the souls toward God remains faithful. When trials like these attack the soul, and one is not cognizant of any infidelity to God, then it is necessary to consult an experienced guide of souls.

There are other ordinary aridities, which we will treat now. First of all, remember they are normal, usual. Often, when a young seminarian or young religious sister first enters the life of God, God gives them sweetness in prayer, sensible consolations in order to detach them from the sensible pleasures they left just recently in the world and to attach them to the spiritual life. Hence, as they contemplate the detailed scenes of the Gospels, they move from one wonderful discovery to another, full of joy. But soon, as they grow accustomed to the scenes, the charm fades, the sweetness is gone. God has withdrawn these sensible consolations in order to virilize the soul, to make it grow up, to see if it is capable of serving Him without being spoiled by these immediate rewards. Now that the soul has sufficiently understood who He is — the height of all perfections! — and what trials of love He has undergone for His creatures — the crib, the Cross, the tabernacle! — the individual should generously spend himself in His service *gratis*. Thus, normally, the trial of aridity has to come sooner or later.

Here are some principles that we must never lose sight of: God merits to be served in all perfection for Himself, not for His gifts. Anyone who gives up mental prayer because of aridity or some similar difficulties gives up by that very act the special favors and the special love of God, who is drawing the soul on through these trials to sanctity. This is the teaching of all the masters of the spiritual life. St Teresa writes:

> The gate through which come the special graces of God is mental prayer or contemplation. Once this gate is closed, I do not know how God can give these graces. In vain will He try to enter a soul in order to take His delight in her and to place His favors within her; the avenues of entrance are closed to Him. In order to give these graces, He must find the soul alone with Him in prayer and desirous of receiving them.

"It is through prayer that all goods come to us," says St. Vincent de Paul. "If we persevere in our vocation, if we do not fall into sin,

if we are saved—all that is the grace of God and through prayer."
The efforts at recollection and at supplication that constitute mental
prayer bear fruit in a million wonderful graces. Without the effort
at recollection, we live fascinated with frivolities of this world. The
effort at supplication brings us the love of God and intimate union
with Him. Never give up mental prayer.

Remedies to the difficulties of mental prayer. First: Make a
sacred and strong resolution to esteem mental prayer as a daily,
sacred duty. This means you will never abandon it, despite difficulties, dryness, desolation. At least you will make of it in those times
a work of reparation to the Heart of Jesus. For priests and religious,
God expects mental prayer as a strict duty leading to sanctity.

Second: Make a daily, diligent preparation for your mental prayer.
Respect for God in whose presence you are going demands this
preparation. Moreover, prudence tells you that being well-prepared
is half the battle in praying well. Fifteen minutes of preparation is
quite sufficient for this resolution. Don't find yourself practicing
confused prayer in the morning because you failed to prepare the
evening before.

Third: Make a judicious use of the various methods of mental
prayer. The best for each person is that which is best for your taste,
that which sustains you more in the battle against yourself and in
the accomplishment of your duties, the method that leads you to
generous acts of love of God and your neighbor. To find this method,
try several of them, and begin by studying the various characteristics
of these methods. Since monotony leads to boredom, and since
individual disposition, physical and moral, vary at times, it is useful
to try different methods for different circumstances. Remember, the
method is not for itself; it is only to help you to pray, to bring you
to union with God; it is a means, not an end in itself. And when
you find yourself easily and profitably in colloquy with God, rest

there, and taste the truths and the good resolutions God gives you. Remember *multum*, not *multa*, is wanted in prayer.

Fourth: From time to time, as grace leads you, make a humble and ardent repetition of one petition—the way our Lord prayed in the garden. You might pray, "Pardon me, O Lord, my past sins!" or "By all means, O Lord, make me humble. Teach me to love You. Give me souls!" These insistent prayers are open to all. Like our Lord, when we see we are in difficulties, let us pray the longer. "And being in an agony, he prayed the longer" (Luke 22:43). *There* is the example to follow. He is our model, our encouragement. In His prayer of desolation, of fear, and of sorrow—what love! What submission to God's will! As did Christ, let us always persevere in mental prayer. Ask Him who spent whole nights in prayer of God to grant you this special favor.

Confer: Pinard de la Boullaye, S.J., *Exercices Spirituels*, vol. 4, pp. 138–153.

THIRD MEDITATION
Hell

IT IS WELL that we should remind ourselves, in time of retreat, how close we live—even those who are called by their state of life to a special profession of holiness—to the danger of eternal damnation. David, at a time when to all outward appearance he was high in the favor of King Saul and in command of his armies, said once to his friend Jonathan, "But truly as the Lord liveth, and thy soul liveth, there is but one step ... between me and death" (1 Sam. 20:3). So it is with us; man in his state of probation walks always at the edge of a precipice. Let's go down into Hell, or at least take a peep over the edge of the precipice, to see the horrible place that mortal sin would lead us.

Already, we have made a firm purpose never to sin again. The contemplation of Hell is meant to clinch this purpose. "Should I forget the love of my eternal Lord on account of my faults, at least the fear of the pains of Hell may help me not to come into sin." Moreover, by contemplating what should have been our punishment, we learn to be humble and to distrust ourselves, to trust only in our Heavenly Father. For we know that we are but brands that He in His love and mercy has plucked from the burning; we deserve to be cast once more upon the flames.

Let us then endeavor to see with the eyes of the imagination the pool of fire burning with brimstone that was prepared for the devil and his angels; to see the depth of the prison house of the damned, the width and breadth of the inextinguishable flames that burn forever and never consume. "For Topheth [Gehenna] is prepared from yesterday, prepared by the king, deep and wide. The nourishment thereof is fire ... the breath of the Lord as a torrent of brimstone kindling it" (Isa. 30:33).

If there was one truth that the sweet and gentle Savior spoke of with terrible earnestness, tried continually to push home with insistence, it was the momentous and disquieting truth that Hell is a fact! On this truth Christ laid tremendous emphasis! If your right eye be a cause of sin, pluck it out; if your right hand scandalize you, cut it off. Far better to lose an eye or a limb than with these to be thrown into Hell, into everlasting punishment, everlasting fire (see Matt. 5:29–30).

The pain of Hell is twofold: the pain of sense and the pain of loss, corresponding to the twofold character of a mortal sin.

The pain of sense. In Hell, the lost soul is merged in the depth of a sea, an ocean of fire; it is encased in fire, as St. Thomas says, it is united to fire as to its body. Fire penetrates to the marrow of its being, courses through its veins, floods through the valves of the heart, fills it entrails, throbs in its temples, makes its eyeballs molten fires, seethes in its brains, and is the air that fills its lungs: it is the impression made by every object in Hell on each specific sense. Fire is a part of a lost being, its body of death.

Every sense and faculty has its individual torture in Hell. The eyes contemplate in horror the sights of demons and other souls hideous in the repulsiveness of their naked damnation. The ears, unfit forevermore for pleasant sound, ring with the coarse, maddened cries of despair and hatred, with howlings and shrieks of demons. The sense of taste and smell and touch, each in the fever of damnation, will suffer appropriate pains. Imagine being cast into a cesspool.

How could we bear the odor, the taste, the loathsome contact of it for a day? Hell is infinitely more loathsome to these faculties. "We fools!" cry out the damned (Wisd. 5:4). However clever, however successful, however rich in life, if all ends in Hell, what fools! They are now in an "unquenchable fire, where their worm dieth not" (Mark 9:42–43). St. Thomas tells us that the "worm" is the worm of conscience, which arises from the tortured depths of the soul and everlastingly points the accusing finger of guilt at the one responsible for all this misery and horror: "You fool! You chose all this freely. You have thrown away eternal happiness with your eyes wide open. You could so easily have avoided this place, but you threw God's graces back into His face; you spurned Him; you would have nothing to do with Him. Now He justly will have nothing to do with you. You fool, you have damned yourself!" And the damned soul will cry out in the words of Job: "Let the day perish wherein I was born, and the night in which it was said: A man child is conceived ... Why did I not die in the womb ... or as they that being conceived have not seen the light" (Job 3:3, 11, 16).

The pain of loss. This is the greatest pain of Hell. We know that the soul was created for blessedness and the happiness of possessing God. God has put an ineradicable impulse in our nature for Him. This craving in this life is drawn off by the distractions of sensible objects. But when we die, the soul leaves the world of sense and enters into solitude, where nothing is left to make her happy but God alone. Irresistibly, with the whole of its immense spiritual energy, the departed soul drives forward toward union with God, the center and joy of its existence. But the soul of the sinner, God's enemy, is driven back by the infinite power of God. Eternally striving to arrive, and eternally being cast back, the soul is eternally miserable in the vast void of frustration. St. Teresa of Ávila, who experienced some of the tortures of the damned, says of this: "Here it is that the soul herself is continually tearing herself in pieces" (*Autobiography* 30:1–10). The lost spirit, an outcast from creation, which it has abused, is now also an outcast from God. It has nothing left but the void, the vacancy of being thrown back upon itself, interned and isolated in self-confinement. Imagine the terrible lonesomeness, the horrible abandonment, the utter despair—and yet withal there remains that infinite desire to possess God, a desire that shall never ever be fulfilled. Can we now realize what a terrible thing it is to lose our souls in Hell? It means to lose God our Father, our eternal Good, forever. To be lost means to know not where we are; to be without bearings; to be in surroundings that are unfamiliar, alien, distressing; to be hopeless, without resources and without prospect of relief. It means that all our operations of mind and body are reversed—the intellect can act, but the intellect of the damned thinks only of falsehood with a mind made for truth. It still can will, but it hates eternally with a will made to love. It can love nothing now; it hates everything. It is no longer *sui juris*; it has no rights; it does not possess itself; it is a slave, the chattel of the enemy of human nature, no longer able to be rescued by the Savior of men whom it hates and spurns.

The eternity of Hell. The eternity of Hell is vouched for in Christ's own words: "Depart from me ... into *everlasting* fire" (Matt. 25:41). Besides, the soul is immortal. The body is corruptible, yet at the general judgment, the souls of the just and the damned shall alike reenter their bodies, never again to be separated from them. These bodies will be perfectly fitted to the souls; glorious bodies for the just, loathsome bodies for the damned. At sight of these tenements for sin, the damned cry out: "Woe is me, wretch that I am, for the Lord hath added sorrow to my sorrow" (Jer. 45:3). And they shall say to the mountains and the rocks: "Fall upon us, and hide us from the face of him that sitteth upon the throne and from the wrath of the Lamb" (Rev. 6:16). The anger of the Lamb shall be a terror to them. "Men shall seek death, and shall not find it: and they shall desire to die, and death shall fly from them" (Rev. 9:6). If they could only get rid of their bodies, Hell would be less intolerable. But the immortal soul shall forever inform the hideous clay. God's decree is final, immutable, and irrevocable.

The souls of lost men, women, children, laymen, and religious go into the house of eternity leaving hope behind. Dante has a terrifying inscription over the gates of Hell. As the lost soul enters, he reads these most despairing words: *Lasciate ogni speranza, voi ch'entrate* (abandon all hope, ye who enter here!). After millions of years of suffering, Hell will still have all the time to run that it had before the soul entered it. There is no end, no terminus, no progress, just one eternal *now* of suffering. Suppose you were told that after as many years had elapsed as there are atoms of matter in the whole universe of solar system, planets, stars, and constellations, you would then be permitted to leave Hell and to do penance for a million years for your crimes and to choose at the end of that period repentance or obduracy, Hell would at once cease to be Hell for you, for you would have the hope of another chance. But, you see, this will never be for a soul in Hell. The soul is lost irrevocably.

Here I think of the souls that have perished before the coming of our Blessed Lord, during His life, and since His coming. And I thank our Blessed Lord for having spared me in His mercy and love so frequently and even to this day. And I thank Him for His pity and love of me, and I promise to hate and detest sin as the worst evil in the world and to repay His love and mercy with fidelity to His laws for the rest of my days.

Confer: Timothy Broshnahan, S.J., *Searchlighting Ourselves.*
Cuthbert Lattey, S.J., *Thy Love and Thy Grace.*

THIRD DAY

Purpose: To realize more profoundly the depth of Divine Mercy toward sinful mankind

Patron: St. Paul

Points for Self-Consideration:

- Do I cultivate great purity of heart so that I detest all sin?
- Do I pray for an abiding sorrow for sin?

Suggested Readings:

Luke 15

Imitation of Christ, bk. 2, ch. 1

Spiritual Exercises: General Confession and Communion

Aspirations:

"But the mercy of the Lord is from eternity and unto eternity upon them that fear Him." (Ps. 102:17)

"Hear, O, Lord, my prayer: give ear to my supplication in thy truth; hear me in thy justice. And enter not into judgment with thy servant: for in thy sight no man living shall be justified." (Ps. 142:1–2)

FIRST MEDITATION

Mercy

HAVE YOU EVER tried, in prayer and recollection, to live a scene in the Gospel? It is a wonderful experience that brings you close to Christ and to God. When you become proficient at this kind of prayer, you will find that you can speak to Christ with joy, with ease, and with naturalness, the way the apostles did as they walked with Him through the streets of Judea, climbed mountains with Him, fished with Him in the Sea of Galilee, or picnicked with Him in the desert.

Tonight you are invited (with our dear Lord) to attend a dinner at the sumptuous house of Simon the Pharisee (see Luke 7:36–50). The time is six o'clock in the evening.

Simon is a wealthy Pharisee. You know it as you recline at table and appraise with a pleased eye the Grecian beauty of his spacious dining hall. You know it as you watch the guests arrive, all the bigwigs of Jerusalem's high society. You know it as you sip the imported wines that grace his table. It is always nice to be a guest at Simon's.

Tonight's dinner is in honor of a certain new prophet — Jesus, they call Him. He is reclining about four tables away, eating, drinking, and talking quietly with Simon and those nearest Him. There's something royal about the prophet's handsome, chiseled features, something divine about the light in His large, dark eyes. People call Him "Lord." How appropriately He bears this title! Your eyes move down the long, lamp-lighted hall, seeking a broad perspective of the entire scene. Waiters and servants scurry about tending the guests. A merry hubbub of conversation floats to the marbled ceiling, rebounds and warms the entire atmosphere with the cheer of well-fed guests. You glance through the portico that fronts the west side of the hall. You admire the classic, seven-columned colonnade. Then your eye peers beyond the columns out into the dim street.

Someone is coming up the steps of the portico, moving rather rapidly. You watch, intrigued by the graceful carriage. A late guest, no doubt. Just inside the first column, the latecomer steps out of the shadows and into the light. It's a woman. You stare! "No, no, not that woman! Simon would never invite her! But here she is!" Mary of Magdala is moving swiftly up the hall. And as she advances, the spoken word is frozen on every lip. It's as if a blight had struck the hall; everyone gapes.

Right past your couch she hastens, and it is then that you notice she holds an alabaster vial of precious ointment. Straight to the prophet's table she moves. You can scarce believe your eyes; she is at His feet in a convulsive heap; tears and kisses press the prophet's feet; the woman's long, luxuriant hair entwines them. There's not a sound in the long hall, save her sobbing sighs. You notice Simon's face; he's looking quizzically at this Jesus, as if to say: "This man, were he a prophet, would surely know that this is a woman of the streets."

You hear a sharp snap of broken alabaster; precious nard and ointment pour over the prophet's feet; their sweet perfume permeates the entire hall. It is then that you catch the prophet's eye. His face is serenely gentle; His eyes, extremely bright. He speaks: "Simon, I say to you that her sins, as many as they are, are forgiven her because she has loved much" (see Luke 7:47). Where had you heard such sentiments before? You know your scriptures; think back. Ah yes! It was King David who cried: "A contrite and humbled heart, O God, thou wilt not despise" (Ps. 50:19). The broken vial upon the floor is a symbol of the broken-hearted Magdalene. Its sweet perfumes are scattered abroad to please all men, a symbol of the contrite love of the sinner that brings joy to God, to angels, and to men.

The vilest sinner in the world may be cleansed of every stain of sin if he wills. As long as life lasts, the worst sinner may obtain the cancellation of his guilt and restoration to the favor of God. Why? Because of God's infinite love and mercy toward us, His wayward creatures. "I will have mercy and not sacrifice. For I am not come to call the just, but sinners," our Blessed Lord told the Pharisees who found fault with Him because He was the friend of sinners (Matt. 9:13). God said through His prophets: "Return to me, and I will return to you" (Mal. 3:7); "As I live . . . I desire not the death of the wicked, but that the wicked turn from his way and live" (Ezek. 33:11). And through Isaiah, God says: "Can a woman forget her infant so as not to have pity on the son of her womb? And if she should forget, yet will not I forget thee" (Isa. 49:15). What is this marvelous virtue of mercy that is said to be above all God's works?

Mercy is a heartfelt sympathy for another's distress, impelling us to succor the one in distress to the best of our ability. God has infinite mercy on us because He loves us with an infinite love and because He wants to free us from the terrible slavery of sin into which we have freely delivered ourselves. "For according to his greatness, so also is his mercy with him" (Sir. 2:23). God asks only one thing of a sinner: that he freely return to his Heavenly Father. A sinner ceases to be a rebel as soon as he turns to God and sincerely resolves to repent. At that moment, a change takes place in his soul greater than the change that took place when God first created him. For a soul that is as foul as a devil becomes as beautiful almost as the soul of the Son of God, for God receives the sinner back as His son. God looks upon the repentant sinner with the eyes of a tender mother gazing on the child she loves. To the most degraded sinner, to him whose sins are as scarlet and are as multitudinous as the sands of the seashores, God says: "How great is the mercy of the Lord, and his forgiveness to them that turn to him" (Sir. 17:28). "As a father hath compassion on his children, so hath the Lord compassion on them that fear him, for he knoweth our frame" (Ps. 102:13–14).

I once knew a criminal who was trying to go straight. He had paid his debt to society after spending five years in prison on a burglary charge. Yet ten years later, at the time I met him, he was still a marked man. Oh sure, society had forgiven him, but he had a record. For ten long years, he drifted from one job to another; no sooner was his record known than his services were no longer needed. Not only could my friend not aspire to positions of honor and trust, but he found that society would not allow him to aspire to any steady position.

How vastly different is God in His mercy toward us! We all have "records" in the eyes of God. But the moment we return to Him, He receives us with open arms and forgives and immediately reinstates us. Reinstated! What a magnificent honor! That is the wonderful thing about God's mercy. It not only pardons but restores. The sinner who returns to God may aspire to the loftiest station in God's Kingdom. Augustine was an arch-enemy of God, using his marvelous gifts against the Giver, defiling the temple of his body by lust, and leading many into heresy by his brilliant and bitter assaults on the Church of Christ. But Augustine repented and became a bishop and Doctor of the Church, and he took his place with the Apostle. David of old turned traitor to God, committing adultery and murder; but on conversion, his sins were wiped out, and he was made by God the forefather of the divine Redeemer. Saul of Tarsus persecuted the Church of God, standing as a witness for the stoning of St. Stephen and later dragging Christians in chains to the dungeons of Jerusalem. Yet on his conversion, he became the fiery Apostle St. Paul, one of the pillars upon which the Church of Rome is founded. When God forgives, He forgives. When God forgives, He forgets. His mercy is not half-hearted but entirely generous. The sinner who receives God's mercy starts out in God's service absolutely unhampered. The only effect of his past transgressions is that he is spurred on to greater distinction in the service of His Merciful Lord. No matter how frequent may have been his sins, no matter how serious they may have been, no matter how many were the relapses, once the sinner returns to God and gives up his sin, he is established again in God's favor and may go forward in company with the greatest saints. God does this not because the sinner merits such loving forgiveness but because He loves the sinner for whom His own divine Son died upon the Cross. The sinner need show only the good will to repent, and this, plus the redeeming Blood of Christ on Calvary, touches the heart of God and appeals to His fatherly mercy.

How beautifully our Blessed Lord has told us the story of God's mercy in the story of the Prodigal Son:

A certain man had two sons. And the younger of them said to his father: Father, give me the portion of substance that falleth to me. And he divided unto them his substance. And not many days after, the younger son, gathering all together, went abroad into a far country: and there wasted his substance, living riotously. And after he had spent all, there came a mighty famine in that country; and he began to be in want. And he went and cleaved to one of the citizens of that country. And he sent him into his farm to feed swine. And he would fain have filled his belly with the husks the swine did eat; and no man gave unto him. And returning to himself, he said: How many hired servants in my father's house abound with bread, and I here perish with hunger? I will arise, and will go to my father, and say to him: Father, I have sinned against heaven, and before thee: I am not worthy to be called thy son: make me as one of thy hired servants. And rising up he came to his father. And when he was yet a great way off, his father saw him, and was moved with compassion, and running to him fell upon his neck, and kissed him. And the son said to him: Father, I have sinned against heaven, and before thee, I am not now worthy to be called thy son.

And the father said to his servants: Bring forth quickly the first robe, and put it on him, and put a ring on his hand, and shoes on his feet: And bring hither the fatted calf, and kill it, and let us eat and make merry: Because this my son was dead, and is come to life again: was lost, and is found. And they began to be merry.

Now his elder son was in the field, and when he came and drew nigh to the house, he heard music and dancing: And he called one of the servants, and asked what these things meant. And he said to him: Thy brother is come, and thy father hath killed the fatted calf, because he hath received him safe. And he was angry, and would not go in. His father therefore coming out began to entreat him. And he answering, said to his father: Behold, for so many years do I serve thee, and I have never transgressed thy commandment, and yet thou hast never given me a kid to make merry with my friends: But as soon as this thy son is come, who hath devoured his substance with harlots, thou hast killed for him the fatted calf.

But he said to him: Son, thou art always with me, and all I have is thine. But it was fit that we should make merry and be glad, for this thy brother was dead and is come to life again; he was lost, and is found. (Luke 15:11–32)

In this wonderful story, our Lord declares to us that He longs for the return of the sinner. He does not regard the evil of the wrongdoing after it is given up but only the changed heart of the wrongdoer. He not only forgives but He rejoices to forgive. He not only reinstates the sinner in His favor but honors him besides. He is not only willing to receive back the erring one but He longs for his return. He does not wait for him but on seeing him approach runs out to meet him.

But Christ not only spoke of God's mercy in His parables, He also displayed God's mercy in His actions. We have already seen how He lifted Magdalene the sinner to make her Magdalene the saint. And to understand the thoroughness of His forgiveness, He not only forgave her but made her the companion of His Mother, Mary. At the foot of the Cross stood side by side Mary the sinless and Mary the sinner that was. Nor was this an isolated case. On another occasion, a woman who was taken in adultery was brought to Jesus. This was a dreadful sin among the Jews, and its penalty was stoning the adulterer to death. The wretched creature was accused to Jesus by the eminently respectable scribes and Pharisees. It seemed to be a case in which there was no hope for the woman. She did not deny her guilt; she made no excuse. She felt so hopelessly condemned that she did not even make a plea for mercy.

She stood before Jesus awaiting sentence. Doubtless, as she stood in the presence of the All Holy One, the enormity of her evil life came before her. By the grace of God, which always radiated out from Christ to those of good will, her heart sorrowed for the wrong she had done. Jesus saw her sorrow and was moved by this change of heart; this was her act of contrition. On the instant, pardon went out to her. Christ became at once not only her Savior but her champion. Her sin was great, but not too great for His mercy. Christ, who knew all things, saw in her accusers men who were guilty of grievous sins and yet ready to condemn sinners. When He saw their false and hard hearts, speaking not a word, but bending to the ground, He traced, I believe, their sins with His finger in the sand. One by one, as their sins were recorded, the hypocrites shamefacedly slunk away. Finally, Jesus looked up at the repentant woman who stood alone. "Woman," He said, "where are they that accused thee? Hath no man condemned thee?" She answered: "No man, Lord." And Jesus said: "Neither will I condemn thee. Go, and now sin no more" (John 8:3–11).

The mercy of Christ toward sinners was so frequently manifested that the scribes and Pharisees found fault with Him for it. St. Luke tells us:

> Now the publicans and sinners drew near unto him to hear him. And the Pharisees and the scribes murmured, saying: This man receiveth sinners, and eateth with them. And he spoke to them this parable, saying: What man of you that hath an hundred sheep: and if he shall lose one of them, doth he not leave the ninety-nine in the desert, and go after that which was lost, until he find it? And when he hath found it, lay it upon his shoulders, rejoicing: And coming home, call together his friends and neighbors, saying to them: Rejoice with me, because I have found my sheep that was lost? I say to you, that even so there shall be joy in heaven upon one sinner that doth penance, more than upon ninety-nine just who need not penance. (Luke 15:1–7)

Like the tenderest of mothers, Christ rejoices more at the recovery of the spiritual health of one of His sick children than in the continued health of the rest of the family.

If any should have any lingering doubt of the mercy of God, let him go to Calvary and stand in the throng that is blaspheming the Son of God dying in untold torments for their souls. Let him listen in astonishment at the infinite love and mercy present in these words: "Father, forgive them, for they know not what they do" (Luke 23:34). Forgive them for their ignorance, for their malice, for having sworn falsely, for acting with cruelty and against justice. To add to His sufferings and disgrace, they placed Him between two criminals, who were crucified with Him. Amidst the roar of blasphemy from the raging multitude, one of the condemned hears the repeated prayer: "Father, forgive them; Father, forgive them." This plea for forgiveness touches his heart. The goodness of Christ makes him reflect on his own vileness. He sees his own life as one long trail of violence and crime. For a moment, the weight of his sins appalls him. Then, in the light of Christ's goodness, he regretted his whole misspent life. He was keenly sorry and confessed his guilt. Speaking for the other thief and himself, he cried out: "We indeed are under condemnation justly; but this man has done no evil." It was his act of contrition. Then he said to Jesus: "Lord, remember me when you shall come into your kingdom." And Jesus said to him: "Amen, I say to thee, this day thou shalt be with me in paradise" (see Luke 23:41–43). The thief nailed to the cross a sinner was taken down from it a saint. God saw that his heart was moved away from sin and back to Him. That was all that was needed for the mercy of God.

Do I hear anyone object: "But I am a very great sinner. God will not hear me." If God will not hear you, why did He praise the publican in the rear of the Temple who struck his breast, saying: "O God, be merciful to me a sinner" (Luke 18:13)? There were two sinners on Calvary. One was saved because he asked to be forgiven; he died a saint. The other did not ask to be forgiven; he died a sinner. Has not our divine Savior said: "Come to Me all you that labor and are burdened and I will refresh you" (Matt. 12:28)? And who is more heavily burdened than the sinner?

Do not refuse our Lord the chance to shower His Mercy upon you. Do not stunt your spiritual life by always looking at your faults. Look to His love and mercy. Accept His outstretched hand and He will raise you up. Never despair! Not until God ceases to be infinitely merciful and you begin to be infinitely wicked have you a right to be hopeless. "Be converted to me, and you shall be saved," God says (Isa. 45:22). "If your sins be as red as scarlet, they shall be made as white as snow" (Isa. 17:18). "The bruised reed he shall not break, and smoking flax he shall not quench" (Isa. 42:3). For "the Lord is sweet to all: and his tender mercies are over all his works" (Ps. 144:9). God loves you.

SECOND MEDITATION

The Kingdom

SO FAR IN our retreat, we have been appealing to the dry light of
reason as we have studied the truths about our relationship to God;
our purpose in life; sin and what an ugly reality it is in itself; Hell,
the punishment of sin; and mercy, the outstretched hand of God.
All these truths indeed convince us in the mind, but because of
their abstract nature, they do not easily move us. We are creatures
of flesh and blood and need to have our abstract ideals clothed in
flesh and blood before we can be moved to a generous, enthusiastic acceptance and practice of these ideals. Our Heavenly Father,
who knows so well every inarticulate yearning of our nature, has
met this need and has sent His own divine Son to earth to display
the goodness of God in His own human thoughts and deeds. The
King who has come enlists our generosity, loyalty, combativeness,
imagination, taste, and ambition by standing before us in His winning lovableness and inviting us to share in His noble mission by
imitation of His selfless deeds. Our chief concern in this meditation
is to greet our Heaven-sent King, to swear Him our homage, and
to fight generously under His banner to a sure victory.

The call, a parable. Suppose a temporal king, elected by God
Himself, possesses all those kingly qualities that are attributes of
the greatest men of all times: he possesses the genius and personal

attractiveness of a Napoleon, the sanctity of a St. Louis, the power of a General MacArthur. Say he has a large heart and is capable of great self-sacrifice. His wisdom and prudence are like that of King Solomon. Now this wonderful king, chosen by God, goes about the villages and hamlets preaching, and he issues an address to all people announcing: first, that it is his will to bring beneath his gentle sway all those who lived in the darkness of error and despotism, to extend the blessings of peace and prosperity to those enslaved by the vicegerents of the powers of darkness; second, that those who are willing to enlist in his mission or enterprise must be ready to put up with the same inconveniences in food and apparel, in marchings and weariness, in watchings and want of sleep that he, the king, will endure; and third, that after undergoing the labors by day and the vigils by night that the king himself would undergo during the campaign, his followers will, on the glorious issue of the campaign, share in the glory, honor, and rewards of victory—the plaudits and gratitude of those they had redeemed from ignorance, slavery, and misery; the dignities and emoluments of the kingdom of peace; the reverence and respect of their fellow citizens—in proportion to their share of sufferings, labor, and devotion for their king. To such an appeal all but cowards would eagerly respond. The man who would refuse to answer such a call would be looked upon as a poltroon, a selfish wretch. The man who refuses to sacrifice self-interest at the call of high duty to his fellow men, the man who refuses in an extreme moment a service to a fellow citizen, will merit universally the withering reprobation that Dante bestowed on him who made "the great refusal" when he said: "I will not serve!" Given such a noble cause and such a magnificent king, only caitiffs and recreants can refuse allegiance and service.

The parable applied. We have a King who is a man such as we are, like to us in all things, sin only excepted, with a human heart to sympathize with all men in sorrow, disappointment, and depression: a heart full of boundless love, of gentleness and humility. And that King is living today, now, here in our midst. St. John, the beloved disciple, tells us how he saw our King one day when he fell into a vision on the island of Patmos. Inspired by the Holy Spirit, he wrote:

> And I saw heaven opened, and behold a white horse; and he that sat upon him was called faithful and true, and with justice doth he judge and fight. And his eyes were as a flame of fire, and on his head were many diadems.... And he was clothed with a garment sprinkled with blood; and his name is called, "the Word of God." And the armies that are in heaven followed him on white horses, clothed in fine linen, white and clean.... And he hath on his garment, and on his thigh written: "King of kings, and Lord of lords." (Rev. 19: 11–14, 16)

This is our King, Jesus Christ. Royalty is His by His natural birth, for the simple reason that He is God. In Heaven, from all eternity, as we have seen, the Word, the Second Person of the Blessed Trinity, is born of God the Father. On earth and in time, this same divine Person was born of Mary, never ceasing for an instant to be God. He possesses supreme dominion, supreme authority, supreme jurisdiction over all men. Jesus is our King because He is our God. His sovereignty over the world is already absolute. Yet it is a spiritual conquest that He desires, the winning of man through man's free choice. His campaign is an enterprise of love, love for those whom He would subdue, love for those who offer themselves as His comrades — indeed, in these latter, of whom we are, He would establish His Kingdom more firmly.

Yet this campaign is a campaign of suffering too. Now, all the world agrees that a true king reigns over and possesses by right of conquest whatever he wins in a just war, especially if he conquers an unjust and wicked foe at the cost of great personal sacrifice and suffering. But Christ our Blessed Lord, King by birth, became man for this purpose: that He might destroy the power of Satan over men. To win this victory, Jesus Christ had to pay a heavy ransom, an infinite price in personal sacrifice. To win this victory, Jesus Christ, though He was by nature God, emptied Himself, took the nature of a slave, and was made like unto men. And appearing in the form of man, He humbled Himself, "becoming obedient unto death, even to death on the cross" (see Phil. 2:6–8). Behold the King, seen by St. John, going forth to do battle in the cause of righteousness against the powers of darkness! He is clad in a garment deep-dyed in Blood, His own, and He is called the Word of God. Christ is our King because He won us in battle. He ransomed us with every drop of His precious Blood; His death freed us from bondage to Satan. It is right and reasonable to proclaim ourselves followers of this King, to know, to love, to serve Him, to give Him the most of our best, to say to Him from the heart: "Master, go on; and I will follow thee to the last gasp, with truth and loyalty" (Shakespeare, *As You Like It*, act 2, scene 3).

Finally, a really great king so governs that he improves the lives of his people and leads them to a realization of their noblest destiny. How magnificently does Christ do this for us! He calls us to aid Him in doing and carrying the same benefits to other less fortunate souls. At birth, we enter as life enemies of God, children of darkness, outcasts of Heaven. But thanks to our King and His conquest, in the sacrament of Baptism, the brilliant seal and character of our King is indelibly engraved on our souls; sin is utterly destroyed; grace floods the souls and makes us partakers of the divine nature of God. This sanctifying grace puts into our souls a real, physical, supernatural image of the nature of God. The

Holy Trinity now dwells in us in a very special way, with all graces, with all treasures. This makes us adopted children of God, deified persons, brothers to the God-man, our King Jesus Christ. Nor is this the whole amazing truth. Besides making us His brothers, Christ our King gives us His inheritance and makes us joint heirs with Himself of His glory. Now we understand why St. John saw the title, "King of kings and Lord of lords." Who are these other kings? Who are these other lords? We are those kings and those lords if we endeavor to serve our King with greater generosity, if we keep nothing back from Him. Has He not told us, "In my Father's house there are many mansions. . . . I go to prepare a place for you . . . that where I am, you also may be" (John 14:2–3)? Here is the cause to which we must completely devote ourselves, here is our leader in whom we can believe with our whole heart. Here is our King for whom we are ready to live and die. We cannot be content with mediocrity in His service; anything less than our best for Him would be despicable; for Him, we must make our lives sublime! Here is a King who will lead us and all men to the accomplishment of our highest destiny — eternal union with God. To Christ, our King, we desire to cling with utter devotion and to offer Him our best service. How? It is in our own souls that we must establish His Kingdom most firmly, first of all. When He is truly Lord there, His battle will have been won; for He is certain to secure anything that He wishes from those who are wholly His. In this sense, all our zeal for the Kingdom of Christ must be directed to "putting on the Lord Jesus Christ," to "letting that mind be in us which was in Christ Jesus," to "living, not now us, but Christ living in us," to being, with Christ, "nailed to the cross" (see Rom. 13:14; Phil. 2:5; Gal. 2:20; Col. 2:14).

Let us make a complete offering of ourselves to Christ today, to join that great army of Heaven that follows Him. As St. John saw it: "the armies that are in heaven followed him on white horses, clothed in fine linen, white and clean" (Rev. 19:14). We are destined to belong to those joyous, triumphant armies, if we keep our souls white and pure in this life. But we must fight loyally here in His cause if we are to reign royally with our King in Heaven.

The Sacrament of Pardon and Peace

NEED OF CONFESSION. Marie was white with fright as she was wheeled to the operating room. "Mother," she cried, "I hate hospitals." The operation was a success, and two weeks later, Marie was home, happy and healthy.

Dad practically had to lasso Paul and drag him to the dentist. "Dad," he howled from a swollen jaw, "I detest dentists." But within a week, Paul was smiling with normal, rosy cheeks.

It is a pity we need hospitals, but we do. It is a pity we need dentists, but we do. Because our bodies get sick, we need hospitals and doctors. Because our souls get sick, we need the confessional. In all three cases, it is tough going in, but it is wonderful coming out. Our Blessed Lord knew that the human heart has great need of revealing its troubles to others. Modern psychologists have rediscovered this truth. They have found that many nervous breakdowns can be traced to suppressed worries, fears, and guilt complexes over unconfided sins. Sin is the great soul-wrecker. It tears souls from the embrace of God, tortures them with a sense of harrowing guilt, and depresses them with lingering melancholy as long as they are estranged from God. The souls knows no peace until sin is destroyed in it. Suppressed sin, like suppressed steam, is dangerous. It festers in the soul, poisons, and paralyzes it. Confession is the safety valve.

Our Blessed Lord, in His divine mercy, instituted the Sacrament of Forgiveness to give us a chance to get the "load of sin" off our souls, while He at the same time pours grace into our souls and reunites us to Himself and His Father. He made Penance the sacrament of pardon and peace. Confession is simply the hospital of souls, where Christ, the divine Physician, displays His healing art through His priests, who bind up wounds and pour into the soul the oil and wine of His grace.

Confessing isn't pleasant. No one goes to a hospital for fun (unless he's mad), and no one goes to confession for fun either. It is humiliating to reveal our shame to another; the words stick in our throats; it seems awful, shocking. Yet we Catholics know it is not unbearable. We are sure of the strictest sacramental secrecy; we know we are confessing in reality to Christ, the divine Confessor, the friend of sinners. We know, too, that the priest to whom we confess and who stands in the place of Christ has been trained to be sympathetic and to live in imitation of our Lord. Despite these truths, there are some who go into near panic at confession time. Why? Don't they know that to make a good confession is a very simple process? The person with the know-how always finds his job easier. Let's look at the manner of confessing well.

The choice of confessor. The Church leaves to all penitents complete liberty in choosing a good confessor. No authority can prevent us from going to a confessor of our own choosing. However, care of our personal perfection must make us choose a regular and steady confessor, one who comes to know our difficulties, our aptitudes, our progress, and our falls and who consequently can adapt his advice to fit our needs. This confessor should be a man who is solicitous for perfection both for himself and for his penitents. If we belong to a religious institute, we should choose a confessor who is known for possessing a high degree of the true spirit of that institute. Hence, except for a special reason, a confessor approved and recommended by our superiors will be found to be just such a man.

How often should we go to confession? Here is a case in which the quality of confession is more important than the quantity. Certain saints attracted by a singular grace profitably went to confession every day. From their example, we can learn this lesson: their marvelous conception of the ideal of perfection and the care with which they examined their consciences led them to see clearly the disorders and faults of their souls. Sometimes, we mediocre and tepid souls can scarcely find anything to confess even at the end of a week! It is our poor blindness! But for fervent Christians and good religious, a good measure of confessing is at least once and maybe twice a week.

The confession. In order to avoid routine in our confessions, it is very useful, for example, to meditate from time to time on the Sacrament of Penance, on the malice of sin, or on the scenes of the Gospels that show our Savior exercising His mercy. On the day we will confess, it is good to ask in advance for special grace, to have a special intention for this subject in our prayers, in our Masses. What could be more natural? At the altar, we prepare for ourselves that sacred Blood that will be poured upon our wounds in confession. Divine friendship, that priceless treasure that we are seeking in confession, is strictly proportioned to the dignity of the Holy Sacrifice. At this Holy Sacrifice, ask with importunity for perfect repentance and for the generosity to make reparation; doing this, you already prove that you love, and in confession you will surely merit a great increase in the friendship and love of God. The length of your examination of conscience will vary according to the seriousness of your daily examinations of conscience. A few minutes will suffice if it is made with care. In this preparation, avoid two extremes: negligence and a scrupulous picking of conscience. Negligence would come to something like this: "I do not see anything particularly grave!" What lack of delicacy of conscience this attitude reveals! What would you think of the cleanliness and orderliness of a home where the domestics said each day as they considered cleaning house: "Well, well, there's nothing particularly dirty." Sloppy people, eh? Let's not become spiritually sloppy. In order to avoid scruples, if you are inclined that way, just remember that you do not have to confess venial sins at all. Better put your efforts on your sorrow and your firm purpose of amendment for all your deliberate faults, and don't consume your time trying to tabulate their number — a useless and sterile task. Remember, we can never completely free ourselves from involuntary faults and surprise setbacks. Concentrate on all voluntary defects: regret these, repair these, try to foresee these.

What about the actual accusation in confession? Here are some rules: Get rid of all useless accusations; avoid vague accusations; confess in a precise way every voluntary fault. Here are some useless accusations: "I had distractions in prayer, some temptations against faith, charity, chastity ..." The saints themselves experienced these trials. To be tempted is not a fault. To feel an attraction to wickedness is not necessarily to consent to this wicked attraction. Here are some vague accusations: "I have not been charitable enough, mortified enough, modest enough ..." Who ever will be enough of these? Besides, what grave sins are sometimes hidden under these expressions? Here are precise and exact accusations: "I spoke too much of myself by boasting; I exaggerated to the point of lying; I was a little negligent in repelling impure imaginations about three times." Just as the first vague and useless accusation bespeaks a poor examination of conscience without a purpose of amendment, so the precise accusation bespeaks the contrary. The humiliation that this latter accusation causes is voluntarily sought after and is very meritorious for the soul. Some saintly souls seriously seeking perfection are wont to say: "If you wish to make of your confession acts of reparation, if you wish to compensate for the sins you regret, then aim at making your confession cost you in shame and confusion." To do this, first of all tell out the things you are most ashamed of and be blunt: call a spade a spade, using simple and clear terms — boasting, lying, impurity — without exaggeration and without excuse. Then, to make sure your confession costs you in shame and confusion, make use of sins already pardoned in past good confessions, if you find that with the grace of God nothing serious or mortal has to be confessed now. This practice will recall to you your great weakness, will keep you humble and contrite, and will make you prove to God that you detest sin and are heartily sorry for it. This practice will be a sign of your generosity and of your desire to make reparation. Hence, many of the good faithful add to each of their confessions: "I accuse myself of all the faults of my past life, especially for grave scandal, for a sacrilegious communion, for all my deliberate sins against the virtue of purity (or whatever the grave fault may be)." This humble practice has the advantage of assuring you that your confession supplies sufficient matter for the obtaining of absolution.

This practice of rendering our confession humiliating to ourselves is a practice of devotion. Generous souls do this for the following reasons: (1) Each avowal of this kind inspires us with a desire to make reparation to God; it is an act of love indeed, increasing in value with the greater humiliation it costs us; (2) this act binds one down with special care to seek his own perfection; (3) by this act, one can earn many special graces for poor sinners who cannot open their lips to confess in time of serious sickness; (4) by imposing upon ourselves more humiliation than is necessary, we obtain for ourselves and others very special and indispensable graces; (5) we help in this way to save more souls than are saved by so many futile sermons.

Here is some practical advice as to how to recall past forgiven sins to our own shame and confusion. Avoid all details of them; give a generic accusation — sacrilegious communion, grave faults against the sixth commandment, etc. Moreover, if you see that, in confessing the same one, routine has set in, choose another that will make you realize your great sinfulness. Do not go back on these faults with apprehension.

What are the fruits of a generous and humble confession? Since the sacrament works *ex opere operato*, each time one receives it with the proper dispositions and without any obstacles, the soul of the penitent is flooded with sanctifying grace, however unworthy the minister of the sacrament may be. He is given a right to those special graces for which our Blessed Lord instituted the sacrament. Since we know that the amount of grace conferred depends on the dispositions of the penitent, then, to be sure, the generous soul who makes the perfect and humiliating confession of reparation receives far more grace because of his excellent disposition. Peace, a return of love, the friendship of God, the light-hearted freedom of the children of God — these are some of the most magnificent fruits of a good confession. Remember, then, this small rule to confess well: Be blunt, be brief, and be gone. Be blunt: Tell the exact kind and number of sins in simple, clear language, offering your shame in reparation. Be brief: Tell only those details needed to let the priest know the seriousness and species of the sin. Tell only your sins, not those of other people. Be gone: When you have done your best and have sincerely made your act of contrition for all your sins, rise from your knees with joy and peace. You are pleasing, in the sight of God, for you have been cleansed in the Blood of Jesus Christ, who died for you. Do not worry about the goodness of that confession. Should you later remember a mortal sin you forgot to confess, it is forgiven. True, you must mention this as a forgotten sin in your next regular confession. But in the meantime, you can peacefully receive Holy Communion. What a marvelous blessing to be able to hear every week the consoling words of the divine Confessor: "Peace be with you ... I absolve you ... Thy sins are forgiven ... Go in peace, and God bless you."

Confer: Pinard de la Boullaye, S.J., *Exercices Spirituels*, vol. 4., pp. 37–54.

THIRD MEDITATION

Incarnation

Now we are to consider in this contemplation the tragic plight of the world without Christ, so that we may appreciate to the best of our ability the marvelous meaning and the divine love that decreed the Incarnation of the Son of God to save the world. Still walking in the company of the three divine Persons, we are to look through the eyes of these lovable Persons upon the world that was in the power of Satan. We take God's view of the world's abominable condition. Seeing things with God's light always leads to a true evaluation and a healthy appreciation of all things.

St. Paul gives us a good description of what God saw when he explains the pagan world of his time, which was just beginning to hear the word of Christianity. Here is that horrible picture:

> For [the pagans without God] professing themselves to be wise, they became fools. And they changed the glory of the incorruptible God into the likeness of the image of a corruptible man, and of birds, and of four-footed beasts, and of creeping things [the rank idolatry that existed before Christ came]. Wherefore God gave them up to the desires of their heart, unto uncleanness, to dishonor their own bodies among themselves. Who changed the truth of God into a

lie; and worshipped and served the creature rather than the creator, who is blessed forever. Amen. For this cause God delivered them up to shameful affections. . . . And as they liked not to have God in their knowledge, God delivered them up to a reprobate sense, to do those things which are not convenient; being filled with all iniquity, malice, fornication, avarice, wickedness, full of envy, murder, contention, deceit, malignity, whisperers, detractors, hateful to God, contumelious, proud, haughty, inventors of evil things, disobedient to parents, foolish, dissolute, without affection, without fidelity, without mercy. (Rom. 1:22–26, 28–31)

Such was the world before Christ; with the people, as St. Ignatius says, wounding, killing, dying, and going to Hell. On this gruesome and repulsive sight looked the ever Blessed and loving Trinity, and in Their love and mercy, They determined that the Second Person should make Himself man in order to save the human race. This stupendous decision of God's love is beautifully expressed in the exordium to the dogmatic bull on the dogma of the Immaculate Conception:

God, the Ineffable . . . foreseeing from all eternity the tragic ruin of the whole human race that would be brought about by Adam's transgression, decreed in the mystery hidden from the world to complete the first work of His goodness by a still more hidden mystery, through the Incarnation of the Word, so that . . . what had fallen in the first Adam might be more blessedly raised up in the second Adam. (Pius IX, Apostolic Constitution *Ineffabilis Deus*).

All this vast and accumulating heap of sin was utterly abominable in the eyes of God and calculated to call down God's righteous wrath upon the entire race of man. And yet God, for all His infinite holiness, turned to mercy. He need not have done so. He might have exacted the last farthing of the debt of sin and condemned to eternal torment all who had incurred grievous guilt, without providing any special help to save men. God is not bound to remove obstacles to man's eternal destiny that have arisen through man's own fault. Or again, God might have freely pardoned all the past and forthwith have provided for a far ampler store of graces for the future. But where would be the great dignity of having the human race take part in its own restoration to God? How would the human race render to God an infinite apology for an infinite offense, an infinite reparation for the infinite fault? No, in His amazing goodness and justice, God determined to restore man to greater glory than that from which he had fallen. The new Adam would be God and man. By the Incarnation of the Son of God, the human race was elevated to an immensely higher plane than that on which it stood prior to his sin. Grace will no longer flow into the race merely from without, from God to man; now, with Christ as one of us, the race has received a right to grace, and it nurtures its principle within itself. Human nature, united to the divinity of Christ, receives a new head, with all the infinite dignity of that head, so that now the human race is able to discharge its infinite debt to God for sin in full and, at the same time, offer God infinite glorification.

Only in the realization of these truths does the mystery of the Incarnation appear in all its grandeur and in its full sublimity. The mystery of the Incarnation is not in the least perceptible by reason. The infinite love of God alone could conceive this plan, bring it into execution, and reveal it to us poor creatures. The God-man is not merely a supplement, a substitute for the first Adam, supplying for the deficiency caused by Adam. The God-man is a complement to the first Adam, pre-ordained by God as one who should be and do infinitely more for the race than the first Adam. To be sure, Christ was to supplement Adam, because He was to repair the havoc wrought by Adam in himself and the race and to supply for the deficiency of grace that thus arose. But this function is absorbed in His higher, more comprehensive function as complement. Since the God-man can and should be and effect immensely more for us, He can and should make good what Adam lost. Beyond our wildest desires and thoughts, God has revealed the depths of the divine tenderness for man. Let us lose ourselves with grateful hearts in the flood of divine riches and ask for an interior knowledge and love of the Lord, who for me has made Himself man, so that I may love Him the more and follow Him.

Our Blessed Lady. We now look to earth to see how marvelously God accomplished the Incarnation. We contemplate our Blessed Lady and the angel Gabriel and contrast their words and actions with those of Eve and the fallen angel who tempted her. For the Redemption is after the forms of the Fall; the actors in each are an angel, a woman, and a man. A rebel angel announced the primal lie that destroyed Paradise and turned the earth into a vale of exile and misery. His lie is involved in every sin. It is a lie that says we shall attain freedom and power by showing contempt of God's commands. A loyal angel, Gabriel, "the strength of God," announces the supernal truth on which the supernatural order is reestablished and fallen man enabled to become like unto God: the truth that blessedness consists in union with God. "Hail, full of grace! The Lord is with thee; blessed art thou," he said to Mary, and through her, to us (Luke 1:28). Blessed are we when God is with us, and in proportion as He is with us and we with Him. Eve, though not herself the direct agent of the ruin of the human race, was nevertheless by her seduction of Adam most intimately engaged in bringing about that ruin. So, too, yet in a far higher manner, Mary, the new

Eve, cooperated most closely and intimately in our Redemption with her Son Jesus, who is the new Adam and the One Redeemer. It was through Eve that sin first disfigured God's visible creation; her soul was the first to be stained by sin, thus fitting her to be instrumental in the overthrow of the supernatural order. It was, therefore, through Mary that primeval grace was again introduced into the world; her soul was the first since the Fall that was absolutely sinless and so fitted to be the anti-type of Eve, the helpmate of the Second Adam in the work of the Redemption.

Yet we may say with the Doctors and saints of the Church that the new order that Mary helped to found raised man from his guilt, his degradation, and his impotence to a dignity higher than that which he lost in paradise. St. Paul tells us that the gift is not like the offense, "For if by the offense of one, many died; much more the grace of God, and the gift, by the grace of one man, Jesus Christ, hath abounded unto many" (Rom. 5:15). Therefore, our Lady is far more closely and intimately connected with our Redemption than Eve was with the Fall. It was to the young, humble woman of no great wealth or power or accomplishments that the mighty archangel brought the plans of God for the Redemption of man through the Incarnation. And Mary, spotless from her conception, when told of the mystery that the Holy Spirit would work in her, dedicated and consecrated her virginity and motherhood to the accomplishments of God's sublime plans: "Behold the handmaid of the Lord; be it done unto me according to thy word" (Luke 1:38). In this overwhelming humility and obedience, the second Person of the Blessed Trinity was conceived as man. A heap of apparent impossibilities and contradictions took place, performed by the power and love of God for us men. The Creator became man; the eternal is born in time; the unchangeable begins to grow; a mother remains a virgin. As the old hymn has it: Strength is made weak; Immensity becomes small; Eternity is born. What wonders You have done, O Jesus, for the sake of man, whom You loved so ardently, outcast from Paradise.

Christ the Incarnate in Mary's womb. At Mary's loving consent to be His Mother, the second Person of the Blessed Trinity leapt down from His heavenly throne and was conceived in Mary's virginal womb. Infinity in bonds: He emptied Himself, taking the form of a servant; being made in the likeness of men — nine months in the womb — the life of Christ's patience began. As a man might sit in a darkened room, having at his command the electric light but refusing to use it, so Jesus in Mary's womb. All His life as man He had at His command the glory of the Godhead, the glory of the only-begotten Son of the Father. He only once displayed this glory in His Transfiguration. Then He put it away from Him and effaced Himself for the love of us.

We must learn from Jesus in Mary's womb the power of lowliness and the strength of love. We must learn that other arms of our warfare, essential as they may be — wisdom, learning, eloquence, the graces of refinement in speech and manners, ability to lead and inspire men, or whatsoever else — would be useless in our hands unless he who wields them is inspired with the humility, lowliness, and love of the divine Son, who willingly effaced Himself for the love of His Father and His brethren.

Pray to follow and imitate our Lord Incarnate. Ask especially that the divine purpose of the Incarnation may always be accomplished in your life.

Confer: Matthias Joseph Scheeben,
The Mysteries of Christianity, pp. 353–356.

FOURTH DAY

Purpose: To inspire the purified soul with a strong love for Jesus Christ and an intense desire to follow Him generously and without fear of the cost

Patron: St. Ignatius

Points for Self-Consideration:

- Poverty. Have I grown in the spirit of poverty as well as in the external observance?
- Am I glad when I feel the effects of poverty?
- Do I try to have few needs and to get on with little?
- Am I attached to comforts, conveniences, and superfluities?

Suggested Readings:

Hebrews

Imitation of Christ, bk. 1, ch. 1

Spiritual Exercises: Rules for Scruples

Aspiration:

> *"I am the way, and the truth, and the life. No man cometh to the Father but by me." (John 14:6)*

FIRST MEDITATION

The Nativity

IN THIS CONTEMPLATION, St. Ignatius takes us in spirit and imagination to the birth of the God-man. He wants us to be present, to see the places, to watch the persons, to hear their words, to enter into their emotions, to speak to them, to become a living part of the great drama of our salvation.

Imagine yourself, then, on the road to Bethlehem one fine, clear, starry night. You join Mary and Joseph just as you enter the town. At the caravansary, the town inn, you are told that there is really no more room. Hundreds of others had been brought to town by the second great census of the Roman Empire, and they have crowded the inn to bursting. Hence, you need not suppose any fault on the part of those who turn you and the humble couple away. Still, a place has to be found. Joseph tells you that his wife is due to have her baby. In a moment, you are solicitous to help the gentle couple; even before He is born, your heart goes out to the Child. Finally, after much effort, a cave is found. It is a stable of sorts, and inside there is a manger. Here Mary gives birth to the divine Infant and lays Him in the straw of the manger, wrapped in swaddling clothes. On either side are Mary and Joseph adoring the Infant; and you, with a heart full of joy at this most blessed event, join them in prayer and adoration. With the holy parents, you are "making melody in your heart," for the desired of the nations has come (Eph. 5:19). He who was foretold by the prophets, called the Messiah, is in your midst a living, lovable Child, come to bring back His people to the bosom and company of God.

The Child. The happiness of Mary and Joseph has been experienced all the world over for centuries, and it is still pressed into the hearts of men on each anniversary of His birth. Why? You will notice that no matter how tired or worried people are, no matter what fears of wars or rumors of wars torment them, when His birthday comes around, when His holy night shines forth again, a quiet happiness glows deep in the hearts of all good men. And this happiness is due to the old story, the true story, the story whose telling never tires us.

The great happiness of this Silent Night not only filled human hearts, but all creation thrilled at the tiny magnificence of the Child. It is recorded that legions of gloriously resplendent angels broke through the vault of Heaven to carol the arrival of God Himself as man. And His proud Father and ours, to celebrate this truly blessed event, hung a bright star in His sky to let everybody know, from the simple shepherds on the hills to the wisest kings of the Orient, that their little divine brother was born.

Thus it was, in the stillness of that wondrous night, that the Word was made flesh and came to dwell among us. Thus it is that each Christmas we remember the prophecy of Isaiah: "A Child is born to us, and a son is given to us, and the government is upon his shoulder: and his name shall be called, Wonderful, Counselor, God the Mighty, the Father of the world to come, the Prince of Peace" (Isa. 9:6). And we gather around our little brother to gaze adoringly upon Him. It is not mere poetry or sentimental fantasy that makes us call the divine Christ our brother. It is the plain, glorious fact that a portion of the flesh and blood of each one of us is in our Christ Child.

The saints of all ages gazing lovingly, even as we do now, upon God in our flesh enthusiastically tell us over and over again with St. Cyprian that "what man is Christ wished to be, that man in turn might be what Christ is." Or as St. Augustine so forcefully expressed: "God has become man that man might become God." And as St. Cyril exclaimed:

> Christ is called the new Adam because by sharing in our nature He has enriched us all unto happiness and glory. Thus by dwelling in one human nature, Christ dwells in all, so that His human nature being made the Son of God (in power), the same dignity now passes to the whole human race.

Even as the Christ child became man by putting on our flesh, even so we become God by being incorporated into His flesh.

Yes, the Feast of the Nativity is a family day of rejoicing because it is the birthday of the youngest Son. On that day, all over the world, the human family is gathered around His crib in loving adoration. His gift to every one of us is His own divine nature. He offers us a real, physical sharing in the intimate life of the Most Holy Trinity begun here in this life. "I am come that they may have life and may have it more abundantly" (John 10:10). The life of which Christ speaks is the life of God.

Now we all know how our hearts fill up with unspeakable joy as we gaze through the big window of the hospital nursery to see our own flesh and blood held up for our first look at our most precious heart's desire. And we know how much greater is our joy when we are able for the first time to take our little son into our own arms and hold him as our very own. "My boy!" says Dad. "My baby!" says sister. "My brother!" says Johnny. "My child!" says Mother. Whenever we view the manger, Mary holds up our youngest for our adoring gaze. And He comes not just into our arms but into our inmost hearts, there to live in love with us forever. No merely human infant can share his life with us so intimately; no merely human infant can make his home within our hearts so completely.

The guests. In the hills about Bethlehem, simple shepherds were watching their sheep at the moment of our Lord's birth. Suddenly, the resplendent heavens were aglow with streams of heavenly light. St. Luke tells us:

> Behold an angel of the Lord stood by them [the shepherds], and the brightness of God shone round about them; and they feared with a great fear. And the angel said to them: Fear not; for behold, I bring you good tidings of great joy, that shall be to all the people: for this day is born to you a Savior, who is Christ the Lord, in the city of David. And this shall be a sign unto you. You shall find the infant wrapped in swaddling clothes and laid in a manger. And suddenly there was with the angel a multitude of the heavenly army, praising God, and saying: Glory to God in the highest; and on earth peace to men of good will. And it came to pass, after the angels departed from them into heaven, the shepherds said one to another: Let us go over to Bethlehem, and let us see this word that is come to pass, which the Lord hath showed to us. (Luke 2:9–15)

The shepherds were men of good will, the true representatives of the Old Testament. They led a pastoral life of simple faith. Doubtless they went to Jerusalem at the fixed times and with overflowing heart sang praise and thanksgiving unto God amid the glories of His Temple. In their ears rang the warnings and invitations of the prophets, and on their lips were the sacred psalms. Theirs was a simple and righteous life. God saw their faith and their love and blessed them for it. They truly represented the Jews and all that their religion could do for them. These were the men of God's good pleasure. When the shepherds had found the Infant and His parents, they understood what had been told them concerning this Child. "And all that heard wondered ... at those things that were told them by the shepherds" (Luke 2:18). We, too, will understand this Child if our hearts are humble, simple, and full of faith in God and of love and reverence toward Him.

The Magi. The other guests at the birthday celebration of Christ our Lord were the wise men from the East. It is a most consoling thought that God chose wise men to represent the Gentiles at His Son's birth. Much as we would have preferred it, we couldn't be there ourselves, since our pilgrimage on earth was decreed for the present time. Yet could the Lord have chosen better representatives for us? The wise men were perhaps of Babylonia, learned astronomers of the Orient. Now the Jews had been in Babylonia in captivity, and even at that time there were still a large number of Jews in those parts. Perhaps these Jews told the wise men of the star that should arise out of Jacob. Anyway, they were acquainted with the prophecy that a great King promised by God would be born among the Jews. They knew this tradition was handed down among the Jews, and they knew that the heavens were to announce the great King's coming. They no doubt studied the books of the Jews carefully to see that the prophecy was no fraud but the genuine words of the ancient prophets. Satisfied as to this, they believed the prophecy wholeheartedly; quite literally, they put their faith to work, searching the sky for the promised sign. It came in the brilliant, burning star of Bethlehem. Quite forcefully, their hope to see the King drove them over field and fountain, moor and mountain until at last they came to the newborn King. They had not come empty-handed! Faith had stirred them to believe; hope had driven them forward to seek; but love had prompted them to take treasures along to offer to the new King. And what royal treasures they offered the Child! Gold to crown Him while they acknowledged His dominion over all; frankincense to honor His divinity as they bowed to adore Him; myrrh to symbolize His future sacrifice as they rejoiced in His present infancy. Had we been present, could we have done more? Can we do anything better today than follow the Christ Child with the strong faith of the Magi; rejoice in Him with their exceeding great joy; love Him with their total generosity? The wise men are our representatives; the wise men were given to be our example. It must be that God wants us, in imitation of their example, to become wise with His own wisdom, with the possession of His own divine Son.

Let us turn to our Lord and thank Him for undergoing so much deprivation and humiliation in order to make us happy by His coming. Let us congratulate Mary on her wonderful Child, pleading with her as the Mother of God to give us the graces to grow in love and holiness with Him all the days of our lives. And let us ask Joseph, the silent one, to teach us to cherish the Child and all the wants of His heart so that we may be ever as devoted to Him as he was.

Reflect that Christ did all this for you. Ask yourself: what am I doing for love of Him now? What have I done in the past? What shall I do for Him in the future? Is there anything He is asking of me for the future? If so, let me generously and with full love offer this to the Son of God as I contemplate His complete offering of Himself there in the manger.

SECOND MEDITATION

The Two Standards

ST. IGNATIUS PROPOSES to us a parable. In this parable, we learn of our Lord's campaign to win souls and of the campaign of His great adversary. Each bears his own standard and calls souls to rally round. We have to fully realize that there is a war going on: "The life of man upon earth is a warfare" (Job 7: 1). In this war, no one can be neutral: "He that is not with me is against me" (Matt. 12:30). Much as we may pine for peace, we cannot put our heads in the sand and hope to avoid the battle. "The devil goes about like a roaring lion seeking whom he may devour" (see 1 Pet. 5:8). And unless we repulse him with the strength of God, we shall inevitably be devoured by him. He is far too powerful and cunning for the unaided resources of us poor, weak men.

It would be an error to imagine that in this contemplation St. Ignatius proposes to us the choice between the standard of Jesus Christ and that of Satan. We rededicated ourselves solely to Christ in earlier meditations. No, this contemplation is meant to enlighten our minds, to make us familiar with the principles and techniques of Christ and Satan so that we may use our precious information in making wise decisions and choices throughout our lives. It is an appeal to the intellect to appreciate that wisdom of God that is foolish to men. Commitment alone does not suffice. His wisdom must help us to discern the principles of Christ and those of Satan, especially when Satan's principles seem to bear a resemblance to those of Christ, when the tempter would appeal to us in the clothing of "an angel of light" (2 Cor. 11:14).

The *mise-en-scène*, to be worked out more elaborately as the contemplation progresses, is two-fold. Think of it this way: Near Jerusalem, Christ marshals His followers in a great field. At another camp, in the region of Babylon, Lucifer marshals his forces. The cities chosen are the City of Peace and the City of Confusion. Our prayer is for a thorough knowledge of both leaders and of their respective strategies. Satan's wiles we must understand, for many a battle is lost because the enemy is underestimated or not known for what he is and for what he is seeking. Even in recent times, communists have won many political battles simply because diplomats are ignorant of the inherent wickedness of their diabolical doctrine. Some have believed they could compromise with the communists, and as a result, they were inevitably enslaved. Even so with the devil; there can never be any compromise with him, no talking things over with him. He's our sworn enemy; to dicker with him is to become his slave. There can never be a truce between us, never an armistice, never any peace feelers of any sort. It's a fight to the death. We simply have to learn his methods of battle in order to conquer him. On the other hand, we must learn Christ's methods because He is the seed of the woman who has crushed the serpent's head. He has never been under the dominion of the Evil One. Hence, He has given us the perfect formula for the victory over Lucifer. Following His life, imitating His campaign of battle, we are bound to bring our whole lives to a glorious victory over Satan and all his forces of evil.

Satan and his principles. We come then to contemplate Satan upon a throne of fire and smoke in the region of Babylon. What a horrible figure to behold!

The fire signifies the destruction he has wrought upon himself and upon others, the destruction he is scheming to impose upon the whole world. True, God allows him to use his power against us in order to try our love. Yet God does not suffer us to be tempted above our strength but bestows abundant grace and easy victory on them that call upon Him with humility and trust. In utter reliance upon God, we have for Satan the contempt that God has for the renegade angel. The fire also reminds us of Satan's rage and frenzy to destroy us.

The smoke signifies the darkness in which Satan shrouds his evil designs. His victims must be kept in ignorance and perplexity; they must not be clear in their own minds nor yet go to others for instruction and counsel. Only the children of light are safe against him, for they leave no dark places in their souls for him. Desiring to know themselves as God sees them and knows them, they are not ashamed to call in one of God's ministers to help them expose both Satan and his wiles within their souls.

What is Satan doing unceasingly every moment of time? He is sending his devils everywhere, to every country, every town, every person; none are too high for him, nor any too low for him. Long ago, St. John Chrysostom told us that each of us has one particular demon who is laboring assiduously for our damnation and who will hang around us until in the strength of our Savior and in His imitation we shall shake him off at the hour of death. So the devils are out with "nets and snares" because they are the sworn enemies of human nature. By destroying us, they hope to take their revenge against their Creator for having cast them out of Heaven. Jealous of us who are called and destined for Heaven, they are determined to drag us into their own misery and thus sate their malicious hatred toward God. The Wicked One addresses his subordinates, harshly, in a torrent of hate, like a Hitler wildly raving: I want victories! Bring me damned souls!

Yet there is cunning and a definite plan to the campaign, which the wise old rebel maps out. True, his subordinates hate their seducer, yet they have to admire his superior craftiness, and they willingly accept his help for their common design of evil. There is an expert distribution of his resources. All of his agents have had thousands of years of experience since Adam and Eve, and though they were obliged to change their tactics since the coming of Christ, they have learned in the last two thousand years how to lead men and nations astray successfully. Look at the fall of a Luther or Henry VIII, and again at the fall of such Catholic nations as England, Germany, and Scandinavia.

St. Ignatius tells us that the devil first tempts us to covetousness for riches, in order that we may more easily come to vain honor of the world and afterwards to ever-growing pride. The first step may be riches, the second honor, the third pride; and from these three steps, he leads on to all the other vices.

Why does St. Ignatius put the root of all evils in riches? Because riches represent at bottom all that can be sought in the world apart from God, and the power to enjoy creatures. Wealth attracts us on the side of the comfort and luxury it promises us. Moreover, wealth fascinates us for the respectability that goes with it. We know well that the craze for honor — or worse, for notoriety — haunts our age. Therefore, not comfort and pleasure so much as honor is the theme of abnegation in his parable of the Two Standards. Riches lead to vainglory. It is an easy step; we possess things worth having and feel self-complacent. This self-complacency is increased by the deference that others show us for our wealth. Sure of ourselves, we turn inevitably away from God. Having turned to creatures, we forget God and become satisfied with our possession. Pride, of course, is the climax of this turning away from God. We become so pleased with ourselves, and others so feign to have the same pleasure in us, that we become independent of God. This is pride. No wonder Christ said: "It is easier for a camel to pass through the eye of a needle than for a rich man to enter into the kingdom of heaven" (Matt. 19:24). And remember: no great wealth is needed for all this, but only the possession of something that can yield satisfaction and is recognized by others as such. The teaching and even the scenery of this part of the Two Standards is no mere invention of St. Ignatius. It is found in the Gospel of St. Luke 6:12–26. There our Lord calls His disciples up the mountain where He has been praying through the night. He picks out twelve of them, whom He calls apostles. Then He descends and stands on a plateau on the lower hillside, Himself, like a general surrounded by his staff, with His apostles around Him. At a little distance, the rest of His disciples; further off, a multitude of the Jews and Gentiles, representing the world at large. Looking at His disciples, for it concerns them most of all, He pronounces four benedictions: on the poor, on the hungry, on mourners, and on men whom other men hate because of their justice. Then the true "shepherd and bishop of our souls" (1 Pet. 2:25) pronounces woe to the rich, to them that are filled, to them that laugh, to them whom all men speak well of. These are they whom the devil has caught in his nets and chains of riches, vain honor, and pride.

Christ and His principles. And now we turn to Christ, who stands lovely and lovable amid His followers without any kind of external display. It is important to observe throughout the Two Standards how Christ, "the Sovereign and True Leader," behaves with the quiet, unassuming grace of one who is conscious of His rank beyond dispute, while Satan shows all the fussy pompousness of an upstart and pretender. "Why, Majesty is so manifest," says St. Teresa, addressing our Lord, "that there is no need of a retinue or guard to make us confess that Thou art King." St. John Chrysostom tells us that truth is tranquil and unpretentious; pride has all the restlessness of falsehood. Truth marches with humility, whereas deliberate systematic lying, to gain a prize to which one is not entitled, is the natural issue of pride. The gentle Christ, too, dispatches His angelic ambassadors throughout the world to save all men and win them for Himself. But here we dwell on His ambassadors among men, of the race of men.

And note the campaign of Christ. It is diametrically opposite to the devil's. First, Christ would bring all to spiritual poverty: that deep and lively sense of the supreme importance of salvation, our inability to obtain it alone, and the need to detach ourselves from the things of the world. To help man attain to this detachment and freedom from the things of this life, Christ would have His followers love to suffer actual poverty, even reproaches and affronts. This is the beginning of a turning away from creatures, and a casting of oneself upon God: it means a loss of all interest in creatures, save insofar as God can be loved in them and they in God. This is a high ideal and must be attained by degrees. One step is patience and meekness under affronts. Another is braving human respect. Another step is a staunch adherence to an unpopular cause when it seems to be the cause of God. Another step is the practical conviction that what we call "snubs" are often better for our spiritual advancement than compliments, failure more profitable to the soul than success. Another step is not to be jealous but rather to rejoice when others have a following and we have none. These practices will lead us to those "inflamed desires of wearing the livery of Christ" in the shape of "insults, slanders and injuries, and being accounted a fool," which St. Ignatius sets so much store by that he refuses to admit into his society any postulant who does not at least "feel the desire of feeling these desires" (*Examen Generale*, ch. 4, nos. 44–45). St. Thomas tells why Christ has called His followers to humility:

The reason why Christ has particularly commended humility to us is because thereby is removed the chief obstacle to man's salvation. For man's salvation consists in tending to things heavenly and spiritual, from which he is hindered by striving to magnify himself in earthly things. And therefore, for the removal of this obstacle, our Lord has shown by examples of humility how external grandeur should be despised. And thus humility is a predisposition to man's free approach to spiritual and divine goods. (*Summa Theologiae*, IIa–IIae, q. 161, art. 5)

Notice how often that the final stage of an active and honored life is often a bed of sickness and nursing, of helplessness and ignominy. This is the last probation for Heaven.

We ask for one thing absolutely in this contemplation — that we may be received under Christ's standard in absolute poverty of spirit. We ask a second thing conditionally (and I do mean conditionally) — that we may be received to actual poverty if it should so please His Divine Majesty. Conditionally also in undergoing affronts and injuries, the more to imitate Him in them, provided only that we may undergo them without sin of any person or displeasure of His Divine Majesty. Having thus accepted Christ once more with increased loyalty and understanding for our holy Leader, for our eternal King, we return to the contemplation of His life, there to see how beautifully He lived out in His own life His own plan of campaign against the devil, and there to draw more light, more inspiration, and more love so that we may become more like Him every day.

Confer: Joseph Rickaby, *Spiritual Exercises of
St. Ignatius Loyola*, pp. 113–117.

CONFERENCE

Mary

MANY SUMMERS AGO, a priest friend of mine and I were down
in lovely old New Orleans. To be exact, we were standing in a long
line, waiting to be admitted to hear the NBC Toscanini-conducted
Symphony Orchestra at the Municipal Auditorium. It was a hot
evening, and a tropical torrent was just beginning to drench the
streets. A green Ford eased to the curb where we stood.

"Father Tom," called the driver to my companion, "take these
two tickets and have a nice evening." "What about yourself, Nick?
Aren't you going to the concert?" "Sure enough, Father. Mary and I
got two extra tickets from our friend in the ticket office. Here, take
these; get out of the rain. Good night, Fathers."

So Father had a friend who had a friend, and I now had these
friends also, two people whom I had never met. You notice in life
that everybody has friends who fix things for them. Mother has
a friend who got her a television set wholesale; Dad got business
information from phoning special contacts. And Junior got a great
summer job at the ballpark because he knows the right people. Even
the most lonely people know someone from whom they can borrow
a hammer or a can of coffee in a domestic crisis.

The trouble is, we very often fail to appreciate and evaluate our
friends. One of the most shamefully undervalued human friendships

in all the world is between each one of us and the Mother of God. St. John relates the perfect picture of how good a friend she is in his story of the wedding feast of Cana (John 2:1–12). Were you to ask the host of that feast what he thought of Mary as a friend, he would tell you that she is the best friend he has ever met in his life.

In order to renew our devotion to Mary and to convince ourselves that we can attain perfection through her, let us consider (1) the affection that Mary has for each of us, (2) the power she wields in our favor, and (3) the place Mary ought to enjoy in our lives.

In Heaven, Mary's love for her divine Son and the regeneration of the world has by no means been weakened. On the contrary, it has been broadened and deepened. From her exalted place where she reigns with Jesus, she looks with love upon all the faithful. No matter how poor we may be in virtue, there is a unique reason for which Mary cannot help but shower upon us her love and her maternal protection. It is the last will and testament that Jesus expressed upon the Cross: "Woman, behold thy son" (John 19:26). Was it of John alone that Christ was speaking? Explicitly, yes. But the Church, the only authorized interpreter of the words of Christ, has always held that Christ meant that all His followers should be joined with the beloved John when He gave him to Mary — just as Christ joined us all to John when He gave Mary to him as his mother: "Son, behold thy mother; love her the way I have loved her." Could such a mother forget the dying prayer of such a Son, or even His daily prayer? She loves each one of us, despite our faults; she is anxious to collaborate with us in our own sanctification, in works of zeal for her Son, in order to make us most faithful imitators of her Son. Make no mistake about it, Mary not only desires to preserve us from mortal sin, but she plans and prays to make us saints of her Son.

The power Mary wields in our favor. Our Blessed Lady wants to help us. But can she? Easily. She can do as she pleases. The

Doctors of the Church have told us that she is prayerfully omnipotent. What is the source of this power in Mary? Well, since she gave life to the Savior, she remains His Mother for all eternity. And she not only can ask Him but also, as His Mother, command Him to give her what she wants. Had not our Savior said, "Whosoever shall do the will of my Father . . . he is my brother, and sister, and mother" (Matt. 12:50)? In other words, our obedience to the Father makes us dearer to Him than a brother, a sister, or a mother according to the flesh. He had also said: "Happy is that servant whom the Master will find faithful at his coming; he will put him over all his goods" (see Matt. 24:46–47). To obey in perfection is therefore most efficacious. Mary alone had perfect love and resignation to God's will in her prayer: "*Fiat mihi secundum verbum tuum*" (Luke 1:38). As He loved and obeyed her perfectly in life, so Jesus wills to give her His eminent obedience in Heaven, He who is the ideal and exemplar of all obedience. If Christ would place a faithful servant over all His works, how much more Mary, His Mother, the most faithful of all creatures in the humble service of God.

What is the extent of Mary's power? The words are clear. Christ has placed Mary over all His goods. Mary is all-powerful in prayer because she need only express a desire and she sees it realized. Her intercession is infallibly efficacious. According to St. Bernard and the common opinion among the faithful, God has placed in her hands the right of distributing grace. God will pardon, save, and sanctify whomever His Mother recommends, because He wishes to honor His Mother.

God accommodated himself to our weakness when He made Mary, our Mother and His, an all-powerful advocate for us. For He knows that sometimes we are frightened by His justice and by the fact that Jesus is to be the strict Judge of the living and the dead. So in case these truths paralyze us into fear or expecting pardon,

He gave us His gentle and holy Mother to be our advocate so that she might bring us back to Him and to our own peace and happiness. St. Bernard has well expressed this truth in his sermon on the birthday of Mary:

> Do you fear to approach the Father? Well, He has given you Jesus to be your mediator. What cannot such a Son obtain from His Father for you? He is your brother! He is of your blood! For you He has suffered all trials, sin alone excepted, in order to show you mercy. But perhaps His divine majesty frightens you, for although man, He is still God. For your affairs before Him, you desire another advocate? So be it. You have Mary as your advocate. She is the purest of all creatures, not only of men but of all creatures. I do not hesitate to say that she will be heard by reason of her great dignity. Yes, the Son will give her whatever she asks, and the Father will give the Son whatever He asks for her.

Mary's place of honor in our lives. Since she is our loving Mother, all-powerful, our advocate, we must love Mary the best after her Son, Jesus. We must conform ourselves to the divine plan that has made Mary the Mediatrix of all graces and seek all gifts — especially the better spiritual gifts — from Jesus through Mary. Unceasingly, we must seek from her greater purity, greater love, greater faith, and greater humility. Make it a habit to ask no gift from God except through Mary. We honor her by doing this, for we express our unbounded confidence in her goodness, and in so honoring her, we honor Jesus, her Son, and give greater glory to God in this manner. We rejoice the Savior, for by granting her petition in our behalf, He receives from us another opportunity of honoring and glorifying His Mother.

This should be a sweet and easy resolution to make and carry out. It isn't necessary that this recourse to Mary be always explicit. It suffices to offer all our prayers, actions, and intentions of the day to Jesus through Mary. Let us tell Mary to help us imitate her virtues in suffering and fidelity to God. We should beg her to prevent us from becoming spoiled children, unable to bear the humiliations and sufferings that God sends us for our sanctification. Ask her to help our weakness in time of trials. We should never despair when we ask Mary for some favor. (Look at Lourdes and the millions of favors she has granted and is granting there!) By continually trusting her, we prove our high esteem and conviction of her goodness and generosity. We are sure to obtain what is good for us if we continue to implore Mary with confidence: "Never was it known that anyone who sought they protection was left unaided!" Never let us hear from Mary's lips that complaint of Jesus to His apostles: "Hitherto you have not asked anything in my name. Ask, and you shall receive; that your joy may be full" (John 16:24). Let us ask Mary for the better gifts of which St. Paul speaks: faith, hope, and, above all, charity (see 1 Cor. 13:13). Ask for the conversion of sinners, the success of difficult spiritual works. Ask to become saints! It is a task above all our forces, yet we are called to it. How much easier this task becomes with the help of Mary the Mother of Good Counsel. She knows how to make us become saints. Ask for perseverance and an ever-increasing love of God and neighbor. If you happen to fall, run to Mary.

In our day, when we lacked the proper leaders to fight against the great enemy of God, communism, Mary came forward through the little ones at Fatima to be our leader. Her plan is: Pray the Rosary daily; live good Catholic lives; consecrate yourselves to her Immaculate Heart. If we do these good things, Russia will be converted. Remember, Mary can fix anything; she is the best friend in the world. She is the woman whose heel has crushed and still can crush the serpent's head. But we must cooperate with her; we must put her campaign into practice. Certainly, she who crushed the serpent's head can easily cause the godless empire of communism to altogether crush and crumble from within, if only we pray with her, live like her, love her, and completely dedicate our lives to her.

Confer: Pinard de la Boullaye, S.J., *Exercices Spirituels*, vol. 4, pp. 125–138.

THIRD MEDITATION
The Loss and Finding in the Temple

IN THIS MEDITATION on the Finding of the Divine Child in the Temple, we have recorded the first message of the King. St. Luke reports faithfully and graphically this important episode in our Lord's life, just as he must have heard it from the lips of the Blessed Virgin. Mary, the bereaved Mother, could not forget one detail of those three days of sorrowing search. And so we see in our mind and imagination the Boy of twelve years — practically a man now, for centuries ago youth in the Eastern lands were considered men when they attained their thirteenth birthday. From that time on, the Jewish boy was subject to the law and held to its full observance — even in the matter of its admittedly difficult precepts, such as the annual fast on the Day of Atonement and the pilgrimage to Jerusalem. Pious parents took the pains to introduce their children to these practices a little before the law enjoined them.

According to the Mosaic Law, every adult Jew had to appear three times a year before Almighty God to worship and offer sacrifices. Unless legitimately prevented, all those within a day's journey from Jerusalem were required to celebrate there the Passover, Pentecost, and the Feast of Tabernacles. No legal obligation bound the women and children. Nevertheless, we see in the Gospel that Mary was in the habit of accompanying her holy spouse, Joseph, and that

Jesus joined them when He was twelve years old. So we see Jesus, Mary, and Joseph traveling the seventy-five miles from Nazareth to Jerusalem in a large caravan of other pilgrims. They are making the pilgrimage in a spirit of piety, not routine; in a spirit of devotion, not custom; they are eager to worship God in His holy Temple. And what of the sentiments of the Boy? How does He enter upon this period of His life?

Since the day when, in His Mother's arms, He had been offered to the eternal Father, Jesus had never gone up to the Temple. Yet He had waited anxiously for this first visit, to pour out His heart to His Father in that most hallowed place and to renew the oblation of that sacrifice that He, the true Lamb of God, would later offer on Mount Calvary. He was eager to see His Father's House, to worship Him there. Already, the zeal of His Father's House had eaten Him up (see John 2:17; cf. Ps. 68:10). Actually, He needed no temples to commune with God; His heart was the true Temple of God: "Sacred Temple of God," "Tabernacle of the Most High," "House of God and Gate of Heaven." Yet the prophet foretold that "the Lord, whom you seek ... shall come to his temple" (Mal. 3:1). Since we are to spend our time with Jesus in this Temple, it will be very appropriate to get a brief picture of that holy edifice.

The Temple of the true God was erected in the middle of a vast esplanade, much greater in area than the Acropolis of Athens or the Capitol of Rome or the sacred wood of Olympus; greater even than the Place de la Concorde in Paris. The foundation of the Temple resembled at a distance a mountain of rock. Within were a multiplicity of galleries, conduits, sewers, and cisterns, making up an inextricable labyrinth. From whatever direction the Temple was approached (except from the north, where there was no entrance open to the public), it was necessary to *go up* to the Temple. It was reached either by long and wide staircases, or by viaducts spanning the Tyropoeon Valley, or by gently sloping avenues leading to the middle of the courts. On arriving there, one was dazzled by the multicolored flagstones and, above all, by the interminable files of Corinthian columns surrounding the immense platform on all four sides. The Royal Porch on the south, with its four rows of 162 monolithic columns — so great in circumference that three men with arms outstretched could scarcely encompass the shaft — gave the impression of the most monumental of basilicas. The ceiling was of carved cedar and lavishly covered with ornamentation in silver and gold.

Everyone, without distinction of race or religion, had free access to the outer courts, but only Israelites and circumcised proselytes could enter the sanctuary itself. This was encompassed by an elegant balustrade upon which, at regular intervals, were placed inscriptions in Greek and Latin forbidding strangers to go beyond it under penalty of death. Beyond the balustrade, a stairway of fourteen steps led to a landing on which was built the wall of the sacred enclosure. This was a lofty structure of great stones polished like marble, its monotony relieved by nine richly decorated gates. The principal entrance for both men and women was at the east, toward the Mount of Olives. This was the Beautiful Gate or Gate of Nicanor, celebrated for its facing of Corinthian brass.

The various parts of the Temple reserved to the Jews mounted one above another in elevation. From the Court of the Gentiles, an ascent was made to reach the Women's Court, and again to reach the Court of Israel. The Court of the Priests, the altar of the sacrifice, and the Sanctuary proper were on still higher levels. The Jews must have drawn their inspiration from the Greek architects, whose temples, rising from a flat coping as from a pedestal, reached up solitary into the blue of Heaven, giving the impression of greater height than they really had.

The dimensions of the sanctuary were fixed by immutable tradition. The Holy of Holies, which the high priest entered once a year, measured about twenty cubits (about six meters) square. The Holy Place, where stood the golden candelabrum, the Altar of Incense, and the table for the showbread, was the same as the Holy of Holies in width but twice as long. These dimensions would have been out of proportion to the rest of the edifice had not this disharmony been remedied by raising the height of these buildings and by enclosing the Holy Place and the Holy of Holies in a group of much more stately constructions. In the front of the Sanctuary stood a pylon, a sort of triumphal arch 100 cubits in height and the same in width. Through the opening of this pylon, the faithful could see the veil that covered the entrance to the Sanctuary and, on its pediment, the decoration of the famous golden vine.

This was the magnificent edifice into which Jesus came to worship His Father. In His later life, when He visits this holy House for the last time just before beginning His Passion, one of His disciples will say to Him: "Look, Master, what great stones and what a beautiful monument!" (see Mark 13:1). But now, as a young Man, He came and saw the layers of stone placed one upon another without cement so artfully that the eye could scarcely distinguish the joinings. The whole structure would have struck His eyes in wonderment; a palace carved out of rock. This Temple of Jerusalem, His Father's House, resting on its gigantic substructures, seemed built for eternity.

Jesus remains in the Temple. After honoring His Father with perfect adoration, bowing before Him, and, as man, giving Him perfect reparation for the idolatry of the human race, Jesus acclaimed His Father in glorious acts of thanksgiving, adoration, and impetration. He offered Himself completely with the sacrifices that were given to His Father, knowing that He Himself was the fulfillment of all sacrifices and that one day He would be in deed and in truth the Lamb slain for the salvation of the world.

After the days of the ceremonies, Jesus remained in His Father's Temple. When the groups of pilgrims were united again according to villages and families for the return journey, as they sat at the evening meal or got ready for the night's rest, what was the dismay of Mary and Joseph to discover that Jesus was not with them! During the journey all day they had felt no anxiety, thinking Him to be with neighbors. Yet it was now too late to go and look for Him. What a night of sleeplessness and anguish! The next day at dawn, while their companions continued their journey, Mary and Joseph retraced their steps to Jerusalem. In vain did they question all the passersby, scour all the crossroads in the city, and knock at all the familiar doors. The whole day passed without the slightest sign of Him.

Finally, on the third day, they went up to the Temple, doubtless to commit their sorrow to God and ask His guidance in their plight rather than in any hope of finding Jesus there. And yet there He was in the midst of the doctors, listening to them and asking questions. The lectures of the rabbis were familiar and informal; they allowed their hearers to question them on obscure points and even of their own accord invited free discussion. This method, they found, enabled them to keep their listeners attentive, stimulate thinking, sharpen wits, and combat passivity.

There was Jesus present at one of those meetings at which the doctors were striving to outdo one another in erudition and subtlety. He was not seated in a high dais in the high posture depicted by some artists; nor was He trying to dazzle His audience with abstruse metaphysical problems or the intricacies of astrology, as the Apocrypha would have it. This would have befitted neither His character nor His age. He contented Himself with listening, asking questions, and answering any questions asked of Him. He fulfilled the ideal of the model pupil as conceived in the teachings of the rabbis: asking pertinent questions, answering carefully, and without anxiety solving difficulties in an orderly way, keeping within the limits of one's knowledge. His questions and answers on religious and moral matters were so intelligent and so apposite that the doctors marveled and wondered whence came to a Child so young such knowledge of heavenly things.

"I must be about My Father's business." Mary and Joseph, witnessing this scene, were also astonished, for they had never before seen their Son manifest this divine wisdom, though they knew its source. When the session was over and the onlookers had dispersed, Mary approached Jesus and gently said to Him: "Son, why hast thou done so to us? Behold thy father and I have sought thee sorrowing" (Luke 2:48). Her words were the spontaneous cry of a mother's heart. What else could a mother say at a time like this? Whether a loving complaint or an affectionate rebuke, Mary's words sprang above all from a desire to know the motive prompting the Boy's conduct, so much at variance with the habits of a Son who had been so completely respectful and submissive and always so anxious to avoid causing His parents the slightest displeasure. Jesus answered: "How is it that you sought me? Did you not know that I must be about my father's business?" (Luke 2:49). They had done no wrong in anxiously seeking Him, and Jesus is far from blaming them for it; but knowing Him as they did, they could have remembered that their Son was not entirely theirs and that His duty was above all to His Heavenly Father's interests. This thought would have calmed their fears and moderated their anxiety.

This is the interpretation commonly accepted today, but several Fathers of the Church are perhaps justified in preferring another translation: "Did you not know that I must be in my Father's house?" From the moment of His unannounced departure from them, the only place He could have been was the Temple, the House of His

Father. They could have found Him there without the trouble of looking elsewhere. So understood, His answer is, at first glance, less sublime; but how much more natural on the lips of the Boy, who utters it with a caress and a smile.

In any case, His words had a mysterious meaning whose depths His parents did not at the time reach. Clarified though their minds were by supernatural light, they grasped only little by little the reason and manner of the plan of the Redemption. Prophetic vision is always part shadow and obscurity, even in the most favored seers. Had Jesus inaugurated His work? Was He going to leave them, to give Himself up completely to the service of the Heavenly Father? And if this was His design, was there no way of carrying it out without breaking His Mother's heart? This is what Joseph and Mary did not at once grasp; and perhaps they could not have suspected that Jesus' behavior was aimed more at our instruction than theirs. It teaches us that God's service supersedes all affections, even the most legitimate. To do God's will is man's all-important duty. In His love and providence, God has planned out the life of each one of us in all its details, with the one object of showing His love for us and drawing us to His heart. Sometimes the course of life fixed for us by God is an ordinary one. We must do His will, glorify Him, and sanctify ourselves in the performance of the simple duties of our life.

Cultivate a great union with God; love your rule; seek after your Heavenly Father's will in all perfection. It may cause pain to you, to your friends, to your loved ones. Be generous and seek God. He will take care of all.

Confer: Ferdinand Prat, S.J., *Jesus Christ*, vol. 1, pp. 119–124; vol. 2, pp. 199–202.

FIFTH DAY

Purpose: To study Christ in the early mysteries of His life

Patron: Mary, the Mother of God and My Mother

Points for Self-Consideration:

- Obedience. Is my obedience supernatural and interior?
- Is it an obedience of the will and judgment, prompt and cheerful?
- Is it regulated by natural likes and dislikes?
- Do I spoil the fullness of my supernatural spirit of obedience by my interior murmuring and by my fault-finding and criticism?

Suggested Readings:

- Matthew 2
- *Imitation of Christ*, bk. 3, ch. 18
- *Spiritual Exercises: Discernment of Spirits for Second Week*

Aspiration:

"To know also the charity of Christ, which surpasseth all knowledge." (Eph. 3:19)

FIRST MEDITATION

The Hidden Life

DURING THE THIRTY years that preceded the public life of our Lord, we have as it were seven glimpses of Him: the nativity, the adoration of the shepherds, the adoration of the Magi, the circumcision, the presentation in the Temple, the flight into Egypt, and the presence in the midst of the doctors at the age of twelve. Thereafter, absolute silence for eighteen years. These eighteen years of His life are summed up in three texts inspired by the Holy Spirit, and they will form the matter of contemplation: "And He went down with them and came to Nazareth and was subject to them" (Luke 2:51). "Is not this the carpenter, the son of Mary?" (Mark 6:3). "And Jesus advanced in wisdom, and age, and grace with God and men" (Luke 2:52).

A life of obedience and growth. The story of Jesus' life at Nazareth from His twelfth year to the beginning of His apostolate is summed up in three phrases: He grew in wisdom and in stature and in grace before God and men; He was subject to Joseph and Mary; His Mother kept all these things in her heart, pondering over them (Luke 2:19). Having come down from Heaven to teach us obedience, Jesus must be the perfect model of it. As St. Paul tells us:

> When he cometh into the world, he saith: Sacrifice and oblation thou wouldst not: but a body thou hast fitted for

me. Holocausts for sin did not please thee. Then said I: Behold I come: in the head of the book it is written of me: that I should do thy will, O God. (Heb. 10: 5–7)

So He offers Himself to His eternal Father, a voluntary servant, freely bowing Himself down to receive the commandments of obedience. He has come to obey all who have a portion of divine authority. Yes, He will make Himself obedient unto the death of the Cross, and the Apostle will be able to say of Him that He learned obedience in the school of sorrow. His whole life at Nazareth is obedience. He was obedient to His parents, subject to them. What a strange reversal of roles! He whom all things in Heaven and on earth obey, Himself obeys and does not command. Mary, the most sublime of creatures, commands and obeys, each in turn; but she commands her Creator and obeys a Man whose merits are far outshone by her own. Joseph, fully conscious as he is of the infinite dignity of Jesus and of Mary's incomparable holiness, commands both of them and obeys only God. Mary found all this an inexhaustible subject for prayer and contemplation. She dwelt on this mystery of the hidden life but could not sound its depth, and she adored in silence what surpassed human comprehension. Here is the sublime example that will move religious to obey their superiors generously and with love. Christ is our model; every act of His is a lesson to be treasured up and lovingly reproduced in our lives so far as circumstances allow. The spirit of His humility and obedience must permeate our minds and hearts.

Devoting Himself to the humble tasks of the household and later to the trade of Joseph, Jesus grew in wisdom, in stature, and in grace before God and before men. His moral and intellectual development kept step with His physical growth. The latter was real and easily perceptible. As regards His intellectual growth, St. Cyril of Alexandria says: "The Word Incarnate freely allowed the laws of humanity to keep their full validity in case that He might resemble us the more, since sudden growth would have something monstrous about it." The hypostatic union in Christ left the divine and the human nature unmixed and unconfused, adding only the divine personality to the human nature. But Jesus Christ, the Son of God, has a title to the possessions of His Father, that is, to sanctifying grace and the light of glory that is its perfection. This right He had from the moment of His conception; and though His redemptive mission forbade the glory of His soul to overflow upon His body in such a way as to spiritualize it, there was no reason for withholding from the soul itself the actual possession of the Beatific Vision. Hence, the soul of Jesus, contemplating God face to face, saw in the Word everything produced by the creative activity of the Word. All this is of faith and cannot be doubted. But it was also fitting that the Instructor, Legislator, and Supreme Judge of the human race, who came to reveal to the world the mysteries and the wishes of His Father, be endowed with a knowledge more in keeping with His role as Redeemer and second Adam. This is what is called His infused knowledge. For all their perfection, beatific knowledge and infused knowledge are not infinite, because they are the adornment of a created nature. Nevertheless, neither of them is capable of increase because they were conferred from the beginning in full measure foreseen and decreed by God. Hence, any progress in Jesus' knowledge must have been only in His acquired or experimental knowledge.

St. Thomas tells us: "We must say that in Christ there was an acquired knowledge, conformed to the human manner of knowing." Certainly, the faculty we have of forming ideas with the aid of images perceived by the senses was not inert in Him, or without an object. That would be a curious way to perceive the perfection of His humanity. Despite His higher knowledge of the Beatific Vision and infused knowledge, "Jesus adapted the manifestation of this higher knowledge to the progress of His acquired knowledge. Consequently, His increase in wisdom was at once apparent and real; apparent with respect to His infused knowledge, which could not increase; real, with respect to His acquired knowledge, which was capable of indefinite progress" (Billot, *De Verbo Incarnato*).

The soul of Jesus, hypostatically united to the Word, was the most perfect soul that ever existed. His penetrating intelligence, His quick perception, His tenacious memory, His unerring judgment, and His flawless reasoning were without equal. No hereditary defect blurred His mind, no haze of passion hovered between Him and truth. He saw effects in their causes and causes in their effects, conclusions in their principles and principles in conclusions. Thus, He was able to enrich himself quickly with vast stores of knowledge. It is by the constant application of His acquired knowledge that Christ appears to us as a true man and as a brother; for Him as for us, it is the font of feelings and emotions. This knowledge reveals itself instinctively in His conduct and speech. His words and discourses reflect the blue of the Palestinian skies and allow us to breathe the scent of the Galilean hills, and this it is that gives them charm. Many of His delightful descriptions are of scenes that have been "lived," as we say today. It is impossible to grasp clearly the allegory of the Good Shepherd, the parable of the Sower, or the comparison of the Importunate Friend, to cite only a few examples, unless one is acquainted with local customs. The use He made of acquired knowledge reveals, moreover, the delicacy of feeling in the heart of Jesus. It was not in virtue of the Beatific Vision or of infused knowledge that He wept at Lazarus's tomb; it was at the memory of the warm welcome and affectionate attention He had received in the hospitable home of Lazarus, whom He loved as a friend, a sympathetic companion of sure affection and tested loyalty. Jesus is moved at the sight of the widow of Naim sobbing by the bier of her only son, even as our own hearts would be wrung at a similar spectacle. He is touched with compassion when He sees the multitudes wandering aimlessly like sheep without a shepherd. He takes up the defense of the public sinner accused by the Pharisees; He protects the unfortunate adulteress persecuted by the Jews. Nor is it only moral distress that moves Him; He has pity on all kinds of suffering. He cannot resist the pleas of the blind, the paralytics, and the lepers who implore His help. Twice He works miracles to appease the hunger of people following Him. All His feelings of pity, fear, disgust, sadness, and joy spring from the same source; they have their explanation in the acquired knowledge of Christ. As we read in the epistle to the Hebrews, Jesus Christ "learned obedience by the things which he suffered" (Heb. 5:8). He knew better than anyone else the nature and moral value of obedience; but it was in the school of suffering that He learned its difficulty, its merit, and its price; and this knowledge is experimental knowledge.

Life of work in the Holy Family. In every Jewish family, the woman's first duty was to grind the wheat needed for the day's consumption. The strident noise of the millstone, as she set it in motion at daybreak, filled the air. Then she kneaded the flour, lighted the movable oven, and baked her bread on white-hot stones. Preparations for the meal were not arduous, because the menu was simple and usually the same: eggs, milk, cheese, honey, olives and other fruits, and sometimes fish. These duties done, the mistress of the house did not remain idle. As the valiant woman in the Book of Proverbs, "She hath sought wool and flax, and hath wrought by the counsel of her hands.... She hath put out her hand to strong things, and her fingers have taken hold of the spindle" (Prov. 31:13, 19). Mary did all these household tasks with loving attention and great perfection. The divine Child rendered Mary all the little services a boy of His age could perform, and then, when His strength allowed it,

He joined Joseph in his workshop. Then as now, the workshop was always separated from the living quarters, out of consideration for the peace and quiet of the family—which was thus spared constant disturbances such as the gossiping and bargaining of clients and visitors, who were often loud and ill-mannered.

Joseph worked in wood. He was doubtless both a carpenter and a joiner, because trades had not yet become so specialized that there was any distinction between these two occupations; both are designated by the same in Arabic. In his shop we would see one or two saws, a hatchet, a hammer, a mallet, and a plane, rarely a work bench or horse—in short, very primitive equipment. But it is enough for making the usual things: doors, window frames, chests for wardrobes, winnowing forks, harrows fitted with points of flint to beat out corn sheaves on the floor, and, above all, yokes and plows in the most antique styles. When a new house was built, the carpenter was called to square off roughly the beams of poplar and sycamore that supported the thatched roof and the more or less watertight layer of hard earth spread over it. But Joseph's humble position had nothing degrading about it in the eyes of his compatriots. The majority of famous rabbis had worked with their hands. One of the five principal duties of the father of the family was expressed in the maxim of the Rabbi Judah: "He who does not teach his son a trade, teaches him to steal." The point was not only to honor work but to rout idleness, the most dangerous of vices.

In devoting Himself to these humble tasks at His foster father's side, Jesus sanctified all labor for all time. He is the worker who teaches us to do all our work, no matter how menial, in the spirit of pleasing and serving God in all we do. As St. Justin says so well: "Our Lord did not set much store by the ploughs and yokes for oxen which He made in Joseph's workshop for eighteen years. In themselves they were not worth a God's while; what gave them value was the Person who made them, and the spirit in which they were wrought." God cares less for what we do than for the *way* in which we do and the *intentions* for which we do. How and why we do things makes us what we are, and for this God cares. He who works as His child in the state of grace pleases Him greatly, no matter how menial the task.

One of Satan's commonest temptations, under the appearance of greater good, is to inspire disgust at our present office and occupation as too paltry for persons of our capabilities. Certainly, we should be greater than our occupations, but we should busy ourselves about them with none the less zeal in imitation of Christ the Carpenter. In all the Holy Family did, they were in complete union with God in prayer and loving recollection. Every throb of Christ's heart was a prayer of the most perfect kind to His Father. Quite naturally, He saw His Father everywhere and in all occupations.

At stated times, the Holy Family would have had formal meetings for vocal prayer. Always, Mary's heart and Joseph's heart were at one with Christ as they prayed in common, worked in common, recreated in common, and loved each other more and more daily. In loving their divine Son, Mary and Joseph loved their God. That was the value of their personal love for Christ. And Christ, in loving His parents, loved His Father for whose glory He came upon earth. He loved us, too, for whose salvation He was living this hidden and lowly life. Such was the hidden and holy life of the boy and young man of Nazareth.

Christ constantly gained the admiration and affection of His townsmen, for "He grew in grace," that is, in graciousness and goodness and faithfulness and beauty "before God and men" (see Luke 2:52). Gentle, modest, docile, obliging, and without any of the defects that mar the attractiveness of childhood and young manhood, He pleased everyone who had occasion to see and hear

Him. More and more, too, in our way of speaking, He earned the complacency of His Father, not by an increase of graces and spiritual gifts but by the accumulation of acts of virtue. These multiplied acts could not fail to be pleasing to His Father, and St. Paul tells us they merited a recompense (see Col. 1:19).

Here is our model of humble living, of hard, honest labor for God, of loving submission to God and all who exercise the authority of God. May the humble Christ mold our hearts like unto His in all the works and occupations of our lives. So be it.

Confer: Ferdinand Prat, S.J., *Jesus Christ*, vol. 1, pp. 124–132.

SECOND MEDITATION

The Three Classes of Persons

WE HAVE IN this meditation another parable that St. Ignatius proposes to us. We remember that in the contemplation of the Two Standards, we enlightened our minds and made ourselves familiar with the principles and techniques of Christ and Satan. We understood the plan of Christ that was to lead us by poverty of spirit (actual poverty too, if He is so pleased to call us to it) and by humiliation to humility, and by humility to all the other virtues. In the three colloquies made at the end of that contemplation, we exercised our will, asking our Lady, Christ, and the Heavenly Father to accept us under the standard of Christ in supreme spiritual poverty, no less in actual poverty should this so please God. We asked even to be allowed to undergo affronts and injuries, the more to imitate Him in them, provided only that we might undergo them without sin of any person or displeasure of His divine majesty. Now, in this contemplation, St. Ignatius wants us to test the disposition of our wills, to see whether we are genuinely willing to follow out the lessons of Christ's strategy learned in the Two Standards and to see whether our affective attitude and will toward the end (and means) is what it ought to be: completely generous.

The contemplation of St. Ignatius's Three Classes is an appeal to our wills. It aims to develop in the will the disposition of preferring the better thing to be done for the greater glory of God and the salvation of our souls. Just as in the Two Standards there was never any question of any choice between Christ and Satan (for we had already chosen Christ irrevocably in the Kingdom) but only a study of plans of campaign, so in the parable of the Three Classes there is never any question of the men making a choice between sin and what is good. The matter of deliberation is not anything to which we are bound by the Ten Commandments or, for religious, by a religious Rule. But it is only a question of embracing, as St. Ignatius puts it, "what is best."

The parable. Three pairs of men have acquired a large sum of money, honestly to be sure, but with motives that were too human and not purely for the glory of God. In fact, each man has acquired $10,000. Why does St. Ignatius use pairs of men for the three classes instead of one man for each class? Well, probably to bring out the struggle that goes on in each one of us, for we often seem to be two persons. William James calls this phenomenon "the drama of the divided will."

All the men wish to save themselves and to find peace with God. They each want to rid themselves of the anxiety that this money causes in their souls, especially since they see they are inclined toward it and might become bound to it. They try to imagine themselves in the presence of God our Lord, all His saints, their patrons, friends, and relatives in Heaven. Each asks to desire and know what may be more pleasing to God, and especially to elect what is more for the glory of His divine majesty and his own salvation. They have varying levels of success.

The first class or pair of men wish to get rid of the affection they have for the money in order to find peace with God and save themselves, but they take no measure to accomplish this end. The will of this type is in the pitiable plight of indulging in velleities. The second class or pair of men wish to get rid of the affection too, but in such a way as to still keep possession of the money and to bring God around to their way of thinking, instead of them going to God's way of thinking. This type is the compromiser, the half-hearted wilier. But the third class or pair of men energetically renounce all affection for the money and bring themselves to complete indifference as to whether they keep possession of the money or not, all depending for them on God's good pleasure. This class is willing to make whatever sacrifices are necessary for the greater glory of God and their own salvation.

The hidden treasure of the Gospel. Let's see if we can't adapt these three attitudes of the will to a parable that Christ told in the Gospel, in order to understand better the attitude of our own wills.

"The kingdom of heaven," our Lord said, "is like unto a treasure hidden in a field. Which a man having found, hid it, and for joy thereof goeth, and selleth all that he hath, and buyeth that field" (Matt. 13:44). Let us flesh out the parable. A tremendous sum of money has been hidden in a field, perhaps to protect it from being plundered by an enemy, robbers, or the fiscal agent. Many, many long years roll by. It is impossible to find the owner. One day, a traveler rests on a boulder at the edge of the field and leisurely turns up the clods and stones at his feet with his staff. He sees a jewel and some pieces of gold glitter in the sunlight. Intrigued and excited, he digs deeper, perceives some more gold pieces, and then finds the main treasure: buried chests chock full of golden coins. The entire sum represents ten thousand times the value of his own fortune. To dig it up and carry it off at once is out of the question, simply impossible; and anyway, that would be theft. To loiter around on the scene would be dangerous — the landowner or some other person might happen along at any moment. Quickly, the discoverer effaces all signs of digging, covers his own tracks, and disappears. Yet his mind is made up. He will buy that field.

Immediate execution of resolves. In business, we all know that there is a big difference between making resolutions and putting them into practice. Even when one sees clearly what actions must be taken, one often hesitates or dilly-dallies when the time comes for the transaction. And if some action is called for that demands sacrifice and some pain or loss, the transaction is put off indefinitely. Days pass, months, perhaps years; finally, the golden opportunity passes with them. In reality, what does the situation call for? Certainly no evasion, no delaying tactics. Clearly the field must be bought — the whole field, nothing less! To speak of buying only some interesting acres of the field would risk arousing the curiosity of the landowner or other prospective buyers. True, the field is an extensive piece of land, and it is going to cost very much. In order to acquire the sum needed, the discoverer will have to sell his own home, garden, furniture, and precious keepsakes of the family. What does it matter? The treasure to be gained is priceless. So he sells all he has as quickly as possible for fear that some other buyer may beat him to the transaction. He spares no sacrifice; on the contrary, the more precious the objects are that he sells off, the greater is his joy. "I will have enough money to buy that field," he says. Only one thought occupies and possesses his soul. "I must not arrive too late!" He does not haggle over the price in order to conceal his avid play for the land. And when the contract is written up and all is in perfect order, he is the happiest man in the world. "The field is mine!"

What others think of his conduct. Neighbors, parents, and friends, as long as they do not know his secret, blame him, outdoing each other in condemning him. "What a fool!" "What sudden madness is this!" "To despoil himself of everything for that land!" What does he care for all that ridicule! When the transaction is successfully closed and the good news revealed, those same neighbors, parents, and friends — and even his enemies — praise, admire, and envy him. It was all very well that he had waited in secret, without a care for what people were saying, without delaying, without haggling over the price! He was right in never stopping to consider what his actions would cost him but in concentrating only on the tremendous treasure they would bring him. Why, even his greatest critics agreed that that was the only wise way to act; they'd have done the same in his place.

Application of the parable to our salvation. We are here on this earth to buy, by our obedience to God's laws, a priceless treasure — priceless not only because it will endure beyond all centuries without end but also because this treasure consists in a happiness that surpasses all the strict rights of creatures, no matter how deserving these creatures may be. Regenerated in the Blood of Christ, we are now to be treated just like Christ Himself, as sons of God. Here is a marvelous hidden treasure! Millions of men do not even suspect it exists. Here is an unheard-of treasure! A happiness that is properly divine, exceeding all our faculties to such a point that these faculties of ours must be retouched and heightened, elevated so that they may enjoy this happiness all the more. Here is a certain and sure treasure! God has promised it in the most precise language, and God cannot lie: "If sons, heirs also; heirs indeed of God, and joint heirs with Christ" (Rom. 8:17); "That you may eat and drink at my table in my kingdom" (Luke 22:30); "Where I am, there also shall my minister be" (John 12:26). We Christians who know our religion (and especially we religious) must act wholeheartedly, giving up everything without exception like the man in the parable. We must sell all our attachments and, above all, do it with joy! But do we act this way? Alas, no! All of us without doubt desire this enchanting reward from God. How is it that we act quite against our desire? The answer is that men fall into three classes in relation to attaining what they desire.

First, a good number of men bind themselves to attain their goal by pure velleities. They dream of Heaven without ever deciding to make the necessary sacrifices to attain it. They never make an effort to suppress habits of laziness, of intemperance, or of luxury. They do not break off dangerous or culpable friendships and do not avoid injurious satisfactions. Convinced of the beauty of eternal goods, they nevertheless refuse to sell *anything* to attain these goods. But, you say, they still desire Heaven. Then they must give something for it. Their decision not to decide subtly decoys them from acting on good resolutions. They don't realize that precious time is wasting, that time is getting short, perhaps shorter than they realize; tomorrow only belongs to God.

Second, a good number of people rest contented with half-measures. They consent to sell something, but only those things to which they are not attached or attached to but slightly. They give themselves for some time to the practice of devotion; they'll even impose some restrictions on themselves. But they'll never come to breaking off from indispensable things, to making the energetic changes that protect them from grave faults and damnation should mortal sin and death surprise them. Even experience has not succeeded in teaching them that one never becomes master of one's passions by continuing in a large degree to cajole them. Good sense and reason has not yet convinced them that to be stingy, to drive a bargain, to evade, and to procrastinate only exposes them to the danger of losing a golden opportunity.

Third, there are some generous souls — alas, not enough — who immediately make and execute the proper decisions. They sell all. Do we mean by that, that they renounce every satisfaction? By no means! They renounce all joys that are obstacles or are forbidden by God's law. Yet how many others remain allowed to them, the more noble joys, the more intense joys! They renounce all passions that God condemns because these passions displease God, and they know that these passions are able to drag them down. So they apply themselves to root these sinful desires out of their hearts totally. They don't passively wait for this to happen. They make these decisions with joy, because of the wonderful reward that lies open to them. This spirit of joy and this energetic generosity make their sacrifices less painful. Surely a firm, rapid thrust with a lance makes one suffer far less than a series of hesitating, uncertain slits. Yes, the Kingdom of Heaven is for souls of this stamp, not for the others: "the violent bear it away" (Matt. 11:12).

Application of the parable to God's friendship. There is a treasure in Heaven that is the most exquisite of all the joys of Heaven: the experience of the affection and love of the King of King's for me, to joy forever in the attentions of His infinite tenderness! A hidden treasure — how many people think of it? A treasure without price: to be treated as dear sons, preferred children, not for one day, nor for a century, but for eternity!

There are as many different degrees of joy in Heaven as there are degrees of tenderness and generosity. Those satisfied with velleities, with fine projects that never come to realization because such souls renounce nothing of what charms them, may renounce only that which would lead to grave faults. They may arrive at the good fortune of preserving the state of grace, but they will never — neither on this earth, nor in Heaven — experience the most exquisite tenderness of divine friendship. Others never go beyond half-measures, for they do not attack their passions resolutely. They live in danger of being ensnared by them into mortal sin. The *supreme* tendernesses of the Heavenly Father are not for them because they do not want to pay the price for them. Finally, a small number of generous and heroic souls zealously undertake the battle against their faults and make efficacious resolutions. They may fail even mortally from time to time, but they begin immediately and with energy to fight again, rising to the struggle with renewed generosity. God pardons them their weaknesses, for He sees their generous resolves and efforts. Little by little, they grow strong, correct themselves, and are thus in proportion more and more loved by God. To lead such an austere life, it is clear that one must designate one in the service of God. One may attract blame and ridicule from the tepid. What difference does it make? The man who found the treasure in the field, did he bother himself because he was called a maniac and fool? To mortify one's senses and passions thus means to undergo a sort of martyrdom! Really, doesn't it mean to free oneself? Nothing now can cause disorder to reign in the soul.

We must, therefore, in the spirit of generosity that St. Ignatius holds out to us, make the necessary resolutions that will bring us closer and closer to God. During this retreat, ask God to enlighten you as to what in particular is keeping you back from Him. It may not be some seriously sinful attachment, but something that keeps your heart distracted and divided between Him and some other creature. The bird that is held by a string attached to its leg is prevented from flying, even if the string be the slenderest of silken strands. Even so with our souls: as long as some creature, no matter how harmless it may appear, keeps them occupied, they cannot soar to the bosom and holy companionship of God. Be generous to God and resolve to get rid of all such attachments. Sell all and follow Him.

Ask yourself sincerely just what category of the Three Classes you belong to: velleities, half-measures, or efficacious resolutions? Maybe we have been able to fool ourselves up to the present. Enough of that now. No more temporizing! Time is short. We must now make up for the past. Ask yourself if your present resolutions are to the point. Do they attack *the thing*, the fault that is keeping you from closer union with God? Act as if you were counseling a friend in your predicament; take down your own advice and put it into action. Or suppose some spiritual director whom you respected and loved knew your case and its problems: what would he counsel you, do you think? Take that advice and put it into execution. Or imagine yourself at the hour of death, at the moment of attaining the prize of your sacrifices. That which you hesitate to sell now, would you not wish you had gotten rid of without reserve at this moment of death? Well, take that advice and put it into execution now. To make your resolutions work, renew them often or at stated times — say on first Fridays, during Stations of the Cross, or on a monthly day of recollection. This fixes them in your soul. Don't drop them among your spiritual notes in the bottom of your drawer. Pray to Jesus to give you the strength to fulfill them. "Without me you can do nothing" (John 15:5).

Progress in the Spiritual Life

A MOUNTAIN CLIMBER who begins to scale the slopes of a very high peak can easily take account of his progress. He is not getting dirty as he was when he trod in the muddy valleys below. He is breathing purer and more rarified air. Already his horizons have broadened considerably, and the enchantment of the magnificent panorama delights him. Yet the more he continues to advance upward, the more the summit seems to recede into the heavens. It may happen that he will mistake his way and descend rather than continue to mount upward. It may finally happen that the going will get so rough that he will lose his courage and give up.

We have almost all experienced how easy are the first stages of upward progress in the spiritual life. If we had the misfortune of having offended God mortally, we put that behind us and, by the grace of God, never sin seriously. Deliberate venial sin becomes rarer in our lives as we progress. At this stage, the temptation is to believe that we have attained perfection; or at least, we flatter ourselves that we can now coast a little. So some of us take ways that divert us; others stick to the straight and narrow but measure their progress every day and are alarmed because they feel they are not advancing rapidly enough. Some directors of souls tell their subjects to investigate their lives to see if they are progressing or not.

The essential thing, they say, is to always tend toward the ideal with energy and constancy. Today I'd like to tell you about investigating your spiritual state and will point out necessary cautions. Then I will explain the difficulty of gauging progress and finally explain some authentic signs of true progress.

The cautions about examining our spiritual life. First, there are such examinations that are reprehensible. We all know, of course, that not riches, not position, not power, not talents, but virtues give us true worth and dignity in the eyes of God. We can and often do abuse the former gifts, but virtue makes us like to God. Hence, it is only reasonable and natural that we must be concerned and occupied about growing in virtue. This is an excellent ambition that even the Stoics insisted upon. But unlike the Stoics, we are concerned about growing in virtue not only because virtue is good for us but because through virtue we please and glorify God, who has said to us: "Be ye holy, because I the Lord your God am Holy" (Lev. 19:2; cf. 11:44). And again, our Lord tells us: "Be you therefore perfect, as also your heavenly Father is perfect" (Matt. 5:48).

A Christian who desires spiritual progress exclusively out of a motive of self-love would be blameworthy. More blameworthy still is that foolish vanity that leads one to examine his merits in order to take pleasure in them. Such procedure is like that of vain women who are constantly admiring themselves from hour to hour in a mirror that accompanies them wherever they go. Even if the mirror does not testify that they are paragons of beauty, yet it does tell them that they are not deprived of very much charm. If only mirrors could talk!

Then there are some who, after having read biographies of the mystics and learned to repeat their inflamed formulas, fancy that they too have arrived at perfection, or at least that they are not very far from these giants of virtue, because they too practice one or two of the good deeds that the mystics practiced. Such self-complacency! Such self-deception!

Then we have the sincere ones (and that means most of us) who examine themselves in all honesty yet disturb themselves needlessly because they cannot measure their progress each day. That's as silly as the child who would take account every few hours to see if he is growing. In our early lives, our bodies grow in height and vigor on condition that we are getting good food and sufficient exercise. We don't actually see ourselves grow; yet we are growing. An exaggerated care of health only impairs the body's growth and leads to hypochondria. Don't become spiritual hypochondriacs, melancholically brooding over a progress that you cannot measure. Go ahead and take the means to become holy, and courageously do the good at hand. If you do, don't worry: your soul is becoming virile and sanctified.

True progress of the soul can't be measured any more than true health of the body can. It is only after long periods of time that we see that Johnny has gained thirty pounds and grown five inches. Growth for the soul as well as for the body is not a work of an hour, or a day, or a month; it is the work of years! Certain growing pains are experienced in children; if we paid too much attention to them, we might be led to believe that health was being impaired instead of bettered. So in the spiritual life, certain lively temptations or certain times of desolation give the impression that we are spiritually sick and failing, whereas through these trials, our virtues are being strengthened and we are growing strong spiritually.

The laudable ways of examining our spiritual growth. We should take stock of our spiritual life at intervals spaced sufficiently apart, say every six months or so. Then we should check to see whether we have vigor, fervor, and élan in our spiritual life. We should see if our desire to become holy is ardent—life is so short as it is anyway! Are we wasting our forces in burdensome practices that may have some merit but that bring us little spiritual progress? What are our methods of amending our lives? The more fruitful they are, the more we should employ them and recommend them to others in need.

To answer all of these questions, different religious orders expressly invite their members to talk these matters over with competent directors of souls, say, every six months or every year. This is an excellent way of providing against future failures, for stimulating our zeal, and for preparing us to direct other souls. Every serious review of this kind will clearly exclude the childish illusion that we can in a short time and with little cost catch up with the giants of the spiritual life—who attained such perfect humility, such deep abnegation, and such sublime charity at the terrible cost of untold and excruciating sufferings and heroic sacrifices. We will find that the more we rid ourselves of our faults, the more we will come to appreciate the spiritual ideal of sanctity—and consequently, the more we will see how far we are from it, despite our best efforts. For the more we progress, the more it becomes clear to us how much we still have to progress. Yet, courage! With God, nothing is impossible! If God is with you, who can be against you (see Matt. 19:26; Rom. 8:31)? Our desire for perfection is already a grace from Him. His goodness cannot fail to sustain if we ask Him from day to day in all humility and confidence: "Teach me, Lord, to correct and conquer myself! Help me to love You as much as the poor heart of man is able to love You!"

The difficulty of gauging progress in the spiritual life. Even when we examine these prolonged periods of our lives to seek for progress in virtue, it is a delicate and difficult affair to evaluate our success, if any. This is true not only if we are checking for the correction of such and such a fault, but especially if we are checking for an overall advancement in our spiritual life. What are the reasons for this?

It is hard to tell whether we have ever truly acquired a virtue—that is to say, whether a certain virtue has become a habit rooted deeply in the soul in such a way as never to be lost. (The saints were exposed to humiliating failures the moment they relaxed their vigilance or trusted in their own strength.) Frequently, faults disappear or become rare in our lives simply because temptations have ceased or have been greatly weakened. Consider, for example, that a woman has feathered her nest of a room so that it is up to date and quite comfortable: it might be quite easy to kneel at her prie-dieu and ardently make acts of detachment. Or perhaps a man feels he has finally acquired humility: it might be that for some time now he has experienced no failure, no humiliation, no contradiction, no injustice that would provoke his feelings and the vindictiveness of self-love.

Or maybe you consider yourself more charitable? Perhaps that is due to the fact that your work takes you into the milieu of the better educated, among those of tried virtue, those of good character. For this reason, it is scarcely hard at all to be constantly pleasant and amiable. Then again, you might believe that you have become founded in the virtue of obedience. Could that belief be explained by the fact that you have passed to the authority of a superior or employer who is sympathetic, less exacting, and in general favorable to your views, much more so than your former superior? Just let the circumstances change and watch nature come galloping back into our lives! Real progress cannot be evaluated until we are pitted against temptations and trials. Whoever forgets this truth is in for some surprises in life.

The difficulty of trying to measure the overall progress in our spiritual life results from the complexity of our nature. The faculties of our souls are many; they seem to be able to be perfected singly on their own. Our senses slowly become quiet; the imagination comes to regulate itself; the intelligence becomes enlivened and enriched; while at the same time, the will becomes weak and wicked. The types of activity open to our powers are so multiple and varied that one can, for example, develop one faculty to the point of virtuosity and at the same time ignore more important faculties such as the mind or will—and the overall picture is that one is going down instead of up. A person may make tremendous progress in mortification and at the same time be building up his self-love. Martin Luther is a good example of what that procedure might lead to: attachment to one's views and increasing pride and stubbornness.

In a word, while we are freeing ourselves from one fault or vice, others are developing in us, like sprouts from trees that have been pruned on one side. How shall we decide, then, about our overall progress? First, get rid of all illusions and errors as to what perfection is and learn the basic reforms that are a necessary condition for it. What is perfection? Well, there can be no perfection without complete observance of the laws imposed by God Himself. That means, keep the Ten Commandments and the laws Christ gave us in the Gospels. This very wise Master and Teacher, who is infinitely good, cannot impose any law upon us simply for the pleasure of imposing His authority or going against our will. Each one of His commands has no other purpose than that of leading us to reproduce in ourselves His holiness.

Authentic signs of true progress in the spiritual life. Suffice to say that all exterior signs like modesty, vocal prayers, time spent in religion, increase of theological knowledge, frequent reception of the Sacraments, etc., do not necessarily prove a deep spiritual life, for there may be simulation, many faults, and an improper use of some of these graces. Where shall we look, then, for sure signs? Well, first let us say that even some affective signs such as consolations, tears, etc., do not necessarily prove a deep spiritual life. They may be due to sensibility, as we saw above. But a habitual taste for spiritual things is a pretty good sign—a taste that is in the depth of the soul and not in the senses. It supposes a firm conviction of the vanity of the world and its joys, of the price of eternal things and the divine friendship. Another good sign is an ardent love of the ideal of conquering ourselves. This bespeaks generosity in the soul. Another strong sign is an increase of peace in God's service. It rules out an inconstant character. Peace in the soul tells us that this soul can sustain itself on God in all its trials and contradictions.

Other signs of progress arise from the order of action or deeds. A good sign of progress is when we maintain a general insistence on fighting against ourselves and our faults. Also, an increasing energy in the conquering of sensuality through mortification is a good sign; no saint ever cajoled his senses or looked for his ease. A third sign is increasing success in submitting our will through obedience to authority. This marks a profound disappropriation of oneself to God. A fourth sign is an increasing fight against self-love in all its forms; this attacks the root of all our disorders. All the saints and Doctors agree that self-annihilation is the prime requisite for all holiness. Hence, he who seeks humiliations, or who suffers them joyfully when they come, is making much progress. And if one seeks them in order to be like Christ, one is well on the way to high holiness and a deep spiritual life. Moreover, one who willingly gives up his good reputation and his rights, who refuses to be jealous in any way, who renounces all complaints—this person is living a vigorous spiritual life. One who pardons all faults according to the ideal proposed by St. Paul—"overcome evil by good" (Rom. 12:21)—for the divine love of the divine King, such a one is imitating Christ closely, such a one has put on the mind, heart, and livery of Jesus Christ and is living splendidly in the sight of God. So be it.

Confer: Pinard de la Boullaye, S.J., *Exercices Spirituels*, vol. 4, pp. 210–224.

THIRD MEDITATION

The Forty-Day Fast, the Temptation, and the Public Life of Jesus

WE COME NOW to that part of our Blessed Lord's life with which the Gospels are mostly concerned. We see our divine King start His public campaign to win souls to His Father. St. Ignatius asks us to see with the eyes of the imagination the synagogues, towns, and villages where Christ our Lord preached. Today let us dwell with Him on the high mountain of Quarantania, named thus in memory of the fast and temptation of the Savior. We are in spirit with our Lord on this high, bleak mountain. There are numerous caves cut into the steep sides, and tradition tells us that it was to one of these caves that our Lord retired when He was driven by the Spirit into the desert after His Baptism in the Jordan. Why was our Lord here? Before beginning His active apostolate, He felt the need of extended communion with His Father. The most illustrious Fathers of the Church (such as Jerome, Basil, Gregory of Nazianzus, and John Chrysostom) as well as founders of religious orders (such as Benedict, Francis of Assisi, and Ignatius) and many others have followed His example, seeking inspiration and strength in solitude before undertaking the great deeds they planned to accomplish for God's glory. As we watch our Lord in prayer before His Father, we ask for a greater interior knowledge of Him so that we may love

Him more and follow Him more closely. And as we watch Him conquer the devil, our hated enemy, we ask Him to give us the strength to follow His example in never compromising with evil, but in repulsing it wholeheartedly.

Immediately after Christ's act of humiliation in allowing Himself to be baptized by John the Baptist in order to accomplish all justice, St. Mark tells us: "And immediately the Spirit drove him out into the desert. And he was in the desert forty days and forty nights, and was tempted by Satan; and he was with beasts, and the angels ministered to him" (Mark 1:12–13). Like Moses on Mt. Sinai, and Elijah on the road to Horeb, Jesus observed an absolute fast of forty days and forty nights; but He was so absorbed in God, so lost in ecstasy, that the natural process of living was almost suspended, and He seems to have felt the pangs of hunger only at the end of His fast. The devil took advantage of this physical exhaustion to tempt Him.

It was fitting that the Savior, who had come down from Heaven to overthrow the empire of Satan, should at the outset pit Himself against the prince of this world, the great enemy of the human race, and should win a signal victory over him. It was fitting, too, in the present plan of the Redemption, that He be tried in every way (sin alone excepted), the better to have compassion on our weakness (see Heb. 4:15). "His sufferings and trials," says the Apostle, "enabled Him to come to the aid of those who are tried" (see Heb. 2:18). He, therefore, did not act thus merely to serve as a model for us in our fight against the devils and to teach us how to overcome them, for there are in Him too many perfections that defy imitation. We carry within ourselves the principal source of our temptations, and even when these come from without, they are sure to find in us certain things that aid and abet them. But Jesus knew no inclination to evil, and His reason, which was of perfect rectitude, ruled as master over His lower faculties. In the temptations that assail us, there is always an element of surprise, ignorance, or error. It was the contrary with our Lord. There was not so much as a passing shadow on Jesus' intelligence. The balance between His spiritual and His sensible faculties was so perfect that for us it is difficult to understand not how He overcame temptation but how He could have experienced it at all.

The word "tempt" is used equivocally in Scripture. God sometimes "tempts" the just to test them, to make them aware of their weakness, or to give them an opportunity for merit. Man "tempts" God by small-souled distrust and by presumptuous pride. The devil "tempts" man to seduce and ruin him. What, then, did the devil have in mind or hope to gain by attacking Christ? St. Ambrose comes forward with a happy formula: "he tempts Jesus to try Him, and tries Him to tempt Him." He sees in Jesus an extraordinary human being; he suspects that He may well be the Messiah and Son of God. Were he sure of this, he would not wantonly expose himself to certain defeat. Of this he wishes to make trial. If he succeeds in snaring Jesus, he will know that he has nothing further to fear from Him. If he fails, he at least counts upon forcing Him to declare Himself. In either case, he will learn what he does not yet know, and certainty seems preferable to doubt.

The First Temptation.

When he had fasted forty days and forty nights, afterwards he was hungry. And the tempter coming said to him: If thou be the Son of God, command that these stones be made bread. Who answered and said: It is written, Not in bread alone doth man live, but in every word that proceedeth from the mouth of God. (Matt. 4:2–4)

This first assault of the evil one is not properly a temptation to gluttony. The term fixed for the fast is passed, and there is no

sensuality in wishing to appease hunger when it has become a torment and there is no further obligation to abstain. Disorder would
come from using miraculous power needlessly and at a suggestion
prompted by curiosity or malice. But to work a miracle to prove
oneself a wonder-worker would be sheer ostentation; to work
one merely to satisfy a personal need would be an act of distrust
in God. Then is the time to hand oneself over to God and His
divine Providence, which will provide for our needs in unsuspected
ways. This is what Jesus means by His answer. The Hebrews in the
desert cried aloud for bread. God rained down manna on them,
something they did not expect, "in order to prove," as Moses said
to them, "that man does not live by bread alone but by everything
that happens at the command of God" (see Deut. 8:3). This was
a double defeat for Satan. He had hoped to exploit the state of
starvation in which Jesus found Himself after His long fast and
get Him to perform a useless and inopportune miracle. He was
frustrated. He had wanted to find out whether Jesus was the Son
of God and knew Himself to be such. He learned nothing; Jesus
kept His secret.

The Second Temptation.

> Then the devil took him into the holy city, and set him upon
> the pinnacle of the temple, and said to him: If thou be the
> Son of God, cast thyself down, for it is written: That he hath
> given his angels charge over thee, and in their hands shall
> they bear thee up, lest perhaps thou da sh thy foot against a
> stone. Jesus said to him: It is written again: Thou shalt not
> tempt the Lord thy God. (Matt. 4:5–7)

The picture here is disconcerting to the imagination and confusing
to the mind. It is hard to conceive Satan seizing Jesus and carrying

Him to the pinnacle of the Temple. Was it all done in a vision? Some of the Fathers say that the Savior freely and spontaneously takes up the challenge of His antagonist. As an athlete confident of victory, He leaves to His adversary the choice of arms. He accepts the terrain chosen by the devil and betakes Himself of His own free will to the place of combat. Now, the pinnacle of the Temple was the point of juncture of the Royal Porch and the Porch of Solomon, at the southeast corner of the outside perimeter. This point overhung the valley of Cedron and was a kind of belvedere, giving a beautiful view looking out toward the mountains of Moab over the gulf of the Dead Sea. It was a dizzying experience to lean over the protective balustrade at the edge and look down into the ravine. This is the height from which tradition says James the Less was hurled to his death.

As before, Satan opens the scene with an ambiguous sentence that is a sort of challenge: "If thou be the Son of God, cast thyself down." If You are what You truly pretend to be, You have nothing to fear; angels will receive You into their hands. God Himself assures You of that. The arch-liar is quoting the Scriptures falsely; the text he uses is not messianic. Besides, though God promises His protection to the just who have confidence in Him, He does not pledge Himself to work miracles for the presumptuous. In itself, the trap was obvious. Nevertheless, a brilliant miracle performed at the highest point of the Temple explained before the assembled multitude might seem to be an effective and ready way to win the people and avoid long and painful delays. But by taking this short-cut, Christ would deviate from the line traced out for Him by the redemptive plan of His Father. As in the case of the first temptation, the Savior frustrates Satan with a text from Scripture taken in the literal sense. Christ chooses to remain faithful to His Father's plan of sufferings and humiliation.

The Third Temptation.

Again the devil took him up into a very high mountain, and
showed him all the kingdoms of the world and the glory of
them, and said to him: All these will I give thee, if falling down
thou wilt adore me. Then Jesus saith to him: Begone, Satan:
for it is written, The Lord thy God shalt thou adore, and him
only shalt thou serve. (Matt. 4:8–10)

Back on the top of Mount Quarantania, the devil uses his powers
to parade the images of all the kingdoms of the earth before the
mind of Jesus. It all happens in an instant. St. Luke says that the
vision lasted no more than the twinkling of an eye, and that the
tempter took pains to add: "To thee will I give all this power, and
the glory of them; for to me they are delivered, and to whom I
will, I give them" (Luke 4:6). The Father of Lies is boasting; he
is not the absolute master of all this and cannot dispose of it at
will. "The earth is the Lord's and the fullness thereof: the world,
and all they that dwell therein" (Ps. 23:1). Yet after the sin of
man, the devil has free access to the world and dwells in it as in
his fief, and he has some title to being called "the prince of this
world" (John 14:30). He will give it, he says, to the one who
bows down and renders him homage, as a subject to a king or
a vassal to a suzerain. He deliberately uses an ambiguous word,
meaning both adoration and homage, for fear of setting in too
violent revolt the conscience of a man whose virtue he well knows.
Nevertheless, the artifice is so plain that it is difficult to explain
it. Perhaps stunned by his two defeats, the tempter loses his head
and strikes out blindly, risking his all like a gambler angered by
bad luck. Perhaps he has ceased to believe in the Messiahship of
Jesus and thinks that he is dealing with an ordinary man who
cannot fail to be dazzled by such vistas of grandeur. As a matter

of fact, this time he does not say, as in the first two temptations: "If Thou art the Son of God."

The Savior rebuffs him by the solemn Hebrew profession of the faith in the oneness of God: "The Lord thy God shalt thou adore, and him only shalt thou serve." To cut short any new attacks, He adds, "Begone, Satan." The devil withdraws, overcome but not discouraged. The Gospel says that he left Jesus only for a time. We shall find him in Gethsemane and on Calvary, but there his rout will be complete and final.

It is an over-simplification to reduce the devil's attack to the triple temptation to gluttony, vainglory, and ambition. This would be to look at the temptations from the wrong side. In the soul of Jesus, there was no "drama of a divided will." His will was not engaged in a battle between the attraction of evil and the call of conscience, for the proposal of evil could evoke in Jesus only aversion and horror. The temptations of our Lord are called messianic temptations. Their object is to make Him deviate from God's plan for the Redemption through suffering and the Cross. Since Christ cannot be induced to evil, the object of the temptations is to get Jesus to choose an easier and pleasanter path than the hard one that God marked out for Him. Effort and combat were called for on the part of our Lord, though there was never any doubt of the issue. Certainly it would have been desirable for the humanity of Christ to satisfy His hunger by a miracle that was in His power to perform. He might well have exchanged a life of privations, humiliations, and sufferings for the peaceful and glorious existence of wonder-worker, or procured the salvation of the world by a brilliant stroke rather than by paying for it with the price of His Blood. The submission of Jesus to His Father's desires and His glorious acceptance of the plan of Redemption earned for Him an immediate reward. When the devil had disappeared, angels came to serve Him (see Matt. 4:11).

Here is our King exercising in His own person the plan of suffering and humiliation to save souls. "The whole life of Christ," says the *Imitation*, "was a cross and a martyrdom." Here is Christ selling all, refusing to accept the material kingdom and messianism of the Jews over the divine and spiritual messianism of His Father. The Spirit of the Third Class, of energetic action and complete surrender to God, is given us by Jesus. Moreover, He teaches us how to prepare our souls for the temptations of the devil. Forty days of prayer and penance and fasting preceded these temptations. Not that Christ needed this preparation; He could never sin. But He wished to give us a living example of the advice He gave later to Peter and all His apostles: "Pray that ye enter not into temptation" (Matt. 26:41). Let us ask His grace to imitate His wonderful example.

Confer: Ferdinand Prat, S.J., *Jesus Christ*, vol. 1, pp. 155–163.

SIXTH DAY

Purpose: To study Christ in the mysteries of His public life

Patron: St. John the Baptist

Points for Self-Consideration:

- My use of the Sacrament of Penance, especially my regularity and carefulness in preparation.
- Do I avoid routine in confessing?
- Do I have an abiding sorrow for my sin?

Suggested Readings:

Matthew 7

Imitation of Christ, bk. 3, ch. 37

Spiritual Exercises: Rules for Thinking with the Church, 1–10

Aspiration:

> *"I count all things to be but loss for the excellent knowledge of Jesus Christ my Lord." (Phil. 3:8)*

FIRST MEDITATION

The Apostolic Life of Christ

As we contemplate our Blessed Lord in His public ministry, the scene will shift with His movements and travelings throughout Judea and Galilee. Perhaps as good a scene as any to start us in our prayer is to see our Blessed Lord surrounded by His apostles and preaching the Kingdom to the crowds that press upon Him, either the Sermon on the Mount or the preaching from the bark of Peter. The grace we ask is for an interior knowledge of our Lord — as St. Paul says, "Put ye on the Lord Jesus Christ" (Rom. 13:14) — that we may love Him more daily and follow Him more closely. So many scenes could be selected from our Lord's public life that in order not to slight any we will rather treat of His ministry from three rather broad divisions.

The divine mission of Christ as proved by His numerous miracles. We know that every extraordinary messenger from God to men should produce his credentials, and the miracle is the seal of God. After inaugurating His work with two miracles at Cana, Jesus Christ scattered miracles everywhere along His way. The Gospel calls them acts of power because they require supernatural power, and signs inasmuch as they serve to authenticate the mission of the Savior, who appeals more than once to their unimpeachable testimony. He cures a paralytic to prove to the Pharisees that He has the power to forgive sins. He answers the disciples of the Baptist who come in their master's name to ask Him if He is really the Messiah by saying, "Go and relate to John what you have heard and seen: the blind see, the lame walk, the lepers are made clean, the deaf hear, the dead rise again, to the poor the gospel is preached" (Luke 7:22).

Whether they are worked from a distance or not, the miracles of Christ are all characterized by their leaving no room for doubt. Neither the disciples nor the indifferent—nor even His enemies—dispute their reality. In well-disposed souls they engender spontaneous faith. In the merely curious they awaken surprise, astonishment, amazement, a kind of religious fear, and an instinctive feeling that the finger of God is here. In His sworn enemies, determined in advance to shut their eyes to the light, they inspire hate and fright. Unable to deny them, the scribes and Pharisees pretend to take them for the work of Satan, whereas in their heart of hearts they see in them a threat to their own standing and influence. They tell their confederates: "This man works too many miracles. If He be allowed to continue, everyone will flock to Him."

We know that a single miracle thoroughly certified, if done by a wonder-worker as a proof of his mission, is enough to authenticate that mission. But the demonstration has much greater proving force when the divine envoy possesses this superhuman power to be used at will, when and as often as he wishes. This was the case with Christ's miracles. Several times, the Evangelists mention a number of them together. Not counting groups of miracles and all the marvels that have the person of Jesus Himself for their object, such as the Transfiguration, the Resurrection, and the subsequent apparitions, thirty-three miracles are described in detail in the Gospels. Among them are eight contraventions of the laws of nature, six expulsions of devils, sixteen cures of various diseases, and three raisings from the dead. Moreover, there is hardly any comparison between the miracles performed of old by men of God and prophets of the Old Testament and those performed by Christ. When Elisha wanted to call the son of the Sunamite woman back to life, he shut himself up alone with the dead boy and, after long prayer, stretched out over him, mouth on mouth, eyes on eyes, hands on hands, as though trying to bring warmth once more into the little body (see 2 Kings 4:32–35). But notice the consummate ease with which Christ raises the daughter of Jairus: He took her hand and lifted her easily back to life (see Mark 5:22–24, 35–43). Remember the dead son of the widow of Naim? He addressed the dead boy, "Young man, I command thee, arise!" (see Luke 7:11–15). This latter miracle was worked in broad daylight, before a whole town and funeral procession, and in circumstances unequaled for evidence and publicity so that all the spectators were struck with that kind of religious fear that is inspired by a divine apparition. Jesus Christ brings back the dead to life as though it were the most ordinary of actions. He speaks as master to those who rest in eternal sleep. It is clear that He is the God of the dead as well as of the living, never more calm than when He is working the greatest of miracles. The people, when they saw His magnificent miracles, cried out: "A great prophet is risen up among us: and, God hath visited his people" (Luke 7:16). It is obvious from all His miracles that Christ is divine and that His work of establishing His kingdom and saving souls is a divine mission, a work given Him by His Father and one meant to be completed in the eternal vision of the Holy Trinity in Heaven.

The divine Shepherd of Souls. What was the spirit of Christ's apostolate? Here we will see our Lord as the divine Shepherd of souls, zealously seeking out the lost sheep, bringing them back to His Father, and giving His life for them. "I am the good shepherd. The good shepherd giveth his life for his sheep.... I am the good shepherd; and I know mine, and mine know me. As the Father knoweth me, and I know the Father: and I lay down my life for my sheep" (John 1:11, 14–15). Three characteristics distinguish the Good Shepherd from the hireling and intruder: He knows His sheep and is known by them; He watches over the well-being and increase of the flock; He risks His life to defend them. He knows His sheep and they know Him, as He knows His Father and His Father knows Him. This knowledge that the faithful have of Christ cannot be adequate and comprehensive; but it is so intimate that it may be compared to the mutual knowledge of the Father and the Son. This hyperbole is purposely used in the Gospel to bring out more feelingly the close bond that unites Christ and the Christian in the communion of the Mystical Body. The Good Shepherd lays down His life for His sheep. Shepherds have been known to risk their lives in defense of their sheep, but recklessly to sacrifice their lives to save irrational creatures would be neither proper nor reasonable. A human life, however, is worth more than that. Yet what an ordinary shepherd cannot and should not do, this the Good Shepherd has literally done. He has given His life for His sheep that they may live; for, in the present plan of divine Providence, they could not have life except at that price.

In all the literatures of the world since the time of Homer and even before him, kings are the shepherds of the people. God called Himself the shepherd of Israel, and in the prophecies, the Messiah has the same title. No symbol was dearer to the early Christians, and the image of the Good Shepherd is profusely scattered among the frescoes of the catacombs. The prophecy of Ezekiel is well known:

> Woe to the shepherds of Israel, that fed themselves: should not the flocks be fed by the shepherds? . . . I will feed my sheep. . . . I will seek that which was lost: and that which was driven away, I will bring again: and I will bind up that

which was broken, and I will strengthen that which was weak.... And I will set up one shepherd over them, and he shall feed them, even my servant David: he shall feed them, and he shall be their shepherd. (Ezek. 34:2, 15–16, 23)

Jesus has done all this for His sheep. His compassionate kindness to the poor, the lowly, and all the outcasts of society profoundly scandalized the scribes and Pharisees, who had nothing but scorn for the ignorant common people. What irritated them even more was the interest He seemed to take in publicans, the refuse of Jewish society, and the indulgence He showed to public sinners, whose mere approach was considered a defilement. "I will have mercy and not sacrifice. For I am not come to call the just but sinners," He told His enemies who accused Him of being a friend of sinners (Matt. 9:13). As a matter of fact, the collectors of taxes formed a very numerous caste, more closely bound together by the sullen hatred and affected disdain directed against them by their compatriots. These men were attracted to Jesus by His sweetness, and they were coming around seeking from Him the signs of sympathy that everyone else denied them. The Savior did not repel their advances; had He not admitted one of their numbers into the group of His apostles? When they invited Him to sit down with them at table, He did not disdain to do so. Notorious sinners mingled with them in the hope of obtaining pardon and restoration. The meetings with these unfortunates went increasing in number, and it was said that they made appointments to meet Him. Strange court for the divine King! This preference of His for physical and moral misery was the complaint most often phrased against Him by His declared enemies. In vain had He told them that He had not come to call the just but sinners.

Jesus told three touching parables to reveal the marvels of God's mercy and to teach men at the same time the value of one soul in the eyes of God: the Strayed Sheep (see Luke 15:4–7), the Lost Drachma (see Luke 15:8–10), and the Prodigal Son (see Luke 15:11–32). They show the Good Shepherd feeding His sheep. But even more by His actions than by His stories did Jesus show Himself the Good Shepherd. Witness His acceptance of Magdalene in the house of Simon the Pharisee: "Many sins are forgiven her, because she hath loved much" (Luke 7:47); His defense of the woman taken in adultery (see John 8:3–11); His healing of the lepers (see Luke 17:12–19); His compassion on the multitude because they were as sheep having no shepherd, and His miraculous feeding of them on two distinct occasions (see Matt. 14:14–21; 15:29–38); His healing of all the sick that were brought to Him (see Mark 1:32–34). Here was the Good Shepherd literally fulfilling the prophecy of Ezekiel. He undertakes immense and often thankless labors and hardships for the sheep of Israel. Perhaps He had a home at Capernaum, headquarters for His public ministry, but He was often away from it, seeking His lost sheep, evangelizing in Galilee, or working beyond its confines. He had no place whereon to lay His head (see Matt. 8:20). And frequently, the very attraction of His preaching made it impossible for Him to eat. Never did He spare Himself fatigue; He was so tired that He scarcely sat in Peter's boat when He slept through a squall, which frightened His apostles nearly to death. Nor would He ever give into discouragement, despite the hatred and opposition of His enemies, the disheartening weakness and dullness of His apostles and disciples, and the fact that after three years of utter self-giving, He seemed to be a complete failure. Such was the love and zeal of the Good Shepherd for His sheep.

His moments of triumph. But despite His hard and laborious life of suffering, Christ our Lord did have His moments of triumph in His public ministry. There was the time when the heavens opened and the Holy Spirit in the form of a dove descended upon Him while

His beloved Father gave eloquent testimony to the well-beloved Son: "This is my beloved Son, in whom I am well pleased" (Matt. 3:17). Certainly, our Blessed Lord's soul was filled with joy even as we are filled with joy at the approbation of our loved ones. Then there was the Transfiguration on the mountain, when Jesus seemed to be enveloped in a dazzling cloud. He was not gleaming with borrowed light, like Moses on Moreb reflecting the divine splendor. His whole person flashed forth light: His face shone like the sun, and His garments were resplendent with the dazzling whiteness of snow. Moses and Elijah spoke to Him, and then a luminous cloud enveloped them all, and the voice of the Father spoke: "This is my beloved Son, in whom I am well pleased: hear ye him" (Matt. 17:2–5). Years later, St. Peter recalled this incident:

> He received from God the Father honor and glory: this voice coming down to him from the excellent glory: This is my beloved Son, in whom I am well pleased; hear ye him. And this voice we heard brought from heaven, when we were with him in the holy mount. (2 Pet. 1:17–18)

But, of course, the great day of triumph is the Processional of Palms, or the triumphal entry into Jerusalem shortly before the Passion. It had all been foretold by the prophet Zechariah: "Behold thy king will come to thee ... riding upon ... the foal of an ass" (Zech. 9:9). The enthusiastic crowd strewed their mantles under His feet or scattered leafy branches and flowery herbage along the route from Bethany to Jerusalem.

Others plucked the greening young sprouts from nearby palms and olive trees and waved them in token of joyfulness, acclaiming with unanimous voice the King of Peace who was making His entry into His capital. "Hosanna to the son of David: Blessed is he that cometh in the name of the Lord: Hosanna in the highest!"

(Matt. 21:9). A victorious King mounted upon an ass! What a strange spectacle! What a violent contrast! Yet Zechariah had said of Him: "Behold thy King will come to thee, the just and savior: He is poor, and riding upon an ass, and upon a colt the foal of an ass" (Zech. 9:9). As the multitude acclaimed Him, the Pharisees asked Christ to impose silence upon them. "If these shall hold their peace," said our Lord, "the stones will cry out" (see Luke 19:40). It was His figurative way of telling the Pharisees that the truth will shine forth in full daylight, whatever the efforts to stifle it in the shade. Yes, He was the King of Israel! And the children took up the cry louder, singing "Hosanna to the Son of David!" In vain, the Pharisees attempted to silence them. "Yes, I hear them," said Christ, "but have you never read in the book of the Psalms: 'Out of the mouths of infants and sucklings thou hast perfected praise, because of thy enemies, that thou mayst destroy the enemy and the avenger'" (see Ps. 8:3).

Yet what is this we see in the midst of such rejoicing? The Good Shepherd, the divine King is weeping, and these are not tears of joy, nor merely tears of sorrow. They are tears of bitterness. As He looks from the crest of the hill down upon His beloved city of Jerusalem, Jesus sees a terrible future for His people:

> If thou also hadst known, and that in this thy day, the things that are to thy peace; but now they are hidden from thy eyes. For the days shall come upon thee, and thy enemies shall cast a trench about thee, and compass thee round, and straiten thee on every side, and beat thee flat to the ground, and thy children who are in thee: and they shall not leave in thee a stone upon a stone: because thou hast not known the time of thy visitation [the hour when the Lord came to offer grace and salvation]. (Luke 19:42–44)

Let us turn to our Savior and offer ourselves anew to Him forever and completely, asking Him to make us imitate His life of devotion to God's cause and the salvation of souls. Let us ask Him to help us take the sorrows and hardships of life the way He accepted His, with joy, courage, and faith in the Heavenly Father. And let us also accept the joys God sends us the way Christ accepted His, with humility, as occasions to glorify the Father.

Confer: Ferdinand Prat, S.J., *Jesus Christ*, vol. 1, pp.
236, 248; vol. 2, pp. 67–73, 185–196.

The Three Modes of Humility

WE COME IN this meditation to another distinctive Ignatian exercise: the three modes of humility. Now, the book of the *Spiritual Exercises* does not present the three modes of humility as a formal meditation. It invites one to reflect on them during the day and especially to concentrate on the third mode of humility. Nothing, however, prevents us from taking this exercise as a formal time of prayer and to adapt the exercise to a meditation or contemplation. As a matter of fact, we can get much good out of the exercise taken this way in a group retreat. What are the three modes of humility? Briefly, as St. Ignatius gives them to us:

The first mode is the humility necessary for eternal salvation. This humility allows me to so humble myself that I obey in everything the law of God in such sort that I would not seriously entertain the thought of any mortal transgression even if my life were at stake.

The second mode of humility is more perfect than the first. I have it if I find myself in such a state of mind as not to wish for, or be drawn to having, riches rather than poverty, honor rather than dishonor, a long life rather than a short one. Further, neither for all creation nor for a threat to take my life would I seriously contemplate the commission of a venial sin.

The third mode is most perfect humility. Here, for the better imitation of Christ our Lord and the more actual likeness to Him, I wish and *choose* poverty with Christ poor rather than riches, reproaches with Christ laden with reproaches rather than honors, and I desire to be accounted a good-for-nothing for Christ's sake—who before me was held for such—rather than wise and prudent in this world.

These three modes of humility correspond to submitting oneself to the good pleasure of God by avoiding mortal and venial sin and by sharing the trials imposed upon the Savior. Hence, the three modes of humility are nothing more than three modes of imitation according to the respective vocation of the common faithful. We are all called to avoid at least every grave fault. Close friends of Christ will give up every deliberate offense, no matter how small or slight it may seem. Some few intimate friends of Christ will follow their good Master as closely as possible.

The three degrees of humility correspond to three degrees of union with Jesus, the Friend who has said: "Abide in me, and I in you" (John 15:4). He who is the mystical spouse of souls desires a union that is at once affective and effective. He desires a union of compenetration that is more and more intimate, where there is more and more an increase of sanctifying grace. He desires a progressive transformation and assimilation and divinization of our souls in Him.

A note to religious: We religious long ago rejected mortal sin and deliberate venial sin. We have chosen and have decided for the third mode of humility. Or rather, Christ has chosen and has called us to be His favorites, to imitate His life most closely—like the apostles, the good women, and His Holy Mother, all of whom shared His sorrows and His joys. Hence, in this hour of prayer, let us emphasize this highest mode of living with Jesus so that we may renew our knowledge of the supreme beauty and importance for us of the third mode of humility, that we may give ourselves to its generous practice of our daily lives.

We are the favorites of Jesus Christ. Among the friends of Jesus, we can distinguish three classes: (1) those who hold themselves to the strict duty of never committing mortal sin; (2) those who go further and are faithfully striving to avoid every deliberate venial sin; (3) those who prefer only what Christ prefers, notably poverty and humiliation because *He* has preferred them. These last, being far more loving toward Christ, are in turn more loved by Him. They are His intimates, His favorites.

Let us study the motives of action to obtain the third mode. Let us study the privileges and the pitfalls to be feared. In doing so, we will appreciate the high perfection to which Christ calls us.

The motives for practicing the third mode of humility. Consider the enthusiastic disciples of a philosopher like Socrates. His followers admit all his opinions, often without verification. They imitate his manners, even his hobbies. Why, they rejoice to be despised or hated by the same people who hate and despise their idol. They show their love by having something to suffer for him.

How much more in our case, we who have been privileged with the grace and love of Christ? How much more should we have one thought: to imitate our Savior, to become as much as possible like Him in all things? Why? There are four good reasons among many others.

First of all, honest pride leads us to imitate Him. Since there resides in Jesus the plenitude of the divinity, complete wisdom, and all holiness, we could not receive a greater honor than to live with Him, to experience the same affections that throbbed in His heart, the same hatreds for sin, and to suffer finally the same trials that were chosen for Him by His Father and that were His meat and joy to fulfill out of love for us.

Secondly, we should desire to give our Savior perfect homage. If we wish to proclaim to the whole world that we have perfection itself and supreme goodness for a living ideal, what better way to do in deed than to give ourselves to Christ to be ruled in all things by Him? To pay Him homage, we must dedicate ourselves to His personal and loving ideas. We must adopt in all things His ways of evaluating things. We must efface ourselves; as the Apostle says, "let this mind be in you, which was also in Christ Jesus" (Phil. 2:5). In doing this, we cooperate with the plans of the Eternal Father, who has given Christ to us to be our Wisdom, our Model whom we must imitate in all things, even when we cannot understand the reasons of His actions.

Thirdly, we desire to imitate Him in order to enjoy the certainty of living united with Him. That is how the apostles reasoned. "Let us also go, that we may die with him," cries St. Thomas the apostle (John 11:16). "I am ready," protests St. Peter to our Lord, "to go with thee, both into prison, and to death" (Luke 22:33). To bind his lot to the lot of His Master: what a splendid homage! And what tremendous consolation for the loving disciples who always remained with Him! It is the will of the Heavenly Father that Jesus continue to live even unto the end of time as the poor man, the unknown, the contradicted, the persecuted. Where, therefore, ever since He came, have we the opportunity of finding Him except in poverty, humiliation, and contradiction? The saints feared and suspected wealth; they preferred those things that no one else wanted. Moreover, they were uneasy when they were honored and praised. But they rejoiced in contradictions; trials were a sure sign that Jesus was with them.

Fourthly, we imitate Him in order to give our Blessed Lord love for love, sacrifice for sacrifice, gift for gift. If He preferred for Himself poverty, humiliations, and suffering, certainly it was not because these were indispensable for our salvation. As God, the least of His actions had infinite value to save us. But He preferred to reveal to us the most certain way to salvation and to save us from long and involved reasonings and investigations to find it. He wanted us to see what He was capable of enduring out of love for us. He wished that our desire to prove our gratitude to Him would make us choose sacrifice, without which we cannot break away from our disordered nature and its mediocrity. Strengthened by the thought that they were giving Christ in return love for love, the apostles rejoiced in their first persecutions: "they indeed went ... rejoicing that they were accounted worthy to suffer reproach for the name of Jesus" (Acts 5:41). The saints have tasted the same consolations in their most bitter trials.

The privileges of His favorites. Those who suffer for the love of God console the heart of their good Master. What a poignant sorrow for Christ to see the multitude of the slothful who betray Him, of the tepid who follow Him from afar, always whining! At Capernaum, with what anguish did He not ask this question: "Will you also go away?" (John 6:68). At the Last Supper, on the contrary, what accents of gratitude tremble in His words: "You are they who have continued with me in my temptations" (Luke 22:28). Again, what sadness in His complaint: "The hour cometh, and it is now come, that you shall be scattered every man to his own, and shall leave me alone" (John 16:32). This is the Sacred Heart that rejoices at every mark of attachment and love for it. The sweetness of our living affection compensates in some measure for the affronts that He must suffer. Yes, surely, in order to convince us of this truth, before His agony in the garden had begun, Christ had asked help and company and consolation from His three favorite companions: "Peter, James, John, will you watch with me?" (see Matt. 16:37–38). What consolation He found in seeing His loving Mother and John at the foot of His Cross with the other pious women (see John 19:25–26). Remember, you too can bring Him great joy in accepting cheerfully to share in His humiliations and sufferings. Surely you cannot stop at offering Him mere sighs, sweet words, and only those pains that you cannot avoid anyway. Could you call that loving Him with the third mode of humility?

Generous souls are cherished by our Savior. Every act of abnegation will certainly be rewarded in eternity. No doubt of that. But what reward can be compared to knowing that Jesus Christ showers upon His companions His most intimate love and tenderness? Now He has promised this: "He that loveth me ... I will love him, and will manifest myself to him" (John 14:21). And again: "If any one love me ... my Father will love him, and we will come to him, and will make our abode with him" (John 14:23). If we think more often of these promises, what joy would we not experience in renouncing ourselves out of love for Him! Certainly, we do not wish to be called only fair-weather friends!

Generous souls are blessed above all. They are the ones to whom the Lord commits His choice works of predilection. Thus, all the great works of spreading the Gospel, of reform, of undertaking monastic life, of rekindling the fire of God's love in the Catholic Church have been entrusted to souls of the third mode of humility. They have accomplished great things for God and man because they spoke of Christ, His sufferings, and His love with accents of conviction that has no equal, and because they knew how to stick to their missions under all sorts of trials, where others would have abandoned them at the first difficulties. Souls like St. Theresa of Ávila, St. John of the Cross, St. Ignatius of Loyola, St. Margaret Mary, Mother Cabrini, St. Frassinetti, and many others. To enjoy the privileges of consoling His heart, of experiencing His special love, of assisting Him in His great works, we must pay the price and be like Him in suffering, humility, and abnegation. Mortification, abnegation, and humiliation frighten us, O Jesus! But what a marvelous reward you give in return! Your friendship, Your intimacy, Your assistance! Can we hesitate?

The faults and failures to be feared. Alas, in spite of their resolution, Thomas, Peter, and all the apostles [except John] abandoned their Master! However, for their momentary weakness, they made generous reparation in their later lives. We, too, have similar failures, seeking vain things again, avoiding mortifications. Yet if we are generous, we will deplore these failures and go anew to love

Jesus whole-heartedly. Jesus allows these failures so that we may learn the baseness of our human nature, to humble us and to teach us never to cease fighting. We must especially fear that our failures ever become habitual. Here are some signs to check:

1. A bad sign is when we lose sight of the ideal or consider it a thing of the past, as when a painter or musician has lost all enthusiasm for his art and no longer studies the masterpieces. We must never lose sight of our ideal, Jesus Christ, or cease our close imitation of Him in practical poverty, humility, and lowliness.

2. Are you attempting to avoid sacrifices? Perhaps you bypass the more humble tasks or look for satisfactions of comfort or self-love. Instead of asking: "Can I not refuse this pleasure for love of Jesus?" I find myself saying: "Is it forbidden?" Instead of seeing how far I can go in abnegation without losing prudence, I see how far I can go in other things without sinning. What a change!

3. Complaints and rancor of heart possess us. Instead of rejoicing in trials borne for the good Master, I find bitterness, and I feel criticism against those who cause me to suffer even slightly poverty or humiliations.

What are the remedies for these?

1. Meditate assiduously on the seeming follies of Jesus Christ. Why did He accept such privations, affronts, and tortures? Because He loved me. But then why am I so indelicate as to forget to suffer out of love for Him?

2. Think often on the beauty of the third mode of humility: to resemble Jesus as much as possible, to imitate Him better, to love Him utterly, to destroy your mediocrity.

3. Ask earnestly for humiliations and trials, but ask at the same time for the proportionate graces to bear them. This preserves modesty and diminishes our fears. Such humble petitions keep up our fervor; by their generosity, they merit us God's assistance.

Yes, dear Jesus, reserve for me some of Your Cross! But You know my weakness! Help me! Sustain me! Keep always before me Your wonderful reward: Your tender love, Your intimate friendship, Your loving self.

Colloquy with our Lady: Deign to vivify in me, Beloved Mother, love of the Ideal, the desire of imitating Jesus as much as possible and of suffering with Him. *Fac me tecum pie flere, Crucifixo condolere, donec ego vixero.*

Confer: Pinard de la Boullaye, S.J., *Exercices Spirituels*,
vol. 1, pp. 177–198; vol. 3, pp. 142–150.

CONFERENCE

The Person and Personality of Jesus

JESUS HIMSELF IS both divine and human. For in the mystery of the Incarnation, He is the mysterious union of the divine and human natures that remain distinct and unconfused within the unity of the Second Person of the Holy Trinity, the Son of God. Jesus is rooted from all eternity in the bosom of the Holy Trinity.

The Son of God became man. He did not descend to inhabit a human frame waiting for Him, but He became a man literally, in order that no possible doubt might arise about His assumed nature—conceived and born of the Virgin Mary—and so that it might never be asserted that the Son of God, despising the lowliness of the human body and human nature, had united Himself only with the essence of a holy soul or with an exalted spirit. Scripture had revealed that God had said: "My delights were to be with the children of men" (Prov. 8:31). In Christ, mankind received its greatest "blessed event," the human child as the Son of God and the Son of man. John the Evangelist states this mystery clearly: "the Word was made flesh" (John 1:14).

Romano Guardini, in his masterpiece *The Lord*, writes of the Incarnation of the Son of God in the flesh thus:

> Only in the flesh, not in the bare spirit, can destiny and history come into being.... God descended to us in the

person of the Savior, Redeemer, in order to have a history, to become history. Through the Incarnation, the founder of the new history stepped into our midst. With His coming, all that had been before fell into its historical place.

He dwelt among us — "pitched His tent among us" — as the Gospel of John puts it. "Tent" of the Logos: what is this but Christ's body? It is God's holy pavilion among men, the original tabernacle of the Lord in our midst, the "temple" Jesus meant when He said to the Pharisees: "Destroy this temple, and in three days I will raise it up" (John 2:19). St. Paul, writing of the loving condescension of the Logos to become man in order to serve His brethren, describes the spirit of Christ on the verge of His Incarnation:

> Let this mind be in you, which was also in Christ Jesus: who being in the form of God, thought it not robbery to be equal with God: but emptied himself, taking the form of a servant, being made in the likeness of men, and in habit found as a man. He humbled himself, becoming obedient unto death, even to the death of the cross. (Phil. 2:5–8)

Christ the God-man. Christ, being God, did not — nor could He — take on fallen human nature, for He was to save sinful man from sin, Satan, and supernatural death. Thus, God prepared Mary, His Mother, with a perfect human nature, never subject to the yoke of sin. In Mary's perfect human nature, there was no weakness of concupiscence, no attraction to sin, evil pleasure, or pride in any degree.

Now, there is a vast difference between the perfect human nature of Mary and the sacred humanity of Christ. Mary received her human nature from her parents, Joachim and Anne. Hers is a human nature begotten in the natural way, from creature parents, though preserved from sin, original and personal, by a special grace of God. We do not adore the human nature of Mary; we venerate it as being sinless and full of grace, but yet the fruit of the procreative act of her parents. In the forming of the human nature of Christ, there is a divine intervention. God, the Holy Spirit, forms the human nature in the virginal womb of Mary. Thus, the humanity of Christ is the sacred humanity of God. That is why Catholics adore the sacred humanity of the God-man. That is why they receive the sacred humanity—Body, Blood, soul, and divinity—under the species of bread and wine, as the divine food and life of their souls. Man could never do this with the humanity of mere creatures, for then he would be guilty of the sins of idolatry and cannibalism.

Mary is unique among all women; she was conceived and born full of grace. The whole concentration of her life was to please God and perform His will perfectly. Hence, the distractions of concupiscence, which are the effects of sin, never disturbed her interior or exterior consciousness. God destined her for the unique mission of becoming the Mother of His incarnate Son.

As for her Son, the God-man, He is holiness itself and His humanity is worthy of adoration. St. John the Evangelist wrote that Jesus would give to those who believed in Him a gift He possessed from the moment of His incarnation and birth. What is that gift? Those who believe in and keep His commandments will be born a second time in Baptism in a supernatural and similar way to which He was miraculously conceived by the power of the Holy Spirit and born of the Virgin Mary. They will be born, like Him, "not of blood, nor of the will of the flesh, nor of the will of man, but of God" (John 1:13).

Then, too, Christ had the most sublime of all imaginable missions. "My meat is to do the will of him that sent me" (John 4:34). Thus, Christ was totally dedicated in His divine and human consciousness to becoming the suffering servant of the Lord. He was destined not for pleasure of any kind but for a life of total self-sacrifice, even unto death on the Cross, in order to multiply the family of God in the life of grace. That He accomplished this mission is testified to by His last words as He yielded up His soul to the Father: "It is consummated!" (John 19:30). That is, I have perfectly fulfilled Your will, O Father.

An objection is often raised: Was not Christ subjected to three temptations by Satan? The three temptations recorded were really external attempts by Satan to find out who Christ was; was He really the Messiah? Satan knew he had no sinful control over this man. Hence, the three attempts to draw Him out: Satan tempted Him to eat the way Eve did, on Satan's terms, not on God's; he glamorized our Lord's mission, trying to lead Him from the path of the suffering servant of God, destined for crucifixion; and he tried to lure Him into a position of riches, power, earthly prominence, and authority over the cities of this world. This was in opposition to His work of establishing God's kingdom on earth through poverty, prayer, penance, rejection by His own people, and death at the hands of the Romans. All three temptations were really three external trials that never aroused the slightest interior attraction in the consciousness of Christ. Christ emphasizes the Word of God as man's essential food for life. He will not accept Satan's spectacular approach for beginning His mission. He refuses to bargain with Satan, rejecting the glory of earthly kingdoms for the kingdom of His Father. Christ firmly drives out the "father of lies": "Begone, Satan! ... The Lord thy God shalt thou adore, and him only shalt thou serve" (Matt. 4:10).

Throughout His public life, the Pharisees would continue these attempts to catch Christ. But Christ always gave them the "perfect squelch" in unanswerable rejoinders. None of these tests were temptations that pierced the interior of Christ's consciousness, as if to find an area of weakness there. Christ submitted to all temptations and trials that came His way in order to teach all persons how to deal with the forces of evil. His tactic for conquering Satan is simple: no dallying with the bait, no spiritual theatrics, no deals, no prolonged sterile discussions; just abrupt, quick rejections, following the advice found in Scripture: "Resist the devil, and he will fly from you" (James 4:7).

Christ as the Good Shepherd. *Christ claims:*

> I am the good shepherd. The good shepherd giveth his life for his sheep. But the hireling, and he that is not the shepherd, whose own the sheep are not, seeth the wolf coming, and leaveth the sheep, and flieth.... I am the good shepherd, and I know mine, and mine know me. As the Father knoweth me, and I know the Father: and I lay down my life for my sheep. (John 10:11–12, 14–15)

Christ knows each individual person; each person never leaves His consciousness or infinite love. The life of each person who is in the fold of Christ depends on the knowledge and love of Christ, who gives His life for every one of them. Then we are startled by the words: "as the Father knoweth me, and I know the Father." Here is an astonishing truth. Jesus is saying that the bond between Himself and each of His followers is the same bond that binds Him to the Father. We have here the love of Christ for each of His followers. It is established in the perfect intimacy and understanding of love shared in its entirety with another person. John taught the world that "the Word was with God" (John 1:1). Christ reveals to each of His followers that the Word is with each one of them. This expresses the mutual love, the sharing of the same bliss with them that He shares with His Father. But His knowledge is also His infinite love. Thus, He loves His followers as He loves the Father. As the Messiah, as the Son of man, as the good Shepherd, no one can love as faithfully as Christ loves every human person in a divine and human manner.

Christ the eternal high priest. The whole order of religious
life is regulated by sacrifice. Among the Jews, a sacrifice sealed the
covenant between God and Abraham; it was renewed between God
and Moses for the Chosen People, while Aaron, the high priest,
stood at his side. Now, what is a sacrifice, and what does its liturgy
entail? First, the priest must be chosen by God to serve officially the
people in the things pertaining to the worship and service of God.
The sacrifice itself is the priest's offering of some creature belonging
to man, something precious and without flaw that is removed from
the secular use for man and given away to God, to express the com-
pleteness of God's ownership and the cancellation of man's domain
over the gift. The gift is then destroyed and consumed in a religious
liturgy that honors God. But what in Heaven's name is God supposed
to do with such gifts? Has He not created everything? Does it not
all belong to Him? What use could He, the infinite one, have for
finite things? Well, in the eyes of God, the gift in itself is nothing.
But what of the intention behind it? This is inspired by the spirit of
adoration, thanksgiving, supplication, contrition, and praise. The
act of sacrifice is an expression of man's recognized insignificance
and His will to renounce creatures in favor of the omnipotent God.
Sacrifice is a statement of who God is when offered in this sacred
manner. For it testifies that God alone is all that really is; all created things exist only through His grace. He rules everything and
everyone. Hence, things should be used to enhance God's presence
to men, to clear the way for His glory. This is the spirit of reverence
behind St. John's statement in Revelation: "To him that sitteth on
the throne, and to the Lamb, benediction, and honor, and glory,
and power, forever and ever" (5:13).

Behind the sacrifice is man himself. He is conscious of belonging
to God. Thus, he has expressed this relation even in the historical
idolatry of offering human sacrifices. An intrinsic truth has been

thus demonically distorted, but the truth remains. Christian sacrifice is a passing over to God, an entering into the life of God by renouncing the life of the world.

St. Paul reminds us in the Epistle to the Hebrews that the sacrifices of the Old Testament, though unworthy of God and unable to justify men, prepared mankind for the one infinite sacrifice of supreme validity for the salvation of the world. Jesus was always conscious of His role of being God's victim, the Lamb of God. At the Last Supper, He says, signifying the consecrated bread, "This is my body, which is given for you" (Luke 22:19). And of the consecrated wine: "This is the chalice, the new testament in my blood, which shall be shed for you" (Luke 22:20). The sacrifice of Christ is the sacrifice of all sacrifices, made by the eternal, divine high priest in the immolation of His sacred humanity for the salvation of all humans and the glorification of His Father.

St. Paul expresses this divine-human mystery beautifully:

> Wherefore it behooved him in all things to be made like unto his brethren, that he might become a merciful and faithful priest before God, that he might be a propitiation for the sins of the people. For in that, wherein he himself hath suffered and been tempted, he is able to succor them also that are tempted. (Heb. 2:17–18)

The priest must be one of those He represents; He must share their fate. For this reason, God's Son, a man, like men in all things except sin, had to make His sacrifice go forth from man's midst. Yet He had to be different from all other human priests too:

> For it was fitting that we should have such a high priest, holy, innocent, undefiled, separated from sinners, and made higher than the heavens; who needeth not daily (as the other

priests) to offer sacrifices first for his own sins, and then for the people's: for this he did once, in offering himself. (Heb. 7:26–27)

What John and the three Synoptics so clearly emphasize is Jesus' unconditional surrender to His Father's will. It is demonstrated in His role as victim and priest. For it is not things that Christ sacrifices, not animals, not food or drink, but His own Flesh and Blood, in the very mystery of His literal annihilation, becoming "a worm, and no man," as Scripture testifies (Ps. 21:7).

> But when Christ appeared as high priest of the good things to come, He entered once for all through the greater and more perfect tabernacle, not made by hands, nor by virtue of blood of goats and calves, but by virtue of His own Blood, into the Holies, having obtained eternal redemption. (see Heb. 9:11–12)

Christ offered Himself that God might be all in all. "Thy will, not Mine!" (see Matt. 26:42). Thus the words of sin — "My will, not God's" — are expiated. With this act, Jesus' humanity passes over into eternity. What He sacrifices is returned to Him glorified. The Lord's way to death is His way to glory, and He takes us with Him. By giving up His life as priest and victim, He finds it, as He tells us; and not only His own life, but ours also. As mankind was dragged into destruction and death by Adam's sin, so it is now lifted into divine life by Jesus' death, Resurrection, and glorification. Baptism stands for our death and burial with our high priest, and it also signifies our resurrection with Him to new life.

Here, then, is the mysterious image of Christ glorified. He stands alone before His Father, ever living to make intercession for His brethren before the throne of infinite mercy. In the purity of His

heart, the veracity of His spirit, and the act of His total immolation in love, He faces His Father as the only perfect high priest in
Heaven and on earth. And His sacrifice, though immolated in time,
is celebrated eternally, in the endless present. Beyond time, beyond
human conception, Christ remains standing, holding His sacrifice
before His Father forever. In the eyes of the Father, the millennia
pass away, but the sacrifice of Christ our high priest remains. No
other sacrifice exists. In all eternity, there remains but one true
sacrifice, forever being offered to God through the words: "do this
in remembrance of me."

Christ: the sign of contradiction. Among the truths that Jesus
gave His apostles before sending them out into the world to preach
His gospel are the following:

> Do not think that I came to send peace upon earth: I came
> not to send peace, but the sword.... He that loveth father
> or mother more than me, is not worthy of me; and he that
> loveth son or daughter more than me, is not worthy of me.
> And he that taketh not up his cross, and followeth me, is not
> worthy of me. He that findeth his life, shall lose it: and he that
> shall lose his life for me, shall find it. (Matt. 10:34, 37–39)

When Christ was presented in the Temple as a baby, Simeon proph-
esied: "This child is set for the fall and for the resurrection of many
in Israel, and for a sign which shall be contradicted" (Luke 2:34).
Yet Jesus' message is one of love and good will. He proclaims the
Father's love and the coming of His Kingdom. He invites people to
the peace found in life in obedience to His Father's will.

The more faithful a Christian becomes, the deeper the chasm
between him and those who refuse to accept Christ. When it comes
to a choice between family harmony and Jesus, members must value
Jesus, the divine source of their being and the goal of their eternal

happiness, infinitely higher than the most intimately loved parents, relatives, and friends. This often calls for cutting the bonds at the core of the dearest relationships. This is extremely hard to accomplish. Temptations of a psychological nature drive persons to preserve their dearest ties. But Jesus warns everyone: If you cling tenaciously to your natural life, abandoning Me for it, you shall lose your own eternal life. If you let your natural life go for My sake, you will find yourself enjoying divine, inexhaustible life.

No doubt this challenge is difficult; it is the Cross. We brush here against the most demanding mystery of Christianity: its inevitable arrival at Calvary. Ever since Christ walked the Way of the Cross, it stands firmly planted on every person's pilgrimage through life in this world. For every person has to endure the Cross. Nature revolts against it, tries to escape it or circumvent it. But Jesus' words are unchangeable and fundamental to genuine Christianity. Those who cling body and soul to life will lose life; those who surrender to God's will, taking up their crosses, will find their lives forever in their immortal self, swept up in the ecstasy of love shared with the glorified Christ.

On the way to Jerusalem and His crucifixion, Jesus repeated His warning about the cross: "for what does it profit a man, if he gain the whole world, but suffer the loss of his own soul? Or what will a man give in exchange for his soul?" (Matt. 16:26). Here the line of division about the choice or rejection of Christ runs not between one person and another but between every person and all creature comforts. The lesson of the Cross is the great call to self-conquest; it teaches man that Jesus became man to bring home the terrible truth that everything great and small, noble and mean, the whole of creation with all its parts, material and spiritual, corporal and angelic, is tainted with sin and in need of redemption. This does not deny the existence of the naturally good or of the intrinsic goodness of human nature. But it emphasizes that human existence *in toto* has fallen away from God. And Christ came to open men's eyes to what the world and human life is in its reality. His teachings and His life were meant to give man a new start from which he could begin all over again with the divine scale of values. Jesus does not discover new or hidden creative powers in man. But He refers him to His Father, endows him with grace, and situates him in the center and source of all life, natural and divine, the Holy Trinity.

Jesus actually is the Way, the Truth, and the Life. He is the Teacher, Guide, Physician, Healer, and Rescuer who enlightens, leads, probes, heals, and rescues man from sin. He puts each man back on the only sure course to Heaven, the Way of the Cross. The story of each person's life is pregnant with the salvific message and displays an ocean of graces from the hands of God. With this understanding, we may feel securely loved, even when we follow Christ's difficult command that we lose our life in order to possess His life.

Sacred reality begins with Jesus of Nazareth, the Logos. It grows as divine life by faith in Jesus. It arrives at high sanctity through the living of His teachings and the imitation of His deeds.

THIRD MEDITATION
The Last Supper

WE COME NOW to the Passion of our Lord Jesus Christ. We will contemplate those events that especially portray the lonely struggle of our betrayed and deserted King of Love, who willingly and generously offers Himself as victim to His eternal Father for the salvation of the world.

The Last Supper introduces us to the Passion. Let us put ourselves there on the night He was betrayed. Our Lord and His Twelve have gathered in a spacious room, located on the upper floor of a fine-looking house in the city of Jerusalem. The room is furnished with mats, cushions, and couches. Such a room as this was scarcely ever used except for receptions and special dinners. It was not the simple guest room that Jesus had asked for. The generous disciple to whom Peter and John had come saying, "The master saith, My time is near at hand, with thee I make the pasch with my disciples," said he had reserved for Christ his best apartment (see Matt. 26:18). He also had the delicacy to understand that despite the extreme scarcity of places, he must yield this beautiful Cenacle to Him exclusively, in order to avoid disturbing the intimacy of the feast. As we gaze into our Lord's blessed face, we can sense the truth of St. John's words describing this occasion: "Before the festival day of the pasch [Passover], Jesus, knowing that his hour was come, that he should pass out of this world to the Father: having loved his own who were in the world, he loved them unto the end" (John 13:1).

The grace we ask of the King of Love in this meditation is grief, affliction, and confusion, because for our sins the Lord goes to His Passion.

Though the love of Jesus for His own is always the same, the visible proofs of this love become more and more striking as He approaches the end. It is the instinct of the human heart to reserve for the moment of parting the most delicate and the most touching proofs of tenderness. The human heart of our Savior on the eve of parting from His disciples and all His followers will prove to them exceedingly, even to the folly of the Cross. It is night, and the apostles are gathered around their Master; Jesus takes His place at the table and says to them: "With desire I have desired to eat this pasch [Passover] with you, before I suffer. For I say to you that from this time I will not eat it, till it be fulfilled in the kingdom of God" (Luke 22:15–16).

The institution of the Holy Eucharist. When the Paschal feast was ended and Judas had left, Jesus took into His hand one of the unleavened loaves and, lifting His eyes to Heaven, pronounced over it a formula of blessing. This blessing stirred the apostles and awakened their curiosity, because customarily it was not at the end but at the beginning of a meal that the food was blessed. Then Jesus broke the bread into as many morsels as there were guests present and distributed it saying: "Take ye, and eat: this is my body, which shall be delivered for you" (1 Cor. 11:24). Then, taking a cup filled with wine diluted with water (for it was not customary to drink it pure), He performed the same ritual as for the bread He had consecrated, and He presented it to the disciples, saying: "Drink ye all of this, for this is my blood of the new testament, which shall be shed for many" (Matt. 26:27–28). The eleven apostles drank each from the cup, and our Lord added: "Do this in remembrance of me" (see 1 Cor. 11:25).

In these divinely simple words, the Sacrament of Love was instituted. The apostles, prepared long ago for this great mystery, evinced no surprise. Had not Jesus promised them a year before in the synagogue of Capernaum that He would give them His flesh to eat and His Blood to drink? Had He not told them and repeated it in every way, that if they did not eat His flesh and drink His Blood, they would not have life in them? And when the majority of the disciples, scandalized at this disconcerting manner of speech, had gone away, had not Peter in the name of all his colleagues made protestation of their common faith? And now that they see the Savior's promise fulfilled, they believe more than ever with all their souls in His truthfulness, as they possess Him in their hearts. They believe more than ever in His power and in His love. "To whom shall we go? Thou hast the words of eternal life" (John 6:69).

The institution of Holy Orders. When He said the words: "Do this in remembrance of me," Christ instituted the sacrament of Holy Orders to perpetuate His marvelous sacrifice. St. Paul tells us: "For as often as you shall eat this bread and drink the chalice, you shall show the death of the Lord until he come" (1 Cor. 11:26). In virtue of this command of Christ and this promise, the apostles are made associates of the priesthood of Christ and are created priests according to the order of Melchizedek, to offer in every place the unblemished victim of which the prophet Malachi speaks. Moreover, they are invested with the power to consecrate in their turn other priests, who will perpetuate the same rites even to the consummation of the world, even to the Second Coming of the Son of Man, *donec veniat*. Christ could have remained content with saying: "This is My Body, this is My Blood. Do this in remembrance of Me." And, in fact, it is in this way that the primitive teaching or catechesis summarizes the institution of the Holy Eucharist. If it adds anything, it is to emphasize still more the reality of His true Body and His true Blood and to exclude for every unprejudiced mind all idea of symbolism, of figures of speech, of metaphor. These words of Christ have nothing ambiguous in them. To teach that He is truly, substantially present under the Eucharistic species, that He here gives His Body for food and His Blood for drink, could Christ have expressed Himself with greater clearness? No! Moreover, His words establish a relationship between the sacrifice of the Cross and the sacrifice of the altar.

The two sacrifices. Faith teaches *us* that the sacrifice of the altar is not only the commemoration and the representation of the sacrifice of the Cross but its mystical reproduction. The Church does not rest this dogma on the words of the consecration themselves; but it is a fact well worthy of remark that these words can be applied without strain to both sacrifices. The twofold formula of consecration, like a sword, separates the Body and Blood of Christ. This Body is delivered for us in the Eucharist as on the Cross, and in both ways, it gives life to the world. This Blood, mystically shed for us on the altar as it was shed on Calvary, effects the remission of sins and seals the new covenant, the new alliance of peace between God and man. In both, the victim is the same. The only difference is in the manner of offering.

The Abiding Presence. All through our retreat, we have seen that Christ must be the center of our lives. Here, as He feeds His own at His heavenly banquet, we see how He has established His reign over our hearts through the Holy Eucharist. "Give us this day our daily bread," He had prayed to His Father, and here He guarantees us for the rest of our lives the supersubstantial bread of eternal life. Every day, if we wish, and if we have the right intention of pleasing Him, we may come to Communion and receive Him into our hearts. The Fathers and Doctors of the Church almost unanimously think that our Lord Himself partook of the Communion. They must be right. Was it not expected that Christ, in the celebration of the first Mass, would have wished to serve as an example and model to His new priests, since He was ordaining them to do what they had seen Him do? The Communion is the complement to and the consummation of the sacrifice. This is why the priest communicates before leaving the altar, and why the Church wishes those present, united in intention with the sacrificing priest, to unite themselves with him also in the effective partaking of the immolated victim.

Sorrow in the Cenacle. Even as they were eating the Paschal feast, a certain uneasiness pervaded the little group. What had their Master meant when, as He washed their feet, He had said: "You are clean, but not all" (John 13:10)? Our Lord explains Himself a little more clearly by quoting a saying of Scripture: "He that eateth bread with me shall lift up his heel against me" (John 13:18). When He said these words, "he was troubled in spirit," as He had been troubled a few days before at the prospect of His Passion (John 13:21). And He adds: "Amen I say to you, that one of you is about to betray me" (Matt. 26:21). The poor apostles looked at one another in consternation, but no thought of crime could be read in any of their faces. Judas remained unmoved. Jesus continued: "He that dippeth his hand with me in the dish, he shall betray me. The Son of man indeed goeth, as it is written of him: but woe to that man by whom the Son of man shall be betrayed: it were better for him if that man had not been born" (Matt. 26:23–24). The fright of the apostles was extreme. Yet to dissipate their doubt, each of them began to ask: "Lord, is it I?" Judas, feeling that his silence would be tantamount to an avowal, had the effrontery to ask the same question, and Jesus answered him: "Thou has said it" (Matt. 26:27). Anguish still gripped the apostles, suspended as they were between the desire of knowing and the fear of hearing the answer. Let us hear from the witness who is best informed, since he took an active part in the drama:

> Now there was leaning on Jesus' bosom one of his disciples, whom Jesus loved. Simon Peter therefore beckoned to him, and said to him: Who is it of whom he speaketh? He therefore, leaning on the breast of Jesus, saith to him: Lord, who is it? Jesus answered: He it is to whom I shall reach bread dipped. And when he had dipped the bread, he gave it to Judas Iscariot, the son of Simon. And after the morsel, Satan entered into him.... He therefore having received the morsel, went out immediately. And it was night. (John 13: 23–27, 30)

It was night. These simple words in the circumstances have a doleful sound, and we are tempted to see in them a symbolic meaning. It was night. It was the hour of the powers of darkness; Hell was, for the moment, about to triumph, only to be forever vanquished.

Now the morsel of bread dipped in the sauce was not the Eucharist. God forbid! The Holy Eucharist was not instituted until the end of the meal. One shudders at the mere thought that if the traitor had remained to the end, the Savior would have given to him, as to the others, His Body and His Blood, since he was not yet a known sinner. If Jesus had ordained him a priest, he would have given him the power to profane at will the Sacrament of Love. Divine Providence would not permit such an abominable sacrilege to profane the banquet of farewell. Jesus had spared nothing to reclaim this miserable man. He had multiplied His advances, His warnings, His tender reproaches; He had shown Himself ready to forgive at the first sign of repentance. But nothing could move the son of perdition. Now, at least, his treason, though it will astound the apostles, will not be for them a rock of scandal. They will know that their Master had foreseen it and foretold it; that it was for Him neither a mischance nor a surprise; and that assuredly He went to death of His own free will. Judas having gone, the Savior breathed a sigh of relief. "Now," He said, "is the Son of man glorified, and God is glorified in him. If God be glorified in him, God also will glorify him in himself; and immediately will he glorify him" (John 13:31–32). He will glorify Him by His redeeming death, whose immediate rewards are the Resurrection and the Ascension.

As we view our Savior giving us the greatest token of His love even while He sees the terrible sufferings that we shall inflict upon Him, let us ask for sorrow with His sorrow, a suffering with Him in His Passion, and a resolve to love Him and visit Him in the Holy Eucharist frequently, to receive Him daily with complete love and self-surrender.

SEVENTH DAY

Purpose: To prayerfully and compassionately accompany Christ in the events of His holy Passion and redeeming death

Patron: Our Lady of Sorrows

Points for Self-Consideration:

- Holy Mass. My reverence, my devotion, my active participation in the Holy Memorial of Christ's bloody Sacrifice. My union with Christ, Priest and Victim.
- Holy Communion. Do I appreciate God's exchange of the gift of His Son as my food in return for my gift of His Son as a sacrifice of love and reparation and atonement?
- Do I long for Christ, entertain Him as my dearest Friend in a time of thanksgiving?
- Do I beg for an increase of faith, hope, and love for Him hidden under the species of bread and wine and in my soul?

Suggested Readings:

John 17–18

Imitation of Christ, bk. 1, ch. 12 and 13

Aspiration:

> *"And walk in love, as Christ also has loved us, and has delivered himself for us, an oblation and a sacrifice to God for an odor of sweetness."* (Eph. 5:2)

FIRST MEDITATION

The Agony in the Garden

HERE BEGINS THE drama of the Passion, to which the struggles of the previous days were but the prologue. The Evangelists narrate this heart-rending drama with an impassivity that is disconcerting. The explanation is that the Evangelists are not so much biographers as witnesses. Their purpose is to transmit to future generations what they have seen with their own eyes and have heard from the lips of eyewitnesses. Besides, they are dealing with emotions that cannot be translated into words, emotions that the most vehement rhetoric would only weaken. The Evangelists are conscious of their role as witnesses, and they present the plain facts, knowing that the language of facts is the most eloquent of languages and the most pathetic.

It must have been between ten o'clock and midnight when Jesus left the Cenacle with His eleven apostles. Let us follow Him still, our hearts inflamed with the love He has enkindled in them at the institution of the Holy Eucharist.

Outside the Cenacle, we descend with Christ into the Tyropoeon ravine and leave the city by the Fountain Gate. Turning north, we cross the brook Cedron, while our Lord gives last instructions and encouragement to the apostles. "Simon, Simon, behold Satan hath desired to have you, that he may sift you as wheat: but I have prayed for thee, that thy faith fail not: and thou, being once converted, confirm thy brethren" (Luke 22:31–32); "For it is written: I will strike the shepherd, and the sheep of the flock shall be dispersed" (Matt. 26:31). But good shepherd that He always is, He promises: "But after I shall be risen again, I will go before you into Galilee" (Matt. 26:32).

We arrive at Gethsemane, a name meaning "oil press." It was a country place or garden planted with a variety of trees, chiefly olive, whose fruit was processed on the spot by means of one of those rock-hewn presses that are so often seen in Palestine, especially in Judea. We can picture to ourselves an enclosure encompassed by a wall of loose stones, perhaps reinforced by an impenetrable hedge of cactus. These country establishments on the outskirts of towns were very often large enough to enclose a watchhouse and, sometimes, a more or less spacious dwelling where the owner could sleep on summer nights or refresh himself during the day in the relative coolness. Gethsemane apparently belonged to a friend and disciple of Jesus. Leaving eight of His disciples in the shelter of a cave situated opposite, Jesus went into the garden with His three most intimate friends: Peter, James, and John. He would not present the spectacle of His soul's distress to any but the three privileged ones who had been permitted to contemplate His glory on the summit of Tabor. To them He said: "My soul is sorrowful even unto death: stay you here, and watch with me" (Matt. 26:38). And then He withdrew from them the distance of a stone's throw. They saw Him fall upon His knees, His face pressed down even to the ground. Close as they were to Him in the brilliant light of the full oriental moon shining in a cloudless sky, they could distinguish His every move; they could even hear His words, for the Jews, as we know, used to pray aloud—and nothing in the sleeping city disturbed the profound silence of midnight.

Although we may not know how Christ suffered, since He always enjoys the Beatific Vision, still this mystery is somehow compatible with the truth that St. Paul has taught us. Jesus did not come down from Heaven to teach us stoicism, which steels itself against suffering by proclaiming that pain is not an evil. Wishing to show Himself a true man, and desiring to be a model within our reach, He lowers Himself to our level. He is not ashamed to present to us the spectacle of His distress of soul. He seeks out the sympathy of His apostles; nor does He repel the intervention of the consoling angel. He, the absolute master of the passions and emotions that agitate the human soul, ostensibly abandons Himself to them today; He seems to unchain them against Himself. But this interior tempest will be calmed in an instant when He shall judge it proper. In the present order of Providence, it was necessary that Christ should suffer all the pains that were compatible with His divine Sonship. It was necessary that He suffer them not only to prove to us the immensity of His love and the purifying power of suffering but also to make Him the ideal high priest of a regenerated world. Here we have the assurance of the Epistle to the Hebrews:

> For it became him, for whom are all things, and by whom are all things, who had brought many children into glory, to perfect the author of their salvation, by his passion.... It behooved him in all things to be made like unto his brethren, that he might become a merciful and faithful priest before God. (Heb. 2:10, 17)

It was right that, "And whereas indeed he was the Son of God, he learned obedience by the things which he suffered: and being consummated, he became, to all that obey him, the cause of eternal salvation" (Heb. 5:8–9). Such are, as far as it is possible for us to grasp them, the providential reasons for the agony of Jesus in the Garden of Olives.

What the agony is. The Greeks gave the name *agony* to those contests in the stadium in which the contestants strained every nerve and energy to gain the palm. We call by the same name that last struggle of man at grips with death, in which death always emerges victorious at the end. The agony of Christ is also a struggle against mortal anguish, but it is a struggle from which He will come forth the victor. Prostrate upon the ground, He is assailed at once by fear, by sadness, by weariness, and by disgust. "Weariness," says Bossuet, "casts the soul into a certain vexation that makes life insupportable and every moment burdensome; fear shakes the soul to its very depths by picturing to it a thousand threatening torments; sadness covers it with a thick veil that makes everything seem a death; and finally, languor and exhaustion cause a kind of dejection and prostration of all the forces." There is the picture that the Gospel traces of our Lord's agony.

The first prayer. It is no depreciation of Christ to admit in Him an instinctive fear. Death is the penalty of sin, and Jesus, all innocent as He was, willed to accept it as such. The circumstances surrounding death are often more terrible than death itself. Many criminals regard it a favor to escape by a speedy execution the long preparations for a death presented as a public show. Jesus knew in advance, to the smallest detail, all the atrocious vicissitudes of His own death, and He harbored none of the hopes, none of the illusions that the rest of mortals fondle up to the very end. Bound as a malefactor and haled before one tribunal after another, delivered to the brutality of menials and soldiery, scourged and crowned with thorns, He will fall under the weight of the Cross and will languish for long hours nailed to His gibbet, suspended between Heaven and earth and blasphemed by a delirious mob, and all this under the gaze of His Mother, who will suffer greatly in seeing Him suffer. This somber prospect, presenting itself to Him in all its horror, wrests from Him the cry: "Father, if it be possible, let this chalice pass from me. Nevertheless, not as I will, but as thou wilt" (Matt.

26:39). If His prayer had been absolute, it would have been granted, but it was conditioned and dependent upon the good pleasure of God. And God's will was that He should undergo death with all its frightful accompaniment.

The second prayer. During the agony of their Master, the apostles were sleeping. Jesus approached them and said to Peter, the responsible head of the group: "Could you not watch one hour with me? Watch ye, and pray that ye enter not into temptation. The spirit indeed is willing, but the flesh is weak" (Matt. 26:40–41). Again He withdrew and resumed His communion with God. "My Father, if this chalice may not pass away, but I must drink it, thy will be done" (Matt. 26:42). It is substantially the same prayer as before, but with a special accent upon resignation and filial surrender. And now a still more frightful spectacle assails His imagination. He sees heaping up over the course of centuries the iniquities of men, for whom He is about to shed all His Blood. How many souls through negligence or malice, in every case through their own fault, will still stand aloof from the fruits of His redeeming death! Even in the Church, how many schisms, how many heresies, what scandals and apostasies and sacrileges! He is prompted to say with the prophet: *Quae utilitas in sanguine meo?* "What profit is there in shedding My Blood?" (Ps. 29:10). Men are not only ungrateful, they turn His own benefits against Him; they outrage Him in the sacrament of His love. This torrent of iniquity bears down upon Him; it overwhelms Him, crushes Him. An angel must come down from Heaven to sustain and comfort Him. The angel brings consolation that He needs and has not found in His apostles.

The third prayer. There are the poor apostles still sleeping. It was, says St. Luke, the effect of sadness (Luke 22:45). Great interior disturbances beat the soul down; they produce prostration, a sort of drowsiness of all the faculties. It is not sleep and yet not waking, but a middle state between consciousness and dread. The apostles, confused at their collapse, know not how to excuse their sleepiness. Jesus leaves them once again; again He repeats the same prayer without seeking new formulas. How could He have found a better than the *fiat* of loving resignation? And now He undergoes another trial, the most fearful of all. He feels all the sins of man weighing down upon Him; for "the Lord," says Isaiah, "hath laid on him the iniquity of us all" (Isa. 53:6); and, according to the much more forceful words of St. Paul: "Him, who knew no sin, he hath made sin for us, that we might be made the justice of God in him" and through Him (2 Cor. 5:21). Under the blows of divine malediction that He accepts, He experiences what we ourselves ought to experience when confronted by sin: aversion, shame, horror, disgust, terror of God's judgments. The cup of bitterness is full to overflowing, it surpasses human strength. And then there happens a very rare though not unexampled phenomenon, explainable partly by the greater delicacy of His physical being, partly by His livelier sensibilities, but above all by His keener appreciation of what it is to offend God. A bloody sweat inundates His members and runs down even to the ground in thick drops, like clots of blood (Luke 22:44).

The storm passes, and all of a sudden comes the calm. Jesus rises and goes to rejoin the three apostles. "Sleep ye now," He says to them, "and take your rest; behold the hour is at hand, and the Son of man shall be betrayed into the hands of sinners. Rise, let us go" (Matt. 26:46–47). There is here in the words of our Lord a gentle reproach that might be called irony, but an irony devoid of bitterness and raillery, as if our Lord said: "Come, sleep as much as you will. I will not trouble you. But, no, arise: the enemy is here."

Saying these words, Jesus went out with them and directed His steps to the place where he left the other eight at the entrance to the garden. He had said: "Behold, he is at hand that will betray me" (Matt. 26:47). Perhaps the clank of arms could already be heard and the tramp of a troop on the march; and now a sinister gleam shines through the foliage.

Jesus advances to meet the enemy: "Whom seek ye?" "Jesus of Nazareth." "I am He" (John 18:4–5). And at these words the enemy fell flat to the ground, such was the power of the Lord who went to death willingly. Judas, a past master in the art of hypocrisy, knowing that Jesus was aware of his perfidious intentions, like a true traitor then began to act out his comedy of repentance. The Gospels, if attentively read, suggest this conclusion. Judas was not content with kissing Jesus, as he had contracted to do; he effusively embraced Him. Catching sight of the Savior, whom he pretended to be looking for, he threw himself into His arms and pressed Him to his breast, pronouncing the customary greeting. "Hail, Rabbi!" Jesus answered him: "Friend, is it for this that thou hast come?" or, since the meaning of the phrase is uncertain, "Do that for which thou hast come" (see Matt. 26: 49–50). And then He sadly said: "Judas, dost thou betray the Son of man with a kiss?" (Luke 22:48). Then, dashing forward at the sign, the crowd seized Jesus and brutally bound Him. The apostles make a show of force. Peter seizes one of the cutlasses at hand, strikes out wildly, and cuts off the right ear of one of the high priest's servants, named Malchus. But Jesus heals the ear of the wounded man by a simple touch of His hand, and then says to Peter:

> Put up again thy sword into its place: for all that take the sword shall perish with the sword. Thinkest thou that I cannot ask my Father, and he will give me presently more than twelve legions of angels? How then shall the scriptures be fulfilled, that so it must be done? (Matt. 26:52–54)

Then all the apostles, abandoning Him, took to flight. This universal abandonment on the part of those whom He loved so dearly and upon whom He had laden so many favors was perhaps the blow most deeply felt by the loving heart of Jesus on that tragic night.

Speak to Him the thoughts of your mind and heart, and offer Him yourselves in love and compassionate sorrow as you see Him led away. Here is God, a criminal: Infinite Power in bonds.

Confer: Ferdinand Prat, S.J., *Jesus Christ*, vol. 2, pp. 308–326.

The Way of the Cross

JESUS AT LAST is in the hands of enemies; everything has succeeded according to their wicked plans. Our Savior now has to
retrace His steps in the journey He had taken two or three hours
earlier. The underlings hurried their prisoner along the valley of
Cedron and brought Him to the palace of Annas. Annas had held
the office of high priest for nine years, and even now he was the
power behind that office that was held by his son-in-law Caiaphas.
Why was Jesus brought before Annas instead of directly before
Caiaphas? It was because all recognized that Annas, after a long
period of time, was still accustomed to speak and act as the master,
and he had concocted the whole scheme of destroying Jesus and
had set the measures afoot and had given orders to such extent
that he was now approached as the inspirer and instigator of the
plot. Caiaphas was only a figure-head, a mere agent responsible
to the Roman authorities.

There was nothing official about the interrogation of Jesus by
Annas. There were no witnesses and no accusers. Moreover, the
members of the Sanhedrin were not assembled in strength. The
only ones present were the fiercest and most fanatical who had
accompanied the night expedition to the Garden of Gethsemane.
The others had been hastily summoned, at least those of whom

they were sure; but at that advanced hour of the night, they had to be given time to arrive at Caiaphas's house, where the meeting was to be held.

Let us consider our divine Savior, judge of the living and the dead, as He stands in confusion, bound hand and foot, before this contemptible old priest. And let us ask our Savior for the grace of sorrow with Him who is sorrowful. Let us ask to be broken with Him who is broken. Let us pray for tears and interior pain at the so great pain which He, our Lord and God, suffers for us. Remember, "He loved me and delivered himself for me" (Gal. 2:20).

The religious trial before the Sanhedrin. Like a police official profiting by the confusion that seizes a prisoner at the time of his arrest, Annas was hoping to wrest from his captive some compromising admission. He therefore questioned Christ about His teachings and His disciples. But the answer was not what he was waiting for. "I have spoken openly to the world: I have always taught in the synagogue, and in the temple, whither all the Jews resort; and in secret I have spoken nothing" (John 18:20). Jesus had scarcely finished speaking when a menial of the high priest struck Him in the face, saying: "Is it thus that you answer the high priest?" (see John 18:22). Since there was nothing official about this questioning, no one in the gathering raised a protest against this shameful treatment inflicted upon a defenseless prisoner still laden with chains. Without losing His composure, Jesus said to the aggressor: "If I have spoken evil, give testimony of the evil; but if I [have spoken] well, why strikest thou me?" (John 18:23). What wonderful patience and meekness! (When St. Paul, on the other hand, was struck in the mouth by order of the high priest Ananias, he addressed him in these terms: "God shall strike thee, thou whited wall. For sittest thou to judge me according to the law, and contrary to the law commandest me to be struck?" (Acts 23:3). Here we see how the disciple most anxious to follow in the footsteps of the Master still lags far behind Him.) Annas saw he was getting nowhere, since the prisoner refused to answer. He therefore sent Him still bound to the house of the high priest, Caiaphas.

Jesus before Caiaphas. Since the son-in-law lived just across the courtyard, Jesus did not have far to go. As soon as the assembly was complete, or as soon as a quorum was present, the presiding officer opened the session and false witnesses were brought, ready to make depositions against Jesus that would entail capital punishment. But everything had been done in such haste and disorder that the witnesses had not had time to be coached properly, and hence, having learned their lessons badly, they could not come to any agreement in the court. But the Law of Moses explicitly said that to condemn a man to death, two or three agreeing witnesses were required (Deut. 17:6). At last, two men presented themselves who seemed to have the same testimony. They had heard Jesus say: "I am able to destroy the temple of God, after three days to rebuild it" (Matt. 26:61). The other fellow claimed He said: "I will destroy this temple made by hands, and within three days I will build another not made by hands" (Mark 14:58). But upon further questioning, these two witnesses did not completely agree either (Mark 14:59).

Given the lack of other charges, however, this double testimony about the Temple was too handy for the judges to let go of it. And realizing, in fact, that this last bit of evidence was about to evaporate into thin air, the high priest decided to take things into his own hands. Rising from his seat and advancing into the middle of the assembly, Caiaphas said: "Answerest thou nothing to the things which these witness against thee?" (Matt. 26:62). But Jesus was silent. Several members of the Sanhedrin noisily challenged Him: "If thou be the Christ, tell us" (Luke 22:66). "If I shall tell you," answered Jesus, "you will not believe me. And if I shall also ask you, you will not answer me" (Luke 22:67–68). Then the high priest assumed an inspired and solemn tone and tried again: "I adjure thee by the living God that thou tell us if thou be the Christ, the Son of God" (Matt. 26:63). The moment was in truth a solemn and a breathless one. Christ had been asked if He was the Messiah; that was one part of the question, for the Messiah need not be the same as the Son of God for the Jews. Was He the Son of God—not a son in the theocratic sense, as were all the members of the Chosen People, but *the* Son *par excellence*, the Son of God properly so called? The entire mission of Jesus, all His teaching, would be summed up in the answer He would give the high priest. Faced with the formal summons of the high priest, speaking in the name of the Sanhedrin and of the whole Jewish nation, He can no longer be silent: "Thou has said it" (Matt. 26:64); or, as Mark's Gospel has it, "I am" (26:64). Matthew's Gospel continues: "Nevertheless I say to you, hereafter you shall see the Son of man sitting on the right hand of the power of God and coming in the clouds of heaven" (26:64). In these words, Jesus brings together two famous texts, one from Psalm 109:1, the other from Daniel 7:13, that predict His triumph. Scarcely had the words fallen from His lips when the high priest and all the Sanhedrin rose toward Him in great excitement, vying with one another in demanding: "Art thou, then, the Son of God?" "You say that I am," by which Jesus means, "I am what you said, the Son of God" (Luke 22:70). The high priest shrieked in horror: "He hath blasphemed; what further need have we of witnesses? Behold, now you have heard the blasphemy: What think you?" And with one accord they shouted: "He is worthy of death!" (Matt. 26:65–66).

The whole trial had been illegal, for the accused had been asked to testify against Himself when no witnesses could be found to agree against Him. But in joy, the high priest and the Sanhedrin turned Jesus over to the guards. The moment the guards saw that Jesus was condemned as a blasphemer, they furiously threw themselves upon

Him and overwhelmed Him with blows and insults. They began spitting in His face; then, blindfolding Him, they slapped Him in the face, saying: "Prophesy unto us, O Christ, who is he that struck thee?" (Matt. 26:68). They were at a loss for ways to torture their victim and to satisfy their rage, thinking that no moderation need be observed toward a man who had been convicted of blasphemy.

Throughout the night they engaged in their cruel pastime, until, wearied with their own cruelty, the guards stretched out upon the ground to sleep, leaving Jesus limp and crumpled like a rag, sitting there in abject sorrow.

Jesus before Pilate. The death sentence pronounced by the Sanhedrin could not be carried out without the explicit approval of the Roman procurator, so to achieve their goal, they decided to bring Jesus to Pilate as if they were just opening a new case. They wished to conceal their own judgment and desire to kill Jesus because they feared that Pilate, once knowing their own verdict, would hardly sanction stoning a man to death for blasphemy. This time, they attacked Jesus on political grounds. He was a political agitator stirring up rebellion against the authority of Rome. But Pilate must have been well abreast of the whole affair. He begins by questioning the Jews, much to their amazement and embarrassment: "What accusation bring you against this man?" (John 18:29). They answered: "If he were not a malefactor, we would not have delivered him up to thee" (John 18:30). This was, of course, no accusation at all. It was intended to capture Pilate's good will, implicitly inviting him to trust the accusers and accept their judgment. But the seasoned Roman immediately saw that this was another of their religious cases. "Take him you, and judge him according to your law," but this was just what the Jews did not want, for: "It is not lawful for us to put any man to death" (John 18:31). At once, their real purpose was revealed to Pilate — the death of this man. So it was a serious case, after all. Alright, where were the proofs against this man? "We have found this man perverting our nation and forbidding to give tribute to Caesar, and saying that he is Christ the king" (Luke 23:2). Pilate was not so naïve as to accept the political bait that was being fed him to attain a death sentence against this man. He would question the prisoner himself. Reentering the praetorium, Pilate asks Jesus: "Art thou the king of the Jews?" This was the most critical question of all. It repeated the last charge made against Jesus by the Jews. Jesus answered: "Sayest thou this thing of thyself, or have others told it thee of me?" When Pilate, somewhat irritated, said: "Am I a Jew? Thy own nation, and the chief priests, have delivered thee up to me: what hast thou done?" Jesus answered: "My kingdom is not of this world. If my kingdom were of this world, my servants would certainly strive that I should not be delivered to the Jews: but now my kingdom is not from hence." Somewhat surprised by this answer, Pilate determined to clarify one point: "Art thou a king then?" Undoubtedly, Pilate expected Jesus to deny it. But Jesus did not deny it, for He answered: "Thou sayest that I am a king. For this was I born, and for this came I into the world; that I should give testimony to the truth. Every one that is of the truth heareth my voice." Annoyed, Pilate interrupted roughly: "What is truth?" and after this exclamation, he went back to parley with the Jews. He rendered his verdict. "I find no [guilt] in him" (John 18:33–38). Immediately, violent protests arose from the chief priests. They knew that if they did not brazen it out, their game was lost. Furiously, they hollered: "He stirreth up the people, teaching throughout all Judea, beginning from Galilee to this place [Jerusalem]" (Luke 23:5).

Jesus before Herod. The name Galilee, pronounced at random, was a gleam of light to Pilate. He would send the prisoner to Herod, the tetrarch of Galilee, and thus get rid of the whole affair; at the same time, he could patch up differences with Herod by the courtesy of turning over this case to him. The murderer of John the Baptist and the incestuous husband of Herodias was a sorry character whose instinctive trait was cunning and whom our Lord stigmatized with the name of fox. Superstitious and half-believing that Jesus was John the Baptist risen again, the tetrarch was exceedingly glad when Jesus arrived, for he had heard so much about Him and was hoping to see some miracle done by Him. But Jesus answered none of his questions; the only answer this wretch deserved was absolute and significant silence. Enraged, the tetrarch in his bloated arrogance took his revenge in shabby fashion. He put on an air of profound contempt for our Savior. Then bethinking himself of treating Christ as a tinsel king, he had Him grotesquely clothed in a bright robe, perhaps one of his own, now worn a little and so not used any more. St. Luke depicts the scene in energetic language: "Herod with his army set him at nought, and mocked him, putting on him a white garment" (Luke 23:11). But just like Pilate, he has to conclude to the innocence of the accused; and so he sends Him back to Pilate.

What a travesty of justice: the King of Justice suffers, and all for the love of me, because my sins must be destroyed in His Passion.

Back to Pilate and delivered to the Cross. The laughingstock of Herod's court, Jesus appears again before Pilate with the burlesque honors of a mad king. What humiliation He suffers to teach me to be humble! And now the compromiser, the shuffler, the politician, the worldling in Pilate comes to the fore. Fortified by Herod's approval of his own findings, he will now, to sate the mob and the high priests, mix a little cruelty with the verdict of innocence that he sees must be rendered:

> You have presented unto me this man, as one that perverteth the people; and behold I, having examined him before you, find no cause in this man, in those things wherein you

accuse him. No, nor Herod neither. For I sent you to him, and behold, nothing worthy of death is done to him. I will chastise him therefore, and release him. (Luke 23:14–16)

Then follows the ignominious Scourging of our Lord, so that not a sound spot is found on His body from the sole of His feet to the top of His head. A worm and no man, He sinks into a pool of His own Blood at the end of the horrible ordeal. When the people choose the murderer Barabbas instead of Jesus, our Lord comes forward crowned with thorns on the balcony of the praetorium: "Behold, the Man!" says the Roman Procurator (John 19:5). Yes, behold the Man of Sorrows spoken of by the prophet Isaiah, the most beautiful of the children of men, who no longer has any beauty to charm the sight or draw the heart (see Isa. 53). He does not even inspire the pity that Pilate had hoped for in order to save Him, for at the sight of Him, the rage of His enemies is not one whit sated. "Crucify Him!" "Take him you," says Pilate to them, "and crucify Him." But the Jews argue back: "We have a law, and according to the law he ought to die, because he made himself the Son of God" (John 19:6–7). So at last the real reason was out, now that they got what they wanted: His death sentence. They were out to kill Him because He was the Son of God and had the courage to claim this title and had done the deeds to prove it. Pilate was frightened when he heard these words. For a moment, he tries again to examine Jesus. But Jesus is silent, telling him only that Pilate would have no power over His life "unless it were given thee from above. Therefore, he that hath delivered me to thee hath the greater sin" (John 19:11).

The power that Pilate had was the power of darkness; he was permitted by God to make an attempt on the life of the Just One for the salvation of the world. Still trying to save Jesus, Pilate is conquered by the words: "If thou release this man, thou art not Caesar's friend"

(John 19:12). This threat of being denounced to Tiberius beats down with one blow all his resistance. To lose Caesar's friendship was to lose all. So it is with all who love the honor of this world. Caesar above God. Washing his hands of the consequences in the place called the lithostrotos, Pilate says: "I am innocent of the blood of this just man; look you to it." And the whole people cry out: "His blood be upon us and our children" (Matt. 27:24–25). What a curse to call down upon themselves and their progeny: the Blood of God! "Shall I crucify your king?" Pilate makes one last desperate effort. "Away with him! Away with him! Crucify him," cry the enraged people. "We have no king but Caesar," cry the chief priests (John 19:15). Then Pilate hands Him over to them to be crucified. From concession to concession, Pilate has gone as far as deicide. Not only in the inner court of conscience does he recognize the innocence of Jesus; he has several times proclaimed it aloud. He devises five or six expedients to snatch Him from the fury of His enemies: the sending to Herod; the theatrical scene of washing his hands; the proposal to liberate Christ to celebrate the feast of deliverance; the moving spectacle of the *Ecce Homo*; the horrid scourging—all calculated to disarm the fiercest hatred. But the Jews, witnessing his vacillation and knowing his weakness, redouble their arrogance, even as the devil does with us. And Pilate ends by yielding all.

We see Jesus embrace His Cross and tread wearily the road to Calvary. And as we do, let us ask for shame and confusion at our sins. Let us ask for sorrow with Jesus sorrowing because He goes to die for love of us.

Confer: Giuseppe Riciotti, *The Life of Jesus Christ*, pp. 586–647.
Ferdinand Prat, S.J., *Jesus Christ*, vol. 2, pp. 347–370.

CONFERENCE
The Sacrifice and the Banquet of Peace

"BUT NOW IN Christ Jesus, you, who some time were afar off, are made nigh by the blood of Christ. For he is our peace" (Eph. 2:13–14).

In ancient times, God made an alliance with the Hebrew nation. From the top of Mt. Sinai, above the blare of trumpets, above the roar of thunder, from out the glare of lightning and the mist of a burning cloud, the Lord said to Moses:

> Tell the children of Israel:... You will hear my voice, and keep my covenant, you shall be my peculiar possession above all people: for all the earth is mine. And you shall be to me a priestly kingdom, and a holy nation.... You shall make an altar of earth unto me, and you shall offer upon it your holocausts and peace offerings, your sheep and oxen.... I will come to thee, and will bless thee. (Exod. 19:3, 5–6; 20:24)

Moses built an altar to God and offered animals as gifts. Half of the blood of the animals he sprinkled upon the altar. The other half he sprinkled over the people, saying: "This is the blood of the covenant which the Lord hath made with you" (Exod. 24:8). And the whole people answered with one voice: "All things that the Lord hath spoken we will do, we will be obedient" (Exod. 24:7).

Thus was the Old Testament between God and His people, sealed and signed in blood. Blood upon the altar bound God to protect and sanctify His people, for the altar always stood for God. Blood upon the people bound the people to love, honor, and serve God. It ratified the peace treaty between God and His people. St. Paul tells us, "Without shedding of blood there is no remission [of sins]" (Heb. 9:22).

Even if he had never sinned, the first duty of man would be to surrender himself to his good God, because God is so lovable and our supreme good. He always has the right to command us: "Thou shalt love the Lord, thy God." We owe ourselves and everything to Him. To God who gave us all, love prompts us to give ourselves whole and entire in a return of generosity, gratitude, and homage.

But we men are not pure spirits like the angels, and we must prove the interior gifts of our heart by some outward sign. Like Harry who proudly presents Papa with the latest deluxe meerschaum pipe as a token of his filial love, so we, too, humbly present God some material gift to demonstrate our love for Him. Such gifts are called sacrifices, for a sacrifice is a gift that is made sacred in its official presentation to God.

Even if he had never sinned, man would have offered sacrifice to God. He would have wanted to prove his love for God by acts of acts of adoration, thanksgiving, and petition. Yet with no sin there would have been no death, no need to repair an insult, to requite an injury, to redress a wrong. Hence, sacrifice would have had nothing in it that called for destruction and the flow of blood.

But sin came, and with it, death. Peace gifts now had to be offered to an outraged and insulted God. We still owed God adoration, thanksgiving, and petition, but now we also owed Him an infinite apology for an infinite insult. We had to offer gifts to escape the rigor of the death sentence: a temporal death of a lamb to prevent our own eternal death. And thus the blood of animals had to flow so that the blood of sinners might be spared, for "without shedding of blood, there is no remission" of sins, no peace with God.

As He sat for the Last Supper, Jesus Christ looked at His beloved Twelve and said: "With desire I have desired to eat this pasch with you before I suffer" (Luke 22:15). Then He took bread, blessed it, and gave it to His apostles, saying: "Eat, this is my body, which shall be delivered for you" (1 Cor. 11:24). And with the chalice, He said: "Drink.... This is my blood ... which shall be shed for many unto remission of sins" (Matt. 26:28). "This is ... the new testament in my blood" (Luke 22:20). With these words, the Old Testament dies, and its bloody sacrifices, always insufficient, no longer please God. Christ, the eternal Priest, offers the gift of His own Body and Blood to God. The next day, Christ fulfills and completes the offering of Himself made at the Last Supper by willingly dying on the Cross. At the supper and on the Cross, Christ is both our Priest and Sacrifice.

But it all would have ended on Calvary had not Jesus, "having loved his own who were in the world ... loved them unto the end," unto the very end of His divine power (John 13:1). "Do this," He told the Twelve at the supper, "for a commemoration of me" (Luke 22:19). By this loving command, Christ perpetuated His priesthood and His sacrifice unto the end of time. He gave us the marvelous Sacrifice of the Mass. Now our altars offer up to God not the blood of animals but the precious Blood of Jesus Christ. Our people not only serve God as a royal priesthood but in the words of St. Peter to the first Christians: "You are a chosen generation, a kingly priesthood, a holy nation, a purchased people ... redeemed ... with the precious blood of Christ" (1 Pet. 2:9; 1:18–19).

"He that eateth my flesh and drinketh my blood abideth in me, and I in him" (John 6:57).

St. Augustine tells of an incident that happened to him before his conversion, when he was still a teacher of rhetoric and oratory. He was addressing a large crowd on the art of eloquence. In this art, Augustine was by nature very talented, but besides that, he prepared this speech with the utmost diligence and was delivering it with consummate skill. He won the crowd so completely to himself that in a wild burst of enthusiasm and love they seized him and carried him around on their shoulders. Such was their affection for him, Augustine says, that it seemed they would have eaten him to be united with him. For love is that great driving force that brings peace in the union of the lovers.

From the dawn of creation, our ancestors strove to be united with God. Although unable to see Him, they offered gifts to God. Sometimes it was oil, wine, cattle, or the first fruits of the field. Whatever it was, the gift was made sacred by setting it apart from other things and removing it from the profane uses of man. Such gifts were transferred to the personal ownership of God, to be consumed in divine ceremonies. Special persons were set apart to offer up these gifts in the name of the people. These persons were called priests; their offerings were called sacrifices. Since they were not able to see and hold the invisible God, our ancestors united themselves to the gifts dedicated to God. Hence, very often the priest and the people consumed the sacrifices at a special ceremony in the hope of becoming more god-like and of obtaining some tangible union with God by eating the divine gifts at the divine table. Among the Jews, it was understood that to eat of the sacrifices of the altar was a means of union with God.

Almighty God saw our great need to be united with Him, and so He sent His beloved Son to bring about this happy union. "God so loved the world as to give his only begotten Son" (John 3:16). When He took His human nature from the Immaculate Virgin, our Blessed Lord already joined the human race to God in His own person. But this was not enough for His immense love for us. He would join each and every one of us individually to God. And so when He gave us the new Sacrifice of Peace at the Last Supper, Jesus also gave us the new and heavenly Banquet of Peace. "Take and eat.... This is my body.... Drink, ye, all of this.... This is my blood." We now had divine food at the divine table. For the Mass, besides being a sacrifice, is also a sacrament. In the Sacrifice of the Mass, we go to God through Christ. In the Sacrament of Holy Communion, God comes to us through Christ.

When we eat lifeless bread, we change it into ourselves. It becomes the same substance as our bodies. But when we eat the eternal living Christ, we change into what He is. He does not change, but He takes us to Himself as branches into a vine. He gathers us to Himself to form one body and one bread, as St. Paul says: "For we, being many, are one bread, one body, all that partake of the one bread" (1 Cor. 10:17) With Him our Head, we grow together into His one body. We become Christ-bearers. Or, as St. Peter says, we become "partakers of the divine nature" (2 Pet. 1:4).

How does this marvel happen? Jesus Christ is God and man. As God, He is eternally united to His Father by the nature of the Godhead. As man, He has a human nature like ours, one that we can handle, see, and embrace. Hence, when we receive the God-man in Holy Communion, we are joined through the Body and Blood of the Savior to Himself and His Father, and He, always remaining in the Father, comes and lives in us. See why the Holy Eucharist is called Communion! It is fellowship of the highest degree, for in itself it is a most intimate and real bond. It joins us to Christ, and in Christ it unites us on the one hand with the Holy Trinity, and on the other with all men who receive the Holy Eucharist. We become partakers of the divine nature because we are raised to the intimate life of God, even in this earthly pilgrimage. As St. Hilary so beautifully says: "Christ is in us by His flesh, and we are in Him; and all that we are is with Him in God." It is especially at this sublime banquet that our Lord's prayer for union is realized: "that they all may be one, as thou, Father, in me, and I in thee; that they also may be one in us" (John 17:21).

Behold the heavenly banquet to which we are daily invited by God! Christ is the divine food who nourishes and strengthens the spiritual life of our souls. He unites us intimately to Himself, His Mystical Body, and the Holy Trinity. He increases sanctifying grace in us, weakens our evil inclinations, and promises us eternal glory. "And the glory which thou hast given me, I have given to them, that they may be one, as we also are one" (John 17:22).

Our Faith tells us all these marvelous truths about this Banquet of Peace, for this Heavenly Bread for the most part affects only the soul in its spiritual character, not the body and the life of the senses. "We are now the sons of God" (1 John 3:2), "according to the inward man" (Rom. 7:22); we are transformed into God. But as St. John continues: "It hath not yet appeared what we shall be." And so according to the outward man, we are still like other natural men after Holy Communion. But since our "life is hid with Christ in God," as St. Paul says (Col. 3:3), so this Bread of Angels that nourishes our life must now remain concealed under its natural veil. One day, this veil will be snatched away when the body of our weakness fails us entirely and Christ pours out His divine life upon us in its fullness. He will make our body conformable to the body of His glory and bring our souls into the immediate presence and vision of the Most Holy Trinity, the only source and complete food of everlasting life. "He that eateth my flesh and drinketh my blood hath everlasting life: and I will raise him up in the last day" (John 6:55).

Let us ask St. Francis Xavier, who had a supreme love for Holy Mass and daily Communion, to increase this love in our hearts so that we may frequently and even daily, with God's help, break the Bread of Life and drink the wine of divine immortality at the Banquet of Love and of Peace.

THIRD MEDITATION
Jesus on the Cross

AND NOW WE come to wait with His Holy Mother, St. John, and the Holy Women at the death bed of Jesus: to console Him in His suffering, to sorrow with Him sorrowing, to be broken with Christ broken, to suffer tears and interior pain at the sight of the great pain that our Lord and God suffers for us. The journey from the Court of the Antonia to Calvary would not require a very long time, not much more than a quarter of an hour if taken in a straight line and under ordinary circumstances. Yet because of Christ's weakness and because of the great crowds in the city that pressed in the streets, the progress was retarded. Jesus, worn out by a night of sleeplessness, by physical and mental torture, and by the horrible scourging and the crowning with thorns, was at the end of His strength. The centurion, seeing Him stagger, at once enlisted the services of Simon of Cyrene to carry the Cross of Jesus. At all times, the military authority had arrogated to itself the right of requisitioning people into its service, and they did this especially to the common people and peasants. Simon submitted; one does not resist armed strength. Tradition teaches that later, he and his two sons, Alexander and Rufus, were to become Christians, enjoying a certain prominence in the early church. So great are the graces that the Cross of Christ carries with it.

Calvary. When the procession reached the place called the Skull, the crucifixion was carried out immediately. Wine mixed with myrrh, believed to numb the senses, was offered to Jesus and certainly to the two thieves who accompanied Him. But it had no sooner touched Christ's lips than He refused it, choosing to drink with full consciousness to the last drop the chalice given Him by His Heavenly Father. St. Ignatius tells us to recall how all through the Passion, the divinity hides itself in Christ—how though it could destroy its enemies, it does not do so, but out of love for us leaves the sacred humanity to suffer cruelly.

Stripped of His garments, Jesus lay upon the ground. His arms were stretched along the crosspiece He had carried, and His hands were nailed to it. Next, He was lifted to the vertical beam already set in the ground, and set astride the support, or sedile. Then His feet were nailed. It is the almost unanimous opinion of the ancient authors that four nails were used. Besides, it would be almost impossible to fix both feet of a living man to a cross with one nail without breaking any of his bones, yet we know from St. John that none of the Savior's bones were broken. His Cross was in the middle; the two thieves were crucified one on each side of Him. The irony of the position in the middle is that the motif of King was still being jested about. On His Cross was fastened the tablet describing His crime. He claimed to be a King; they would treat Him as King. The tablet read: "Jesus of Nazareth, King of the Jews."

Their grisly duty done, the four soldiers sat down upon the ground to play at dice, the stakes being the belongings of the condemned above them.

The seven last words of Jesus on the Cross. The last words that fall from the lips of a dying person are piously gathered by friends and dear ones as a sacred heritage and the most precious of memories. Below Him, the chief priests and scribes exult in their triumph.

They vainly try to taunt the Savior into some hostile response by their jeers and insults, their jokes with one another, as they sneer: "He saved others; himself he cannot save. If he be the king of Israel, let him now come down from the cross, and we will believe him" (Matt. 27:42). In vain do the passersby, misled by the priests, nod their heads and repeat: "Thou that destroyest the temple of God, and in three days dost rebuild it: save thy own self: if thou be the Son of God, come down from the cross" (Matt. 27:40). Jesus is silent; not a word of reproach, not a sigh, not a single plaint. The first word that He utters aloud is a word of reproach, "Father, forgive them, for they know not what they do" (Luke 23:34). He prays for all His enemies, yes, even for the chief priests and the Pharisees. Especially for them, since their guilt is greatest. There is always in the sin of man a portion of ignorance and blindness that distinguishes it from the sin of the angels. Jesus, in pleading their cause before His Father, does not ask for their pardon absolutely and unconditionally. He implores for them the grace to repent and a time of delay of God's justice so that they may repent. And His prayer is not in vain. God will wait forty years before delivering this people up to destruction at the hands of the Romans.

The second word. One of the two malefactors blasphemed against Jesus, saying: "If thou be Christ, save thyself and us." But the other malefactor rebuked him: "Neither dost thou fear God, seeing thou art condemned under the same condemnation? And we indeed justly, for we receive the due reward of our deeds; but this man hath done no evil." And then, turning to the Savior, he said: "Lord, remember me when thou shalt come into thy kingdom" (Luke 23:39–42). Probably the good thief knew Jesus of Nazareth by reputation and had heard of His goodness and His miracles and of the Kingdom of God that He preached. And obviously, despite his crimes, there was a residue of goodness left in him. In the face of death, it rises to the surface and covers all his past. The dying man clutches at the last hope left to him, personified in the Just Man unjustly dying with him. And Jesus answers: "Amen, I say to thee, this day thou shalt be with me in paradise" (Luke 23:43). To be with the Savior, to enjoy His company, to share His happiness wherever it be. This was to be his happiness, his true paradise today! Such is the lot promised to the good thief, canonized by the voice of God while he was still alive. Such is the reward of Jesus to those who trust and have faith in Him!

The third word.

> Now there stood by the cross of Jesus, his mother, and his mother's sister, Mary of Cleophas, and Mary Magdalen. When Jesus therefore had seen his mother and the disciple standing whom he loved, he saith to his mother: Woman, behold thy son. After that, he saith to the disciple: Behold thy mother. And from that hour, the disciple took her to his own. (John 19:25–27)

In this last will and testament, the dying Jesus united in John the whole human race to His Mother as her children. The role of co-redemptrix is the principle of the spiritual maternity of Mary. At the foot of the Cross, Mary offers to the Heavenly Father His divine Son, who offers Himself on the Cross for our salvation. Mary offers Him with the authority of a mother whose consent God asks for. Jesus, in dying for us, adopts us as His brothers; Mary, by sacrificing her Son for us, gives us as brothers to Jesus and adopts us as her own children. The *fiat* of the Redemption, pronounced from her heart by the Blessed Virgin on Golgotha, answers the *fiat* of the Incarnation and, in some way, completes it.

The fourth word. Jesus was failing rapidly. Suddenly it began to grow dark: "from the sixth hour there was darkness over the whole

earth, until the ninth hour" (Matt. 27:45) — or from noon until
three o'clock. In the darkness that hung over physical nature, Jesus'
earthly existence ebbed slowly away through an agony that lasted
three hours. His life and strength were bleeding from Him through
His torn hands and feet and the gaping welts left by the scourging.
His head was riddled with thorns; not a muscle of His body could
relax in that position on the Cross. There was no rest as the pain
grew more and more excruciating. In that dark spasm of agony,
only the pinnacle of His soul was serene, lifted in contemplation
of the Father. He hung in silence. Suddenly about the ninth hour
(three o'clock), Jesus cried aloud, saying: "My God, My God, why
hast thou forsaken me?" (Matt. 27:46). Since this is from a psalm,
its full meaning must be derived from the entire composition. This
psalm, in fact, predicts the final sufferings of the future Messiah,
and in reciting its first line from the Cross, Jesus meant to apply it
to Himself. Among other things, the ancient psalm had said:

> O God, my God ... why hast thou forsaken me? Far from
> my salvation are the words of my sins. O my God, I shall cry
> by day, and thou wilt not hear: and by night, and it shall not
> be reputed as folly in me.... But I am a worm, and no man:
> the reproach of men, and the outcast of the people. All they
> that saw me have laughed me to scorn: they have spoken
> with the lips, and wagged the head [exclaiming], He hoped
> in the Lord, let him deliver him, let him save him, seeing
> he delighteth in him.... For many dogs have encompassed
> me: the council of the malignant hath besieged me. They
> have [pierced] my hands and feet. They have numbered all
> my bones. And they have looked and stared upon me. They
> parted my garments amongst them; and upon my vesture
> they cast lots. (Ps. 21:2–3, 7–9, 17–19)

Hence, Jesus' exclamation affirms once again that He is the Messiah and as proof indicates the clear fulfillment in Himself of the prophecy He is quoting.

The fifth word. And as He hung waiting on the Cross, Jesus spoke again: "I thirst" (John 19:28). Given His loss of blood and extreme exhaustion, this was very natural, but it is not the whole explanation of these words. In fact, the psalm that Jesus had just quoted also said: "My tongue hath cleaved to my jaws" (Ps. 21:16). Thirst, then, was also part of the prophetic vision of the suffering of the Messiah. Hence, John calls attention to the fact that Jesus, "that the scripture might be fulfilled, said: 'I thirst!'" This time, Jesus' request, His last, met a compassionate response in one of the soldiers guarding the Cross. The soldier dipped a sponge in a drink called *posca*, a Roman mixture of water and vinegar good for quenching the thirst and still used in Italy today, and on the tip of a javelin, he offered it to Jesus to drink. Jesus took some drops of the liquid with His lips, and having swallowed it, said: "It is consummated."

The sixth word. "It is consummated" (John 19:30). This time all, indeed, is finished. Nothing more in prophecy to be fulfilled; nothing more of type to be made reality; no expiatory act to be added; no new pain to suffer. The work of the Redemption is completed; the earthly career of Jesus comes to a close. The *consummatum est* has its commentary in the words of the priestly prayer: "Father ... I have finished the work which thou gavest me to do" (John 17:1, 4). Then He bowed His head as if to sleep. He did not bow it after death, as other men, but before dying, in order to show that He died voluntarily.

The seventh word. And yet before dying, He gives forth a last cry and breathes out His soul in an act of filial abandonment: "Father, into thy hands I commend my spirit" (Luke 23:46). Again He borrows the formula of the psalmist, adding only the word "Father"

(Ps. 30:6). He was dead. The King was dead. Long live the King of kings! The message from the ruddy throne had been one of forgiveness, love, generosity to man, prayerfulness to His Father, filial resignation to the Father's will, and utter and complete devotion to the plan of His Father for our salvation. This is the King we have sworn to follow. As we contemplate Him dead, a victim of love, let us console His Holy Mother, let us accompany her to the tomb, and let us there weep for all our sins, promising to renew our devotion to His service in doing His will.

Confer: Ferdinand Prat, S.J., *Jesus Christ*, vol. 2, pp. 371–400.

Giuseppe Ricciotti, *The Life of Christ*, pp. 634–647.

EIGHTH DAY

Purpose: To experience supernatural joy at the great apparition of the triumphant and risen Savior

Patron: St. Mary Magdalene

Points for Self-Consideration:

- What is my spirit of joyfulness in the service of My Lord?
- Am I growing in the power and inspiration of my faith in my risen Christ?
- Do I have an audacious confidence in God and in the power and love of Jesus Christ?
- Do I strive to attain to the contemplation of divine love in my prayer life?

Suggested Readings:

John 21; Acts 1:1–12
Imitation of Christ, bk. 3, ch. 49
1 Corinthians 12–13

Aspiration:

*"If you be risen with Christ, seek the
things that are above." (Col. 3:1)*

*"For I reckon that the sufferings of this time are
not worthy to be compared with the glory to come
that shall be revealed in us." (Rom. 8:18)*

The Resurrection

THE RESURRECTION OF Christ contributes to our justification. St. Paul tells us that: "Jesus Christ, our Lord ... was delivered up for our sins, and rose again for our justification" (Rom. 4:24–25). Belief in the Resurrection is the foundation of our faith and the prop of our hope. "If Christ be not risen again," says the Apostle, "then is our preaching vain, and your faith is also vain.... For you are yet in your sins. Then they also that are fallen asleep in Christ, are perished. If in this life only we have hope in Christ, we are of all men most miserable" (1 Cor. 15:14, 17–19).

On the Sunday following Good Friday, at the first glimmer of dawn, a violent earthquake shook the vicinity of the sepulcher, and Jesus came forth glorious without breaking the seals, as He had once before left the chaste womb of His Mother without causing the least injury to her virginal integrity. No one saw Jesus in the act of rising from the dead. Yet we are told that after the earthquake, an angel of the Lord came down from Heaven and rolled back the stone and sat upon it. His countenance was dazzling like lightning, and his raiment was like snow (see Matt. 28:2–3). St. Luke implies that the tomb was already empty, and that was why the stone was removed, because it no longer served any purpose (see Luke 24:2–3). As we contemplate this dazzling scene of glory, let us rejoice with Christ rejoicing, congratulating Him on His victory over death and on the infinite reward and glory heaped upon Him by His Father. As St. Ignatius says: "The grace I want is to exult and rejoice intensely at such great glory and joy of Christ our Lord."

The empty tomb. The extraordinary seismic disturbance and the apparition of the angel dazzling with light stupefied the guards, and knowing that there was no longer any reason for them to stay there, they fled fearfully to the city. Once back in the city, they remembered that their flight was formal desertion of their post of duty and subject to heavy penalties according to Roman military discipline. They had to find some remedy, and they shrewdly perceived that their best hope lay with the chief priests who had the greatest interest in the matter. And so, as dawn gave way to day, they sought out the chief priests and told them the smallest details of what had happened. The priests, in a hastily summoned morning session of the Council, discussed what measures would be taken to deceive the people and to prevent the truth from becoming known. They gave to each of the guards a large sum of money, with strict instructions to say that Jesus' disciples had carried away the body when they were asleep (see Matt. 28:11–15). Fools! What a ridiculous invention! If the guards were asleep, how could they know that the disciples had carried the body away? And if they were not asleep, why had they failed to stop them? The risen Savior was not seen by the guards. He was not to show Himself to eyes unworthy of seeing Him. St. Peter, in his discourse at Caesarea, gives this reason for it: "Him God raised up the third day, and gave him to be made manifest, not to all the people, but to witnesses preordained by God, even to us, who did eat and drink with him after he arose again from the dead" (Acts 10:40–41).

Magdalene and the Holy Women. The sepulcher did not remain alone very long, for a group of pious women was already on its way from the city. It was very early in the morning, while it was yet dark; St. Mark says very soon after sunrise (16:2). They brought spices that they might anoint Him. The burial on Good Friday had been hasty because of the approaching Sabbath. "Who shall roll us back the stone from the door of the sepulcher?" they asked as they approached the tomb (Mark 16:3). But when they reached the sepulcher, there was the stone rolled back.

St. John tells that Mary Magdalene, unable to wait for her slow-moving and busy companions, had run on ahead. Sped by her great love, she could brook no delay and arrived at the tomb all alone and breathless while it was still dark (John 20:1). But she was struck with dismay at the sight. The tomb was empty, and the stone rolled back. He had been stolen; we must tell someone: the disciples! Maybe they knew something about it all. It never occurred to her that Jesus could have risen from the dead. "She ran, therefore, and cometh to Simon Peter, and to the other disciple whom Jesus loved, and saith to them: They have taken away the Lord out of the sepulcher, and we know not where they have laid him" (John 20:2).

Immediately, Peter and John ran to the sepulcher, hope and desire giving them wings, to verify Mary's surprising news. Mary did not go back with them but seemed to delay in order to communicate the news to the other disciples. John, after seeing the bandages lying about, must have decided that no thief would carry off the uncovered body. He must have come to the marvelous conclusion that His Master was risen.

When Mary returned, now alone, she stood outside the vestibule, her face covered with tears; and then instinctively, she leaned down over the low entrance of the tomb and looked inside. What was her surprise and terror when she saw two angels clothed in white, seated one at the head and the other at the foot of the place where the body of Jesus had rested! They said to her: "Woman, why weepest thou?"

and she answered, "They have taken away my Lord; and I know not where they have laid Him" (John 20:13). As she said this, she turned around and saw Jesus standing before her. But her eyes were veiled in tears, and she was so far from believing Him alive that she did not recognize Him. Thinking that she was addressing the man who was gardener and watchman, she made this naïve request of Him: "Sir, if thou hast taken him hence, tell me where thou hast laid him, and I will take him away" (John 20:15). She believes that everyone must be acquainted with the anxiety that obsesses her; she imagines that she is able, by herself, to replace the body of Jesus. Surely in excess of sorrowing love, she no longer knows what she is saying. And then she hears her name: "Mary!" Her name pronounced by that familiar voice wakes her from her dream. She turns her head and looks. It is He! It is her adored Master! She finds but one word to answer: "Rabboni!" — "My Master!" (John 20:16). At once she falls at His feet to embrace them and bathe them with her tears. The reward of sorrowing love and devotion to Jesus Christ. With Mary, let us adore and love our Risen Savior and rejoice with Him.

In St. Matthew's version of that great and eventful Easter Sunday, we read: "In the end of the sabbath, when it began to dawn toward the first day of the week, came Mary Magdalene and the other Mary, to see the sepulcher" (Matt. 28:1). Then he recounts the earthquake, the opening of the sepulcher by an angel who had descended from Heaven, and the terror and fright of the guards. He continues:

> And the angel ... said to the women: Fear not you; for I know that you seek Jesus who was crucified. He is not here, for he is risen, as he said. Come, and see the place where the Lord was laid. And going quickly, tell ye his disciples that he is risen: and behold he will go before you

into Galilee; there you shall see him. Lo, I have foretold it to you. (Matt. 28:5–7)

They straightway departed from the tomb, filled with fear mingled with joy, and they ran to announce these things to the disciples. And behold, Jesus met them, saying, "Hail!" And drawing near to Him, they embraced His feet and adored Him. Then Jesus said to them: "Fear not. Go, tell my brethren that they go into Galilee, there they shall see me" (Matt. 28:9–10).

On the same day, Jesus appeared to Peter, but the Evangelists give us no particulars. The glorious Christ is comforting His followers who had suffered at His suffering, who had lost all interest in life when their Master had seemingly gone down to inevitable defeat.

Today the joy of Christ's victory is ours. It had given us our most precious possessions. What would Christianity be if Christ had not risen? Without the Resurrection, there would be no tabernacle, no altar, no sacrifice, no priests. Baptism itself would lose all its meaning; for by Baptism, we mystically die with Christ and with Him mystically rise again. This is why all the apostles have placed at the foundation of their preaching the Resurrection of Christ as the indispensable complement of the redemptive death. "I delivered unto you first of all, which I also received," says St. Paul to the Corinthians, "that Christ died for our sins, according to the scriptures: and that he was buried, and that he rose again the third day, according to the scriptures.... Whether I, or they [the other apostles], so we preach, and so you have believed" (1 Cor. 15:3–4, 11). "This is the day which the Lord hath made; let us be glad and rejoice" (Ps. 117:24).

Let us thank Christ for His great victory and all the untold benefits it has brought to us. But above all, let us dwell on the glorified Son and rejoice in His happiness. Let us reflect, as St. Ignatius tells us, on "how the divinity now shows itself so miraculously in the Resurrection by its true and most holy effects." Here is our divine Consoler. He shows us how one day, because of our devoted service under His standard, because of our loyalty to Him our King, because we have generously and completely consecrated ourselves to Him, He will be our Consoler in person; He will conform our bodies to the gloriously risen Body that He enjoys today; He will be our reward, our glory, our Resurrection.

Confer: Ferdinand Prat, S.J., *Jesus Christ*, vol. 2, pp. 410–428.
Giuseppe Ricciotti, *The Life of Christ*, pp. 648–659.

SECOND MEDITATION

Apparitions at Emmaus, the
Cenacle, and Lake Tiberias

ON THE ROAD *to Emmaus.* We will follow the shifting scene in this contemplation, noting how our Risen Lord consoles His friends, how He completes the training of the apostles, how He establishes Peter as head of His Church. In all, the spirit of joy pervades the scenes, and the majesty of the Risen Christ is shown in His divine power that glorifies His body and makes it independent of the laws of nature. Let us ask for that intense spiritual and human love that Christ shares with His followers, that benevolent love that makes us exult in His victory and reward.

Two or three hours had passed while the various persons mentioned went back and forth to the tomb. News had come back to the disciples that the tomb had been found empty. The word that Mary Magdalene had seen Jesus had not yet had time to circulate. So two of the disciples left the Holy City at about eight or nine in the morning to return to their homes. One of them was called Cleophas; the name of the other is not given. Hopeless and dispirited over what had taken place, they set out alone for Emmaus, where they lived. As they walked along, they talked to each other about all these things that had happened, exchanging melancholy reflections. And it came to pass, while they were conversing and arguing together, that Jesus Himself also drew near and went along with them. And He said to them: "What are these discourses that you hold one with another as you walk?" (Luke 24:17). Who was this strange wayfarer who thus questioned them, putting His finger, as it were, on the wound in their hearts? Their surprise interrupted their journey for a while. And they stood still, looking very sad.

> And the one of them, whose name was Cleophas, answering, said to him: Art thou only a stranger to Jerusalem, and hast not known the things that have been done there in these days? To whom he said: What things? And they said: Concerning Jesus of Nazareth, who was a prophet, mighty in work and word before God and all the people; and how our chief priests and princes delivered him to be condemned to death, and crucified him. But we hoped that it was he that should have redeemed Israel. (Luke 24:18–21)

What redemption is Cleophas thinking of? It is no doubt the nationalist-messianic kingdom: namely, that Jesus would deliver, with the help of God, the holy people from all foreign domination. But at Jesus' death, the hope had vanished, and so Cleophas continues:

> And now besides all this, today is the third day since these things were done. Yea and certain women also of our company affrighted us, who before it was light, were at the sepulcher, and not finding his body, came, saying, that they had also seen a vision of angels, who say that he is alive. And some of our people went to the sepulcher, and found it so as the women had said, but him they found not. (Luke 24:21–24)

These last words show that the two left Jerusalem before Mary Magdalene's announcement that she had seen Jesus, otherwise they would have mentioned this too, if only to cast the same doubt on it. But when Cleophas had finished, the unknown traveler's manner changed; rather than ignorant of all these things, He now seemed extraordinarily well-informed.

> Then he said to them: O foolish, and slow of heart to believe in all things which the prophets have spoken. Ought not Christ to have suffered these things, and so to enter into his glory? And beginning at Moses and all the prophets, he expounded to them in all the scriptures, the things that were concerning him. (Luke 24:25–27)

The lesson lasted until the end of the journey, but to the disciples it was all much too short. "And they drew nigh to the town, whither they were going: and he made as though he would go farther. But they constrained him; saying: Stay with us, because it is toward evening, and the day is now far spent. And he went in with them" (Luke 24:28–29). It is not necessary to suppose that it was already nightfall. The expression "toward evening" could apply to any time from noon time on, and so if the two disciples had left Jerusalem about nine o'clock and traveled twenty miles, it must have been by now toward two or three in the afternoon.

> And it came to pass, whilst he was at table with them, he took bread, and blessed, and break, and gave to them. And their eyes were opened, and they knew him: and he vanished out of their sight. And they said one to the other: Was not our heart burning within us, whilst he spoke in this way, and opened to us the scriptures? (Luke 24:30–32)

It hardly seems probable that Jesus gave the two disciples the Holy Eucharist when He broke bread, for we do not know whether these two disciples knew that Jesus had instituted the Holy Eucharist; apparently, they had not been present at the institution of the Holy Eucharist, but only the Twelve. Most modern exegetes say they did not receive the

Eucharist; they recognized Him because they had more than once seen Him perform this familiar action of breaking bread, as the master of the household and their Lord. The disciples, full of joy at seeing the Lord, immediately rose and started back to Jerusalem. There, they found the Eleven gathered together and those who were with them saying: "The Lord is risen indeed, and hath appeared to Simon" (Luke 24:34). And they themselves began to relate what had happened on their journey, and how they recognized Him in the breaking of bread.

Apparitions in the Cenacle. While the new arrivals from Emmaus were trying to convince their brethren of the reality of Christ's Resurrection without any success—for St. Mark tells us that doubts arose on all sides and they did not believe them (see Mark 16:14)—Jesus unexpectedly stood in the midst of them. He had made His way through the walls of the closed Cenacle without the slightest noise announcing His coming (see John 20:19). For the laws of gravity and impenetrability that govern material substances do not constrain glorified bodies. "Peace be to you," said Jesus to them (Luke 24:36). But they were terrified and stricken with fear and thought they beheld a spirit.

> And he said to them: Why are you troubled, and why do thoughts arise in your hearts? See my hands and feet, that it is I myself; handle, and see: for a spirit hath not flesh and bones, as you see me to have. And when he had said this, he showed them his hands and feet. (Luke 24:40)

No reasonable doubt is possible any longer; but according to the profoundly psychological statement of St. Luke, excess of joy and surprise made them incredulous. The reality seemed too wonderful; they could not believe in so much happiness, and they wondered if they were not the plaything of a dream of their own wishful thinking. Jesus said to them: "Have you anything to eat?" (Luke 24:41). They gave Him a piece of roasted fish left over from their frugal meal. He took it and ate it in front of them, to complete the effort to convince them that He was not a specter. Then their faith was whole and their joy without alloy.

But He had not solely come to console; He came also to bring to the apostles the complement of the priesthood. He addresses only the apostles as He says: "Peace be to you. As the Father hath sent me, I also send you." Then having breathed on them, He said: "Receive ye the Holy Ghost. Whose sins you shall forgive, they are forgiven them; and whose sins you shall retain, they are retained" (John 20:21–23). Today, the Savior is keeping the promise once made to the apostles regarding their government of His Church.

Now, Thomas was not present that evening. We know not why. Perhaps his stubborn, skeptical attitude kept him away. When he was told by the others of Christ's visit to them, he refused to believe it: "Except I shall see in his hands the print of the nails, and put my finger into the place of the nails, and put my hand into his side, I will not believe" (John 20:25). After all, Thomas was telling his fellow apostles, in effect: You must be reasonable. How could a man rise again when He had been crucified, reduced to a mass of torn and wounded flesh, with His hands and feet pierced and a gaping hole in His side? Mary Magdalene has seen Him? Now what reason could there possibly be for believing a distraught woman, a woman from whom seven devils had gone forth? The other apostles had seen Him, and had especially noticed His hands and feet? Well, those apostles were all fine good men, but they were a little on the volatile side and too easily imagined they saw what they wanted to see! He, Thomas, was the calm, deliberate man among them, just the right man to have around in certain cases; and in cases like this, it was not enough to see—one must touch and feel; only on this condition would he believe! The prince of the positivists and hypercritics remained unshakable in his conviction for eight days, and no argument the apostles might propose could budge him.

But after eight days, the disciples were again inside, and Thomas was with them. Jesus came, though the doors were closed, and stood in their midst and said: "Peace be to you!" Then He said to Thomas: "Put in thy finger hither, and see my hands; and bring hither thy hand, and put it into my side; and be not faithless, but believing." Thomas answered and said to Him: "My Lord, and my God!" Jesus said to him: "Because thou hast seen me, Thomas, thou hast believed: blessed are they that have not seen, and have believed" (John 20:26–29). Yet in Thomas's words, what sentiments of faith, of respect, of humble supplication, of ardent prayer, of repentant love were in that sweeping exclamation: "My Lord and my God!" His eyes revealed to him only a man, but faith led him to adore a God. His words should often be in our heart and upon our lips.

On the shore of Lake Tiberias. After the close of the Paschal season, there being nothing to keep the apostles in Jerusalem, they took the road back to their native country of Galilee. Some of them naturally took up their old profession, earning their living by fishing. They were waiting for that promised visit of our Lord in Galilee. So Peter said one day, with the lake rippling invitingly before him: "I am going fishing." And the others with him answered: "We also are going with you" (see John 21:3). For night fishing, it was better to have a couple of helpers, because they could use the long dragnets. There were seven in all on the trip. They got into the boat and cast their nets, but it was a hopelessly bad night, and at dawn they had not yet caught anything. Simon Peter had known similar nights in the past. So they started pulling for shore again to disembark. When they were about a hundred yards from shore, they glimpsed a figure through the mist; they could not see it at all clearly, but it seemed to be a man waiting for them. Perhaps he wanted to buy their catch. When they were within calling distance, He asked: "Children, have you any fish?" After that long night of wasted toil and effort, the question sounded more than a little ironic, and from the boat came a quick, brusque "No!"—which would normally discourage any further discussion. But the man shouted again through the morning mist: "Cast the net on the right side of the ship, and you shall find [them]" (John 21:5–6). His tone of authority impressed them, and they also knew from experience that a man on the shore is always in a better position to direct the fishing and to give useful advice. One of them therefore seized a loose net and skillfully gave it a wide sweep. The result was as quick as it was unexpected. The net became so full that the combined efforts of the apostles were scarcely enough to haul it aboard without capsizing the boat. Such an astounding prodigy could only come from the Master. John, who got the first intimation of it, said to Peter; "It is the Lord" (John 21:7). In an instant, Peter bound up his coat to swim more easily and jumped into the water to get to shore as quickly as possible. The impetuous love of Peter drove him through the water, and with a few strong strokes, he was at the feet of the divine Master. The loaded boat dragged in behind Peter. When the apostles disembarked, there was a little fire already lit, with fish laid upon it and bread prepared for them. Jesus said to them: "Bring hither of the fishes which you have now caught" (John 21:10). They had caught 153 fishes.

> When therefore they had dined, Jesus saith to Simon Peter: Simon son of John, lovest thou me more than these? He saith to him: Yea, Lord, thou knowest that I love thee. He saith to him: Feed my lambs. He saith to him again: Simon, son of John, lovest thou me? He saith to him: Yea, Lord, thou knowest that I love thee. He saith to him: Feed my lambs. He said to him the third time: Simon, son of John, lovest thou me? Peter was grieved, because he had said to him the third time: Lovest thou me? And he said to him: Lord, thou knowest all things: thou knowest that I love thee. He said to him: Feed my sheep. (John 21:15–17)

Jesus' threefold question, in tactful charity, made no explicit reference to the past, but in its threefold repetition, it was nevertheless linked with a painful past. Three times Peter denied the Master in the hour of darkness, and now, in the hour of light, he three times professes his love for Him. On this occasion, Jesus is confiding to Peter, His representative on earth, the guardianship and care of His whole flock: lambs, little sheep, and sheep. Peter is to discharge the office of pastor in all its fullness. He will guide the flock to healthy grazing lands and will turn it aside from poisonous pasturage. The ideal picture that the Savior, the Good Shepherd, has lived out must henceforth be applied to Peter and his successors. The privilege of papal authority is granted for the Church because the sheepfold of Christ can never dispense with its shepherd. While delegating His sovereign authority to Peter, Jesus is reserving another favor for him, the favor of sharing His Cross. After He had said, "Feed My sheep," immediately, without transition, He adds: "Amen, amen I say to thee, when thou wast younger, thou didst gird thyself, and didst walk where thou wouldst. But when thou shalt be old, thou shalt stretch forth thy hands, and another shall gird thee, and lead thee whither thou wouldst not" (John 21:18).

We, too, have been called to follow Christ. Even on this joyful occasion, Christ reminds us of this great honor. Even as He closed His message to Peter, so Christ closes His message to us as we complete contemplating His life, and the important words are: "Follow Me" (John 21:19). Let us cheerfully and joyfully go after Him, even as Peter and all the apostles did.

Confer: Ferdinand Prat, S.J., *Jesus Christ*, vol. 2, pp. 428–444.

Giuseppe Ricciotti, *The Life of Jesus*, pp. 659–665.

CONFERENCE
Confidence in God

OF ALL THE enemies that can stop our progress in the spiritual life and
dry up our zeal for perfection, the worst is discouragement. Whereas
certain illusions increase our efforts tenfold, discouragement annihi-
lates our powers. Discouragement plays the devil's game, for it leads
us to choose for our part mediocrity and a sterile life. No matter
what the cause from which it springs—difficulties, contradictions,
apparent unsuccess, experience of our weakness, the cooling of our
ardor—we must fight this spiritual disease to the death. Now, as
we approach the end of our retreat in which we have so generously
rededicated ourselves to God, it is most important to fortify ourselves
for the future against this dread and paralyzing disease. And so let
us examine what confidence is; how efficacious a virtue confidence
is in the spiritual life; what must be the measure and degree of our
confidence in God; and what are some practical rules as to how we
may practice this salutary virtue.

The nature of confidence in God. Considered in its effect,
confidence is a more or less firm hope of attaining a desired favor
despite the difficulties that are in the way. Such confidence sustains
courage. It is less a virtue than a condition for virtue; it is a force
of the soul. But considered in its source and principle, confidence,
since it rests in the goodness of God, expresses the firmness with

which we rest upon the promises of God and on His goodness to fulfill what He has promised. In both these aspects or meanings, confidence in God is nothing else than the virtue of theological hope. It is, therefore, that habit of the will, sustained by grace, by which instead of counting upon ourselves and our own resources, we lean upon the assistance of God above all things, to help us attain and accomplish His will and our eternal happiness. Confidence is that virtue that stands midway between presumption (an inordinate esteem of our own powers) and despair (or inordinate distrust of ourselves and of God, a distrust that only looks at our own failings). The point we must always remember is that confidence, like all virtues, resides in the will. It must, therefore, not be confused with a *feeling* of confidence that we experience. This sentiment or feeling consists in a propensity to believe that "all will be well," that somehow "things will straighten themselves out," that success is bound to come. These feelings can be caused from good health joined to an ignorance of the difficulties that must be overcome. This *feeling* of confidence is in no manner an indication or a sign that the *virtue* of true confidence in God is possessed by the soul — just as the Protestant's feeling of faith does not give him the true faith (for the true faith is an enlightening of the intellect through grace, not a feeling or sentiment); just as sensible devotion is by no means the true measure of love of God or of true devotion. And thank God these feelings are not the true virtues that they simulate. Otherwise true faith, true devotion, and true confidence would only exist in gullible persons or people with temperaments tending to tears.

This important difference between the *virtue* and *feeling* of confidence explains why certain timid souls, without ever correcting their native impressionability, still undertake and bring to successful issue the most difficult works. It is said of the Marshal of Turin that before each battle, he would say to himself: "You are trembling with fear, you poor, weak body! Why if you knew where I am presently taking you, you will tremble more!" Was he a coward because his flesh was shaking with cold chills of fear? By no means! He was a brave man, since he took no account of his feelings but ruled them with the courage of his mind and soul. Thus, timid souls often feel their weakness—they may even be weak temperamentally—but throwing themselves resolutely on God, they nevertheless attain full success in the most difficult trials of life. Always remember this distinction in the virtue of confidence too. When we fear we are lacking in confidence because our feelings are not true, despite the fact that our resolution is to count completely on God to accomplish whatever He commands with His assistance, then ignore the feelings. God permits such apprehensions and feelings in order that our confidence may be anchored more profoundly in our will to cling to Him. It is a truth of the spiritual life that no virtue is enrooted in the soul until it is tried and purged in the fires of temptation from the opposite vices. St. Teresa says she experienced this truth in her own life. Hence, never is your confidence in God more pleasing to Him than when you cling to it in your will, despite all your adverse feelings and repugnances. Remember what St. Augustine said about love: "If you will to love, you already love." The same is true of confidence in God: If you will to have confidence in God, you have it, and you have as much as you will to have, for virtue is in the good will clinging to God. All the rest is a matter of feeling and not worth bothering about.

How efficacious is the virtue of confidence? Confidence in God is absolutely and sovereignly efficacious—always on the condition that our prayers are reasonable. Why is this? Let's consider three very good reasons why this is so.

1. Confidence in God gives God the very occasions that He most desires to prove His infinite goodness to us. His very essence is goodness, and it is God's greatest pleasure to multiply His benefits to His children. Goodness is diffusive of itself, and the more opportunity it gets to communicate itself, the happier it is. How infinitely true of God! We can say of God that it is almost a necessity — a spontaneous tendency of His nature — to make all things happy. As a matter of fact, He cannot be stopped in His prodigality toward His creatures and especially us men, except by presumption, abuse of His gifts, malice, and distrust of Him. Hence, we see how our prayers of confidence — asking for things that are needed for our advancement in virtue, the glory of God, or the daily needs of our souls and bodies — cannot but please God and make Him gladly hear and answer them.

2. Confidence in God forces God not to disappoint our high idea of His infinite goodness. Suppose there were two friends: one turns out a pauper, and the other very powerful and rich. The pauper tells his friend in wealth: "I'm down and out. With your help, with your credit, I'll be able to get back on my feet. Only you can help me." The rich friend's name is mud if he refuses, and he knows it. Dare he betray such complete confidence in his goodness? Then look at God. The one attribute He continually boasts of is His infinite goodness. Men must be convinced of that before all His other perfections, above His creative power, above His knowledge, above His omnipotence. The Scriptures continually sing of His goodness, His goodness without measure, His absolutely disinterested goodness, His goodness especially to the poor and downtrodden. If there is one point God is touchy about, it is His goodness. It almost

seems to be a weak point in Him, so that if we appeal to Him for anything through His goodness, He seems to be irresistibly moved to grant the request. Are we exaggerating? No! "Because he hoped in me I will deliver him: I will protect him because he hath known my name" (Ps. 90:14). St. Bernard says that confidence in God will obtain gifts in proportion to its audacity. And St. Thomas says: "If charity makes our prayers meritorious, it is confidence in God that assures them of obtaining what they are after."

3. Confidence in God binds God to keep His promises in their complete extent. Jesus told us: "Ask and you shall receive. Whatever you ask the Father in My name, that I will do. All that you ask in your prayers, believe that you will obtain it and you will see it all accomplished" (see John 14:13–14; 15:7; 16:23–24; Mark 11:22–24; Matt. 21:21–22). These solemn assurances, once given by the Son of God, place the glory of God at stake. God cannot lie, and He cannot fail us. God is faithful and will give you all you ask — provided, of course, you ask with confidence and you seek Him in a good, holy, humble life. After such promises, we must be convinced that so long as we are striving to love and follow God's commandments, there is nothing He will refuse us if we ask confidently and in the name of Jesus. In fact, not to ask, or to ask half-heartedly, would only wound the infinite love of His heart.

What must be the measure and degree of our confidence in God?
The answer is simple. The measure of our confidence must be boundless, infinite. Why? Because the foundation of our confidence in God is infinite. It is the infinite goodness of God. God is charity, love, an ocean of infinite goodness, without limits in length, breadth, or depth of goodness. When He will have poured out His goodness for

millions of centuries, upon millions of creatures, His infinite goodness will be as infinite as ever, not having diminished one least jot. You need only look at the crib, the Cross, the Church, the sacraments to see only some of the ways in which God has proved His love for us. What remains in Heaven with Himself is beyond all human understanding and language.

Some practical rules as to how we may practice this salutary virtue of confidence. In general, it will be very profitable to meditate from time to time on the height, depth, and boundless breadth of the infinite goodness of God in order to arouse and strengthen our confidence in Him. This will fix our wills in confidence, no matter how our feelings may roam. More in particular, every now and then think over your past with regard to confidence and try to foresee your future with this same confidence.

As regards your past: It is good for us to depict the misery in our past. What usually brought us to that misery? Pride. And, of course, we see only a small part of our failings. As St. Augustine says: "I fear very much my hidden sins, which only Thy eyes, O Lord, see and which mine do not see." But then think of the infinite mercy, love, and goodness of God despite all this! Tell God: "What magnificent glory for You, O God, for having championed such a poor creature as I. I hope in You, against every human motive; I will hope against hope in You; I will hope in You above all things." In this way, we make even our failings a cause of salutary confidence in God's goodness. The Little Flower of Jesus had this habit of throwing herself completely upon God. She says that even if she had the misfortune of committing thousands of mortal sins daily, she would throw herself in contrition and complete confidence upon the infinite goodness of God, sure of being received by Him. Therefore, never disquiet yourselves about your past sins and faults, no matter how grave they might have been. If you have confessed them and have been sorry for them, they must not be allowed to prevent you from laying hold of the intimate friendship of God. For God's heart is not small like ours. No, He finds joy in gathering the poor ragged creature from his hill of sin and placing him among the princes of His court. Such is the love of God.

As regards the future: Take the resolution to rejoice in the faults that you will inevitably fall into through weakness or surprise, and each time you fall, renew your confidence in God. Tell Him: "This new fall teaches me to know myself better. It binds me to reparation, to make compensation to your Sacred Heart. You, dear Lord, you always remain the same, ever infinitely good! Despite my failures, in the name of Jesus I beg and request the graces I need to serve you better!" Such an exercise will increase our humility and our confidence in God. In all cases, never give into discouragement; despise the feelings of disturbance and of despair. March forward in naked faith, leaning on the truth that destroys all doubts: God is charity. Remember the promise of our good Master: "Whatsoever you shall ask the Father in my name, that will I do" (John 14:13).

Confidence is a virtue of the will that relies on the infinite goodness of God for what it asks. By its practice, one becomes master of the heart of God and honors Him; and in return, God makes one master of one's enemies, spiritual and material. Remember the boy David, slingshot in hand, advancing against Goliath, a giant armed to the teeth. Yet the boy advanced with confidence in the true God: "I come to thee in the name of the Lord of hosts, the God of the armies of Israel.... This day ... the Lord will deliver thee into my hand, and I will slay thee" (1 Sam. 17:45–46). And so it happened. God cannot fail those who have confidence in Him. Perhaps we tremble, too, at our enemies. "Have confidence," says our Lord, "I have overcome the world" (John 16:33). Let us advance with courage, confident of God, sure of victory.

THIRD MEDITATION
Contemplation for Attaining Divine Love

THE CONSTANT WORKING *and labor of God on my behalf.* God is not idle, like a friend who contents himself with sighing near his friend. In double labor, exterior and interior, He never ceases to work for our happiness.

His exterior activity. God is present in all creatures. He maintains them in existence and collaborates with each one of their acts. True, Scripture speaks of God resting on the seventh day, but our Lord tells us: "My Father worketh until now" (see John 5:17). The infinity of His love permits Him to love each one of us as if we were the only one in existence; He loves me as if I alone existed with Him. He wants me to get such happiness and use out of all creation as if He had created it all solely for me. Our Blessed Lord, speaking to the French mystic, Lucie-Christine, said to her: "My daughter, there is no one but you and I." "But Lord," she asked, "what about all other creatures?" "For each soul in this world," answered the divine Master, "there is nothing but it and I; all other souls and all other things are nothing to each souls except through Me and for Me."

"There is no one but you and I!" What a brilliant light of truth! What a consoling thought of love! What a stimulant to love God alone and all in Him!

His interior activity. "God is closer to my very being than the elements that go to make it up." Besides that, He works constantly in me, even when I sleep, even when I am away from myself and am no longer present to my consciousness. His light, His attractions, His strength, His reproofs are procured immediately for me by Him. I have not a good thought, not a good inspiration that does not come from Him into my mind and heart. There is not a single exterior event, not the least trial, that God does not by His suggestions turn to my profit if I allow Him to be my guide. "We know that to them that love God, all things work together unto good" (Rom. 8:28). There is no friend who works in the way that God does for me, from the first moment of my existence until the last instant of my life here on earth. Where can you find one who serves you with such sweet wisdom? God is infinite wisdom and knows and does all that is good for me. Will you find a human friend to work for you with complete disinterestedness? Hardly. Yet what can God expect from me for His infinite service to me? Can my praises and homage add one whit to His infinite happiness? No! Why, then, does He work so selflessly for a puny creature as me? Out of His benevolent love for me. True, God's work for me brings Him neither fatigue nor suffering, but the Word became flesh and dwelt among us, undergoing the worst tortures, becoming like us in all things except sin. That's what St. Paul means when he says: "the Son of God ... loved me, and delivered himself for me" (Gal. 2:20).

How shall we show our gratitude for such great love? Let us not hesitate or hold back. We must consecrate ourselves to this adorable Master in all our actions to the utmost of our powers. We must use all our efforts to procure His reign over us, individually. We can be assured of the success of our apostolate by working for Him on our personal sanctification.

In short, I must spend myself, use myself up even to the last sigh of my life for "His greater glory." There must be nothing separating Him from me. Every affection of which God is not the principal end would only divide my heart. He must be all in me since I must only act and can only live with the grace of Jesus.

What God is in Himself. "Your innumerable gifts to me, O ineffably good God, Your presence which envelopes, surrounds and penetrates my being, Your incessant activity which sustains and directs me, only give me a slight presentiment of what You are in Yourself.... Give me, therefore, I beg You, an appreciation, however slight, of Yourself." God answers: "I Am Who Am" (Exod. 3:14): I am Being, Infinite Being.

I am Being. That is to say, God is the only one who exists in the full meaning and power of the verb "to be." Because He exists from inner necessity, the very perfection of His nature is to be, so that without Him, no thing could be drawn out of the abyss of nothingness into existence.

I Am Who Am — that is to say, Being without any mixture of non-being, therefore without any imperfection or limitation. Every creature is an image of Me because of what it has received from Me; but by reason of that which a creature lacks, no matter how marvelous it may be, every creature is only a flat, insipid image of My essence. I Am Who Am. I am consequently the fullness of Being, the infinity of all perfections.

The Infinite One. The Infinite One is not an amount, a sum, an addition of all perfections. Were you to unite all that is pleasing in creatures, were you to draw out all conceivably good qualities, were you to attempt to write all these in mathematical numbers, you would obtain a fantastic yet finite number. It would not suffice by far to number the splendors and glories of God. Between this fantastic number and what perfections I am in myself, there would exist an infinite difference. Infinity is not an ideal term above and beyond which it is possible to imagine anything more. It is an abyss without bottom, an ocean without shores, an immensity whose each perfection, far from being limited by the others, comprehends them all and contains each one without limits. What perfection can more arouse your admiration and wonder? The intelligence of God? Well, that is incommensurable too! God's goodness? Incommensurable! The more one contemplates God's perfections, the more one must despair of ever grasping them in their entirety and of ever admiring them as they merit to be admired.

God is infinite joy. Every beautiful thing, every truly beautiful thing will make you thrill. Something beautiful will take you outside of yourself, at least as long as you have discovered no defect. In God there exists, without any defects, He who is infinitely irresistible above all attractions. For anyone to contemplate God without veils, he would not be able to resist the infinite attraction; he could not remain neutral, but he would be thrilled to admiration, exultation, jubilation — all without limit and without end. Such is the beauty of God that he who looks upon God cannot live. Why? Because the soul is irresistibly drawn from the body to the bosom of God. Union with God is ecstasy to the will. Here below, we necessarily love that which appears lovable and perfect. In order to prove this love, we take pleasure in sacrifices, but a few deceptions stop us cold. However, with God no deceptions are possible. All possible reasons for loving Him carry me to the infinitely lovable God. In fact, God puts in me only and all reasons for loving Him. To see God and to love Him completely are the same thing. Because the direct sight of Him would snatch away our liberty, God hides Himself momentarily from our eyes in this life. We are not to remain in this vale of tears, however, and we will see Him face to face if now we show ourselves worthy of

Him. We now have only a short time in which to love Him with a free and meritorious love: this life.

Let us recall to ourselves often who God is, what marvelous sacrifices and sufferings He undertook for us. Let us pray often, "O Beauty, O divine Goodness without measure, I love You." Each second of our existence should make us think of the true life, the ecstasy without end, in the contemplation of the Divine Face! Everything ought to recall to us our powerlessness to glorify God except through obedience and meritorious sacrifices. All things ought to repeat to us: "Love is proved by deeds, by the greatest possible self-abnegation now! Later will be too late!" Each occasion of sacrifice and suffering must tell me: "For that infinite beauty, for the infinite goodness and amiability, let me offer at least this small homage." Take care that you are never diverted from God by anything!

Make a loving colloquy with Mary and all the elect of Heaven, asking: "Draw me to this double ecstasy of intellect and will. Teach me to give in every instant all that I can give; to use to best advantage every opportunity of loving God." To our Lord pray: "O Jesus, model of all your adopted sons, send me Your Holy Spirit of love who made You live only for the glory of Your Father, who taught You to rejoice even in suffering that the Son might glorify the Father." To the Holy Spirit pray: "Come, O Holy Spirit, and enlighten the hearts and minds of us, your Faithful, and enkindle in us the fire of Your divine Love!"

Confer: Pinard de la Boullaye, S.J., *Exercices Spirituels*, vol. 2, pp. 198–208.

About the Author

FR. VINCENT P. MICELI, the son of Italian immigrants, was born in New York City in 1915. He worked his way through school and entered the Jesuit order for training. He was ordained in 1949. His extraordinary career included countless lectures in all parts of the world and many TV and radio appearances in the United States|—|including programs like ABC's "Good Morning America" and CNN's "Crossfire." Fr. Miceli was a teacher for many years, specializing in Theology and Philosophy at the following institutions:

> Loyola University, New Orleans
> St. John's University, New York
> Springhill College, Alabama
> Christendom College, Virginia
> The Angelicum and Gregorian Universities in Rome

Father Miceli's previous books:

> *Ascent to Being*
> *The Gods of Atheism*
> *The Antichrist*
> *Women Priests and other Fantasies*
> *The Roots of Violence*

His two most popular books, *The Gods of Atheism* and *The Antichrist*, are published by Sophia Institute Press.

Sophia Institute

SOPHIA INSTITUTE IS a nonprofit institution that seeks to nurture the spiritual, moral, and cultural life of souls and to spread the gospel of Christ in conformity with the authentic teachings of the Roman Catholic Church.

Sophia Institute Press fulfills this mission by offering translations, reprints, and new publications that afford readers a rich source of the enduring wisdom of mankind.

Sophia Institute also operates the popular online resource CatholicExchange.com. *Catholic Exchange* provides world news from a Catholic perspective as well as daily devotionals and articles that will help readers to grow in holiness and live a life consistent with the teachings of the Church.

In 2013, Sophia Institute launched Sophia Institute for Teachers to renew and rebuild Catholic culture through service to Catholic education. With the goal of nurturing the spiritual, moral, and cultural life of souls, and an abiding respect for the role and work of teachers, we strive to provide materials and programs that are at once enlightening to the mind and ennobling to the heart; faithful and complete, as well as useful and practical.

Sophia Institute gratefully recognizes the Solidarity Association for preserving and encouraging the growth of our apostolate over the course of many years. Without their generous and timely support, this book would not be in your hands.

www.SophiaInstitute.com
www.CatholicExchange.com
www.SophiaInstituteforTeachers.org

Sophia Institute Press is a registered trademark of Sophia Institute.
Sophia Institute is a tax-exempt institution as defined by the
Internal Revenue Code, Section 501(c)(3). Tax ID 22-2548708.